MY WAY

John Wilson

Dedication
To my dearest friends John and Jackie Smith.

First Published in July 2010

© Text and pictures - John Wilson

© Illustrations - David Higginbottom

© Design - Mpress (media) Ltd

Editors - Terry Doe and Rosie Barham

ISBN NUMBER 978-0-9560935-6-1

designed and published by m press (Media) LTD.

CONTENTS

INTRODUCTION

This volume is neither encyclopaedia nor a method manual. Simply an amalgam, and rather diverse I admit, of my personal angling experiences, recollections, techniques, preferences and even hopes for the future of angling, originating from both home and overseas locations. You will note, for instance, that pole fishing is not included despite the fact that during my youth I was an ardent pole angler catching dace, roach, and occasionally even a barbel. Living in North London, as I did until my early twenties, using a traditional Tonkin cane (bamboo) pole, the Rivers Lea and Thames were my weekend retreats. However, it is impossible to include each and every technique, location, species or subject I enjoy in my role as an 'all-rounder'.

You will gather for instance, that I am extremely worried about the current escalation of predators upon our freshwater scene in the UK, in particular cormorants and otters, and this topic raises its ugly head throughout my wanderings. So what you are about to read is very much my personal take, in fact, 'My Way' on a kaleidoscope of subject matter within this glorious fieldsport we call fishing.

Why do we writers continually confuse our readers by sometimes calling it 'fishing', and other times 'angling'? Well, in pure terms, I guess 'fishing' could relate to fishing commercially for food, whereas 'angling' is usually referred to in sporting terms. I make the same mistake as most of my contemporaries, however, by calling it both, and at no particular time, but then you'll forgive us, won't you?

John Wilson MBE
Great Witchingham, 2010

PROLOGUE

I am indebted to Pearson Publishing in Cambridge, for allowing me to reproduce the following chapter I wrote for 'Our Countryside', back in 1996.

Ours is indeed a strange attitude. Within our industrialised western society, the city dweller is perfectly content to purchase from the local supermarket a piece of frozen, headless fish or meat wrapped in Clingfilm, not knowing or even caring from which particular creature it came. Obviously, it had to be killed by someone, yet that same city dweller will subsequently condemn the countryman who shoots a rabbit for his dinner, or who fishes for sport. So, until the men in white coats come for me, I shall continue to hunt where and when the fancy takes me and to fish until I drop.

I guess it is the sheer mystery of it all that continues to capture my imagination after more than half a century of peering into the depths of water, wherever I happen to be in the world. I often think I could even fish happily in a bucket of water providing the bottom couldn't be seen, and there was just half a chance of the float tip bobbing under.

I care not whether the day is swelteringly hot or miserably cold; whether it is blowing a gale or deathly still in the grip of winter. Indeed, with the lake frozen over and crystallised hoarfrost covering waterside shrubbery, there is no finer moment for removing the lens cap from my camera and leaving the rods in the car. Many are the times when half a day spent fishing has included not a single cast, yet I have returned home completely satisfied.

When river margins are frozen over, there is such marvellous magic to see, raw certainly, but beautiful nonetheless. Simply being there, walking along while observing the river's flow patterns without so much as making a single cast is commitment enough, for there will be other times when such information can be put to good use. It is perhaps as close as the fisherman can ever come to the experiences and feelings of his ancestors who, regardless of weather conditions, fished purely to survive. This very same inner feeling is something all fishermen treasure, yet find difficult to explain to our families and friends, who sit at home in comfortable warmth, content in the belief that we all must indeed be certifiable.

To ardent anglers such as me, few moments in time can match that boyish excitement of rising at dawn on a summer's morning with birds in full chorus and clouds of grey mist hugging the river bank. The chill, the unknown quantity, the smell of crushed watermint, the sight of dew-covered spiders' webs hanging from marginal grasses and the disapproving 'honk' of an old heron - the greatest and quietest fisherman of them all - as he takes off indignantly. Bubbles erupting on the surface from deep down suggest fish are feeding earnestly, but is the water too clear? Will they fancy the flavour of paste prepared carefully the evening before?

From nowhere, a kingfisher zooms low along the river like a bolt of cobalt blue lightning, en route from one perch to another. He also has a family to feed. The float tip lifts slowly and a firm strike connects with unseen power. The forearm supporting the rod is jagged down and the sense of mystery that has curdled in my brain since I first wore short trousers is instantly switched on. Is it one of those huge bream I've seen but never managed to hook, or is it merely an aggressively powerful male tench? For a second I ponder, and question the coincidence that Mother Nature should apply such aggression to the males of her species, but that split-second of lost concentration costs me dearly. The monster, alas, has managed to transfer my hook into a long sprig of hornwort, a crunchy waterweed that in certain environments takes on a distinct smell of the sea. I am totally deflated for several seconds but a new piece of paste is pressed on the hook. Thankfully, bubbles are still bursting into the oily surface film despite the commotion of losing a fish. My enthusiasm is instantly renewed and expectation levels are reaching to the point of climax.

There is no conclusion to a fishing tale. Go fishing and experience it for yourself, and do, please, see fishing in its proper perspective, as do the odd two million sport fishermen in Britain who you will be joining. Why Mother Nature made man a hunter, or apples for picking, is for no one on this earth to question, for it will always be so, and a dog eat dog and

Watching the seasons change around my own two-lake carp fishery from spring through summer, then back to a severe, old-fashioned winter, is pure joy.

fish eat fish world in which over-population of certain species has been well catered for by our creator. Can you imagine, for instance, if reptiles, amphibians, fish, spiders, bats and birds did not catch and consume the largest proportion of hatched insects both terrestrial and water borne? The insects would reproduce ten-fold in as many days and the world as we know it simply could not survive.

We are all part of an intricate global ecosystem that constantly changes (remember the dinosaurs?) whether we like it or not, which is why man should never relinquish his basic instinct for hunting. People who preach total vegetarianism, anti-this and anti-that, tend not to understand what they are talking about really, and wouldn't recognise a viviparous lizard from a toadstool if they sat on one. I am a hunter, first and foremost, and

proud of it, and I have been put on this earth as such. It is why I go fishing. It is, in fact, a need in me and is something I could not quash even if I wanted to, any more than I could stem the urge felt throughout adult life for the propagation of my species. They are physical characteristics held in my genes and handed down by my ancestors. I also fish for pleasure because it satisfies all those primal, animal instincts in which we need fulfilment. I do occasionally fish for food in the same way that I might occasionally shoot a pheasant, specifically to feed myself or others, though generally I am content to take enjoyment from watching an adversary swim or fly away; and here, perhaps, lies the sporting element in man.

I cannot alter how I feel towards the field sports of hunting, shooting and fishing, any more than the domesticated dog which sleeps indoors and walks on Axminster carpet can stop itself from walking around in a circle, as it does in the wild to flatten grass, before slumping down into sleeping mode beside the fire. My wife, Jo, and I find

To us country folk, the splendour of the horses and hounds leaving the village green before the hunt is a wonderful sight, so deeply entrenched in our British heritage. Long may it remain so.

constant joy and amusement in our 'Westie' Bola, who tries to bury a pig's ear indoors into the depths of a shagpile rug or into the folds of the bedspread – yes, he sleeps on the bed - constantly prodding, poking and folding material over it, as though soil in the garden. That one saying, 'you can take the animal out of the jungle, but not the jungle out of the animal' is so perfectly true, even in the case of man. For you can take man away from the hunt, but not his instincts for hunting. Those who try and have tried towards their ideal of a 'nanny' state are now paying the price.

A great sadness of our contemporary inner city life is the way in which children now grow up in high-rise flats without gardens or access to wild places and thus have their basic curiosity towards a love of natural history greatly suppressed. Sadly, when their hunting instincts do develop, as they surely will, without water, land and trees to climb and without wild places and animals upon which to vent their pent-up natural aggression, they take it out on, and even hunt, fellow human beings. Look no further than the hooliganism and violence among football supporters. I would wager all that I own on the belief that aggravated crime in the UK is, per head count, far lower in the countryside where teenagers can go hunting, shooting or fishing, than in the streets of an urban, concrete jungle where lager-lout and drug-driven yobs, track down the old and infirm for an easy kill. Yet what are they doing? Yes, you've guessed, hunting!

In truth, there are times when, due to my total involvement with fishing which includes fisheries management, writing and producing programmes for television, I become totally irritated by continually having to substantiate my love of the sport. After all, I have never seen fit during my weekend off, to spend the entire time ensuring that others do not enjoy themselves, which would appear to be the wishes of the so-called 'anti's'; though these I believe we could count in hundreds rather than thousands. It's just that like many minorities, sadly, the media sees fit to give them all airtime. You have certainly got far more chance of appearing on television these days by being bad rather than doing good.

Do we really believe there are more murderers, rapists, or child molesters around now, for argument's sake, than there were 30 years ago? Or is it, as I truly believe, all hyped up totally out of proportion and literally brought immediately to everyone's attention by the media, with goodness knows how many news bulletins on countless radio and television stations, from your local disc jockey to satellite transmitted news industries like CNN?

Sometimes, I even find myself falling under this ridiculous spell, when the oh-so-appealing TV weather girl says there is going to be a severe frost or heavy snow the following morning. I take my tackle out of the car and bung it back in the garage, only to wake up to a beautiful morning when I could, and indeed should, have gone fishing. Boy, could I kick myself, for I should have known better.

Yes, I admit it. There are many times when I do decidedly feel like an angry old man, but fortunately, I'm still getting out there fishing, come rain or come shine, and relishing every minute.

A 4lbs-plus perch, like this monster from the upper reaches of the Great Ouse, is one of the most desirable and fulfilling catches in freshwater fishing. No wonder I'm smiling.

There can be few more evocative and bountiful stretches of running water than the majestic River Wye. A veritable chub and barbel haven, much of its length is the on the border between England and Wales.

AGGRESIVE ALIENS AND PLUMPER PERCH

When my younger brother, Dave, and I were in our teens, which is certainly some time back, 50 years ago to be precise, we used to love catching crayfish from all the clear-flowing streams of Hertfordshire, within motorbiking distance of our then home in Enfield, North London. In fact, crayfish were and still are a superb, natural bait for catching summer chub, particularly the larger specimens. Simply hooking once only through the last tail segment with a size 4 hook, tied directly to 6lb reel line and 'freelining' through the swim, was the way to catch chub in those days. Of course, it is now illegal to use any species of crayfish for bait in the UK - dead or alive.

These baby signal crayfish - note their red claws - provide a rich, extra food source upon which perch and chub reach monstrous proportions. Sadly, their alien status negates their use as bait.

More often than not when seeking chub, Dave and I actually left home without any bait. I wonder how many anglers today would even consider doing that! We knew full well, that with the aid of a small torch, we could easily gather enough crayfish by turning over old logs and large pieces of flint in the shallows, during that last hour of darkness prior to dawn breaking, for a morning's stalking session after chub.

At this time though, sadly, 50 years of water abstraction has taken its toll. These were lovely, sparkling, enchanting little rivers like the Rib, the Beane, the Upper Lea, the Ash, and the blue-clear Mimram, which seemed to breed slightly larger crayfish than all the other rivers.

The crayfish then was, of course, our native white-clawed crayfish. Grey in colour, they are quite distinguishable from the very much larger and more aggressive American signal crayfish, which is now colonising many river systems throughout the country, having been introduced originally, back in the 1980s by trout farmers to clear up dead fish from the bottom and thus provide a secondary crop from their stillwater fisheries. What a monumental mistake by our then Ministry of Agriculture and Fisheries in allowing this to happen!

Yes, having adult signal crayfish constantly attacking your ledgered lobworms intended for big perch does sometimes make you want to cry, but you can get your own back by eating them.

CRAYFISH

The sad outcome is that the signal has all but ousted our native white-clawed crayfish, recognisable by a white dot on the underside of its claws, by a virulent fungal disease that it carries, but to which it is immune. If not this, then by sheer aggression upon the smaller, indigenous, white-clawed crayfish with which Dave and I used to catch those chub so many years ago. Sadly, the white-clawed species is fast losing its battle for survival and is in devastating decline, although there are still isolated colonies left in river systems that are yet to be invaded by signal crayfish.

There are four other alien species of freshwater crayfish now thriving in Britain, according to the Environment Agency. They are namely, the narrow-clawed Turkish crayfish, the Louisiana red swamp crayfish, the noble crayfish, and the spiny-cheeked crayfish, all imported for the pet fish trade. Fortunately, these have not yet spread like signals, nor are they as aggressive or as large.

In the long term, signal crayfish can only be viewed as a total disaster to our river systems, and not only to the angler who is continually suffering false bites from signals pulling on his bait, especially worms. Whenever you are inexplicably missing what appear to be perfectly hittable bites on the quiver-tip, suspect signals, immediately! The delicate invertebrate life in British running water, which due to four decades of agri-chemicals continually being fed into the land, and now continually leeching into the rivers, is having trouble enough reproducing. An adult signal can reach weights of up to half a pound, but colonies of large crayfish, which average around five or six to the pound, do little to promote healthy propagation of our indigenous freshwater fish. Moreover, signals consume vast quantities of fish spawn and fry - as if cormorants aren't bad enough!

However, together with the alien mitten crabs which are common in the lower Thames and also fall into this category, signals have created an entirely new food source for certain freshwater species, perch in particular. From many river systems around the country where signals have become prolific, adult perch are not only reaching heavy weights more quickly, but also growing 20-40 per cent larger than angling records suggest they should. Scale-to-growth rates research by the Environment Agency has confirmed that perch of just four years old can reach weights of up to 4lbs; staggering statistics these. Perch are not known for regularly hoovering up high protein pastes, pellets and boilies, as are tench, barbel, bream and carp, so in certain environments it can only be high protein intake of a giant crustacean diet, namely, signal crayfish, that is creating real numbers of huge perch, and quickly.

BIG PERCH

Take the River Great Ouse, for instance, in its upper reaches between Buckingham and Bedford where 30 years back all previous angling records suggested that big Ouse perch topped out at around 3½ lbs, with the very occasional monster over 4lbs, but such fish were exceedingly rare. The British national perch record in 1976 was just 4lb 12oz - incidentally, believe it or not, the tench record then was just 9lb 1oz; barbel 13lb 12oz and bream 12lb 14oz - whereas today, 4lbs-plus perch are common occurrences all over the country, but especially in the Lower Thames and the Upper Ouse. With the national record

at the time of writing getting on for 6lbs, and bound to surpass this figure in the years to come, these are truly astounding increases for a predatory species, whose weight is in no way linked to manufactured high protein baits, as are the chub, tench, barbel, carp and bream records.

My own wanderings along the Upper Great Ouse, below Buckingham, in search of big perch during the past 15 years have produced some previously, totally unimaginable results. At the time, I thought I'd died and gone to heaven. They included two separate catches that included no fewer than four perch over 4lbs apiece, the best being a catch of five perch totalling 20lb and half an ounce. Of course, one very good reason I was able to account for such monsters, apart from their extra diet of crayfish, is that largely, only shoals of perch, together with pike and the occasional big chub actually existed where I fished, and still do, incidentally. I guess that all the small to middle-sized perch dace, roach and chub had simply been ravaged by cormorants over the years. I cannot think of another plausible explanation.

It's interesting to note that parts of the Upper Great Ouse riverbed seem to be paved with crayfish. Continual attention to ledgered lobworms proves this on most sessions when there is real predatory aggression in the swim, from numbers of big perch and several pike, all purposefully seeking the broken lobworms catapulted in. When this happens, those crayfish become conspicuous by their absence. This suggests that even though they possess huge claws, big perch when all fired up make short work of even the average, large-sized signal crayfish. This fact is borne out, often by finding the remnants of part-digested claws in the bottom of my holding tube, upon returning big fish following a photography session at the end of the day.

*Part of a dream Upper Ouse perch catch of five
fish totalling 20lb ½oz, which included three
over 4lbs, from back-ledgering lobworms during
a mild winter spell in the late 1990s.*

Incidentally, don't let a crayfish play with your worm for too long, or you'll find, upon retrieval, that it has retreated to its burrow in the bottom. It could be a couple of feet long and you might then even need to pull for a break.

With perch, and particularly big river perch, I pay much attention to the barometer, weather patterns, and air temperature. I look for those days when for the previous two or three nights, usually due to a mild, south-westerly airstream, winter temperatures have not dropped below 6-8 degrees C. If I can match such a day to the river fining down nicely, but still holding colour following severe flooding, then so much the better. During the preceding days, a mountain of worms will have washed into the river, and as it clears, those big 'stripeys' will be on the lookout for more.

It makes sense if you think about it, which is why large, juicy lobworms are my all-time favourite bait for big perch. Live baits such as gudgeon, bleak, small dace or roach, and artificial lures, will always have a part to play, especially in clear water conditions when big perch become super-wary, but a much higher proportion of bites are missed using live baits, say, than on the humble lobworm. You'll know when river perch are really on to your worms when, paradoxically, you hook into more pike than you would expect, because both are competing in the same swim. Contrary to popular belief, pike do specifically target worms when continually introduced, a fact that is often proven by the wodge of broken lobs you see down their gullet when removing the hook.

Strangely, I have never noticed big perch to be put off when they have to share a glut of loose fed worms with pike, so don't be tempted to use a wire trace should the odd pike bite you off. They get rid of a size 4 single hook easily, but should you switch to

wire, bites from perch could immediately come to an end. They do not like the harshness and stiffness of a wire trace. Let's face it, how many times when live or dead baiting for pike using a wire trace, does a big perch grab hold? I've honestly had just one in my entire angling life.

BACK-LEDGERING

While the techniques of long trotting, stretpegging (see chapter four) and even freelining lobworms have each provided me with some memorable catches of these big Ouse perch between 3 ½ and 4 ½ lbs - I've now clocked up getting on for 20 monsters over that magical 4lbs barrier - I rate back-ledgering as most effective of all.

This is a technique I developed specifically, through trial and error, for searching the Upper Ouse and the Claydon Brook, where groups of big perch seem to be moving about constantly and rarely concentrate in one area for any length of time. In a river system full of perch grub, though, where the bottom is literally crawling with signal crayfish, why should they? It revolves around using two, soft quiver-tip rods - in all but the most confined swims, when one rod suffices - with 6lbs test mono and a simple, fixed paternoster ledger on each. A 12-inch length of line, the link, is tied 20 inches up the reel line, using the incredibly neat four-turn water knot. A size 4 wide gape hook goes on the longer link and between one and three 2XSSG or 3XSSG shots on the shorter, link. What could be easier to construct?

Now, there are two main reasons back-ledgering is so effective, particularly in clear water conditions when continual casting progressively further down the swim could easily scare spooky fish. Firstly, far fewer

The technique of back-ledgering demands total concentration, regular casting, and broken lobworms constantly catapulted into the swim. Using bobbin indicators provides minimal resistance and 'sail-away' bites.

casts are actually made, but the entire swim is nonetheless thoroughly searched, simply by casting one rod, say, halfway down the run, and the second right to the very end of the swim. Maybe, where you expect perch could be situated; perhaps close to an overhanging willow or sunken bush, and if that is 50 or 60 yards away, then fine. Secondly, when you raise the rod tip to lift each bait from the bottom, after, say, a 5-20 minute wait, and wind the reel a turn or two. Any big perch sitting there, looking at the worm as a cat might a mouse, daring it to move, invariably slams into it providing an unmissable bite. So, always be on your guard; relaxed, but expectant. My old pal, the late Fred J Taylor MBE, always said when fishing the Upper Ouse, 'concentrate as though you had just missed a bite' - and he was so right.

Methodically, you keep bringing each worm back up the swim toward the rods in increments of two to four feet, say - hence my terminology of back-ledgering - until a bite materializes. A hit could come at any time due to that fluttering movement of the worm as it lifts attractively, as you raise the rod tip and wind, and when it falls through the water to settle on the bottom. It is a totally fascinating, and thorough 'searching' method of location helped along to a large degree by catapulting broken lobworms into the run, following each repositioning of the baits. This helps to create predatory aggression in the swim. So, you need a good supply of lobworms when locating perch using this method. I wouldn't arrive at the river with less than a 100 or so, and have actually got through 200 on some days.

In strong currents I usually rely totally on bite registration from soft quiver tips, with the rod tips angled upward and out at an angle of 45 degrees. In slow currents, though, I prefer to have both rods pointing directly downstream at the two baits, and use low-resistance, bobbin indicators clipped on to the line, on a 15-20 inch drop, between reel and butt ring. This is because in clear, slow water conditions, big perch can prove incredibly sensitive to resistance, even the pressure build-up from a soft quiver tip. Believe me, there are occasions when bobbin indicators pointed directly at the bait make all the difference between seeing a whopping great perch on the bank, and not.

Those specializing in zander fishing in the slow water of the Fens will experience exactly the same phenomenon. On some days, zander will happily pull a lightweight bobbin up to the butt ring, but conversely, they will let go of the bait, due to resistance, long before the line is pulled from a drop-back indicator; a point well worth remembering.

I know full well that bobbins may not appear as fashionable as the latest drop-back indicators, but it's a fact that they are far more sensitive. So my advice is, do not use drop-back indicators when zander fishing. If the flow is sufficient to keep dragging the bobbins upward every few minutes, I pinch a shot or two on to the retaining cords, immediately below the bobbins. It's a lovely way of waiting for the bite from a big perch, which sometimes starts with the bobbin giving a preliminary 'jingle', followed immediately by it going steadily, in a most authoritative manner, up to the butt ring. On slow days, I even incorporate an electronic bite alarm, which allows me to totally relax without missing out on what could be the only bite or two of the session.

Occasionally, should the perch decide to swim upstream, having gobbled up the lobworm, the bobbin will perhaps jingle momentarily, before suddenly falling back

completely slack. The perfect drop-back bite no less, to which I respond by winding down quickly, before lifting the rod steadily and firmly into the fish. Heavy, 'sweep-the-rod-back' strikes are simply not required when perch fishing in little rivers, whatever the bite, and could easily cost you fish that come off because the hook has been wrenched from that soft membrane holding the perch's jaws together. So, beware; there needs to be a shock absorber somewhere in the set-up - one reason I like to use soft-actioned, quiver tip rods, and always prefer monofilament for my reel line. Using braid will almost certainly cost you fish.

Of course, in those pre-commercial fisheries, pre-high protein pelleted food days, when rivers had a healthy biomass and a strong pyramid of all species, with millions of fry at the bottom leading progressively upward to a few natural monsters at the top, no one species got all the grub. This is completely different to most situations today. The systematic decimation by cormorants of silver shoal fish populations is bad enough, but we now also have the continuing and catastrophic problem, created by so-called do-gooders, in the form of otters. Stupidly, they have been introduced into delicately balanced river eco systems that are already decimated by predators and the otters are eating their way steadily through the small concentrations of huge, specimen-sized adult fish that are left. Remember, these adult monsters can be anything between 15 and 25 years old and are truly irreplaceable fish, because as we all know, there is nothing in the pipeline coming through.

Cormorants have eaten all the 'middle order' fish, those that would occupy the middle of a healthy pyramid of year classes. It is an incredibly worrying state of affairs because, even if there were a few medium-sized fish coming through, they would be decimated by otters long before reaching specimen-sized adulthood; the huge 20lb-plus, once-record barbel, found dead and part-eaten by an otter at Adams Mill on the Great Ouse being a prime example. Another is a near-20lb barbel found partly eaten on the banks of my local River Wensum, not a mile from the house. Again, another potential British record fish wasted by a creature that, because it kills a 20lb fish simply to consume just a pound of its flesh, can only be classed as a wanton, indiscriminate killer.

In my local pub, the Bridge Public House in Lenwade, for instance, which lies adjacent to the River Wensum, is a preserved 16lbs barbel in a glass case that gave historic pleasure to several local anglers before it was found one morning in the shallows with half its head eaten away by an otter. Okay, so the otter is furry and looks cuddly, but then so is a grizzly bear, and we can do without both; but more of otters at the end of this chapter.

SIGNAL CRAYFISH

Meanwhile, down on the very bottom of the river, the exceptionally aggressive signal crayfish is wiping the floor clean, when not helping perch to grow even larger, or providing those who gather them with a tasty meal. Yes, signal crayfish can indeed be harvested to eat. For me, it's definitely a primal 'hunter-gatherer' syndrome. Once or twice each year, I also enjoy a pheasant drive, where I can hunt, kill, prepare, cook, and subsequently eat my own food. I deem it an all-important part of living in the countryside, as indeed is gathering tasty ink-cap and shaggy, parasol mushrooms whenever I can find them, which is probably why many people who live in London's metropolitan area have trouble relating to us country folk.

Finding irreplaceable creatures such as this 16lb River Wensum barbel, dragged up on to the bank where its wanton killer, an otter, had eaten a mere pound of its flesh before abandoning the carcass, makes my blood boil. Fortunately, a local taxidermist came upon it before it was scavenged by a fox.

BARBEL 16lb 2oz
R WENSUM LENWADE NORFOLK 29th NOV 2001

The small plate contains the tails from no fewer than 42 signal crayfish that have been boiled. It's a lot of work, but they do taste marvellous, with far more flavour than prawns.

Alternatively, you can simply take home those huge signals still hanging on to your worm when you retrieve it while fishing for perch. You are supposed to kill them anyway. In fact, it is now illegal to return signal crayfish to the water, whether alive, dead, or even used as bait. They must be taken away and eaten or destroyed, which is kind of sad because it means that even small signal crayfish can no longer be used to catch chub or perch. Pike, of course, love em', too.

Can you just imagine, in this day and age, walking down Oxford Street with a broken 12-bore across the crook of your arm, and a brace of plump rabbits tied with baling twine hanging across your shoulders? The RSPCA would be inundated with irate calls from old dears who think you are cruel to kill what you are about to eat. Yet, so long as it's wrapped in Clingfilm and labelled 'food' when displayed on Sainsbury's shelves, it matters not to whoever consumes it, whether it was killed humanely or suffered a battery existence, so long as the price is right. Cynical? Of course I am.

If you wish to trap crayfish, specialist traps are readily available and a licence, which is free, can be obtained by applying to the Environment Agency, Bromholm Lane, Brampton, Huntingdon PE28 4NE. The Agency simply likes to know in which area you are trapping them. Their national phone line is 0870 850 6506, and if you wish to know more about crayfish in Britain, you can request a most comprehensive 'crayfish pack' from the agency.

Signal crayfish, when boiled in water for five minutes, turn a lovely lobster-red and I know there is a lot of carapace rubbish to dispose of for such a small nibble, but the succulent tail segment can be removed from the shell and served cold on a crisp rocket salad with a light dressing just like prawns. Crayfish tails possess far more flavour, though. Or they can be breaded and deep-fried like scampi, and further complemented by making up a chilli sauce for dipping. You need at least 20 good-sized signals for scampi for two, and twice as many for a salad. Every one you eat is one fewer left to chew at your ledgered lobworm intended for big perch in the future. I cannot think of a better way of getting your own back. Incidentally, those who take the bother of applying for a license to trap crayfish in rivers can expect up to a kilo or two of signals per trap when left overnight. Like everything else to do with the Environment Agency, though, it's a bit of a rigmarole.

Once boiled, hold each crayfish in both hands, with your thumbnails touching, and gently twist to separate head and carapace from the tail end. Then, using a pair of scissors, snip through the underside casing of the tail, and separate the meat from the shell. This leaves the tail with a dodgy-looking dark, end that cannot be eaten. Simply pull it backwards towards the narrow end, with the red side facing upwards, and its alimentary canal should come out all in one piece. Don't leave any of it in or it will taste like the worm you caught it on. This is referred to as 'dead man's finger' to those who dress crabs.

Rinse each tail under the tap and put it into a bowl before popping it into the fridge while you decide how to eat them. You can, of course, make up a quick, tangy sauce from mayonnaise, tomato sauce, or puree, lemon or lime juice, plus black pepper and a little salt. Then, mix them into a giant glass along with chopped tomato, lettuce, and red onion, as a sort of de-luxe crayfish cocktail. There's nothing like impressing your friends. Or, and I do admit to this being my favourite, you can knock up a tempura batter and fry your cray tails, just like those starters you get in Thai restaurants, along with some vegetables such as button mushrooms, slivers of carrot, broccoli florets or anything else you find in this delicious battered vegetable dish. I've even used florets of elderflower when in season, and it's all scrumptious.

Make up a tempura batter by beating an egg yolk with eight fluid ounces of iced water, most important this, and then sieve four ounces of plain white flour into it. Mix well and don't worry that the resulting batter appears lumpy. Heat your vegetable oil to around 180 degrees in a wok, two inches deep should do, and after dipping each tail in the batter and shaking off any excess, lower in a few at a time, cooking each for just two to three minutes. Drain on paper napkins and keep warm until you're ready to eat them.

Lastly, make up a plum/chilli sauce of your choice for dipping. All that work of separating tails from shells will have seemed worth it after all. Incidentally, the 40 or so crayfish in these photos all came one ridiculously mild November day on the Ouse while perch fishing. Half were caught in my fish-baited trap, which I sling out and bring in when leaving, and the rest came to ledgered lobworms, slowly wound in and lifted out, straight into a waiting carrier bag. I didn't catch any perch – I don't always succeed you know - but I did lose two sizeable pike during the dawn to 2pm session. Both felt like reasonable doubles and were taking line when we parted company. By then, I'd had enough. I know they were pike because both bit through the line. Just goes to show how many crayfish there must be on the bottom of the Upper Ouse though, doesn't it?

Is this getting your own back on signals, or what? Tempura-battered crayfish tails, button mushrooms, and broccoli florets with buttered French bread and two different chilli dips. It was all wonderfully delicious.

No wonder we anglers call cormorants the 'black death'. They are fast becoming a worldwide problem as larger and larger concentrations of small sea species are removed commercially, making these predatory sea birds hunt further inland.

CORMORANTS

Now for the creature that, in my book, is the most aggressive alien of all. Along with abstraction and the leeching of farming chemicals that have made the upper rivers over-eutrophic, and thus choked with weeds during the summer months so there are few sandy-bottomed or gravel runs to hold roach, cormorants have largely destroyed the very reason I came to live in East Anglia 40 years ago. The area was then a haven for big river roach, but cormorants have been steadily eating their way through our silver shoal fishes. Conservative MP, Mr Norman Tebbit, once proposed that any cormorant further inland from the coast than five miles should be shot, and how right he was. Why, oh why was this never passed as law!

Until a couple or three decades ago, this ravenous seabird was only seen inland occasionally because, by and large, it is an ocean and estuary bird and far too effective a predator for the cyprinid species inhabiting our clear-flowing, lowland river systems. However, because we - yes the royal 'we', which means each and every country - are slowly raping the planet's seas of small fish, we have only ourselves to blame for the huge and ever-increasing numbers of the 'Black Death' working their way over to Blighty from Europe. Mark my words, even in my own lifetime, the cormorant will eventually be seen as the world problem it already is. Please believe what I'm saying.

I think I first became aware of the devastation cormorants can inflict on our fragile coarse fisheries in the late 1970s when out pike fishing on Ranworth Inner Broad. It is a wildlife reserve and this, I guess, is why the Black Death has been allowed to kill many of the trees surrounding the Broad, through their guano, and to continue to rape the area of its fish. Pike anglers, would you believe, were only allowed to fish there during the last few weeks of the season.

On my first visit, I could not comprehend the sheer number of cormorants roosting in the trees. I even started counting them. I gave up when I got to 300, but pondered that if each bird took but one roach or small bream a day – which is a gross under-estimation of the true number - over 300 fish were disappearing daily. The writing was on the wall, even then, but most of us were blind to the consequences. Nowadays, we know the outcome only too well.

As I write this is early 2010, there has never been more of a case for imposing a national cormorant cull. Obviously, not to totally eradicate this supreme predator, simply to reduce its numbers - a reduction of 90% should do - so that our indigenous silver shoal fishes have a chance to re-establish their numbers, particularly throughout river systems. Surely homegrown shoal fishes have more right to exist than immigrant predators; if not, then we may as well all whistle 'Dixie'.

Believe it or not, I do not hate the cormorant. In fact, I even admire, and rate it very highly indeed as a predatory creature. It is of course too efficient. Would you put a wolf into a pen full of lambs, or a shark into a lagoon full of bream? For those not really convinced of its devastating impact on the demise of silver shoal fish, let's talk numbers. After all, everyone involved, Government and angling clubs alike, requires firm proof of its capabilities, although that wonderful HSBC investment banking advert on TV, where an old Chinese boat fisherman uses a tame and trained cormorant to fill his basket with quite sizeable fish, 1-2lbs carp, is photographic proof enough of how devastatingly effective this predatory seabird is.

According to the RSPB, whose headquarters are in Bedfordshire, Tel: 01767 680551, and the BTO in Thetford, Tel: 01842 750050, the two main organisations covering movements of wild birds throughout the UK, there are around 9000 breeding pairs of cormorants living inland. Now, that may not sound many, but that's some 18,000 birds that each consumes around 1½ lbs of fresh fish daily. Remember, they don't feed on peanuts or fat balls, but live fish. Sadly, this number, despite anglers culling them when and as they can, is actually on the increase. The cormorant population for instance between 1988 and 2002, increased by some 15%, according to the RSPB, but for argument's sake, lets stick to 18,000 birds. They are more than enough, though additional flocks of the Black Death are flying over from Europe to our shores along the east coast, daily, like squadrons of WW2 German bombers.

Also, for argument's sake, let's assume that the 1½ lbs of fish they eat daily - RSPB figures - are 6-7 inch roach weighing around three ounces each. Each cormorant could account for eight roach, daily. Multiply that by 18,000 birds and you arrive at the staggering number of 144,000, three-ounce roach, or the equivalent, being taken from our inland, UK waterways every day!

If that's not catastrophic enough, contemplate if you will, what happens in one calendar year, or when you multiply 144,000 by 365. Those 18,000 strong cormorants will have consumed annually, from our inland waterways, 52,560,000 three-ounce roach. Yes, that's over 52 million small roach, or the equivalent of 26 million six-ounce perch or bream, or over 6 million 1½ lb chub, barbel, roach, or bream. It is truly horrendous and quite frightening, any way you work these figures.

By complete contrast, how many fish do you think are actually stocked by the Environment Agency that we pay our licence money to, trusting they will look after our interests, which, by the statutory law of the land, they are supposed to be doing? Well, taking the country as a whole, in 2009 they stocked just 1,515,000 fish, a large proportion of which were salmonids, over one million, in fact. So if you are a coarse angler, and the majority of the people who buy licences are, a paltry fewer than half a million coarse fish, less than a week's food for the UK's resident 18,000 cormorants, were stocked by the Environment Agency from their fish farms on your behalf during 2009. It's like pissing into the wind, and makes you wonder, doesn't it? Why is it that coarse anglers are continually being made to feel second-class countrymen? Well I'm not, I'm not scared of saying so, and I dearly wish to be long-trotting again for quality roach in my local River Wensum before I pop my clogs.

It would certainly make more sense, and undoubtedly create more prolific fishing, simply to give everyone working for the EA a shotgun and a couple of hundred cartridges. Yes, for all the good this department does, I'm deadly serious. Were they to account for just 1000 cormorants in a year, it would result in nearly three million more three-ounce roach, or 1 ½ million six-ounce roach, bream or chub still alive in our rivers and available to be caught. Make no bones about it, the Environment Agency as it stands at present, with its willy-nilly, head-in-the-sand approach has not got a snowball in hell's chance of ever compensating for the amount of fish

consumed by cormorants now living inland in the UK - hence my plea for a nationwide cull.

For goodness sake, you guys working in Westminster, take this national problem away from the man on the bank, who purchases his license in good faith every year, so we can have some silver shoal fish back in our river systems, for the next generation of our children's children to catch. The present escalating situation is nothing but scandalous; twitchers are not made to buy a licence for their passion, incidentally.

Many of the cormorants live and roost on the islands situated in many of our large man-made reservoirs. Rutland for instance, owned by Anglia Water has over 300 breeding pairs down at the nature reserve end, where their numbers could be reduced easily. Over the years, the existence of these birds has come to affect drastically the quality of even manufactured and stocked fishing, such as in our trout reservoirs.

Nowadays, small trout, that used to grow big and strong on the rich, aquatic insect life, so that by the following winter those not caught would become large, over-wintered bars of silver, are simply not stocked for fear of almost certain cormorant predation. So, for the most part, those lovely, golden days of beautiful, fully-finned, hard-fighting silver fish are gone and have been replaced by much larger, cormorant proof - well almost - stew-fed trout of between 2-3lbs. It's just not the same. The effects of the Black Death are indeed far reaching, leading eventually to there being next to no fry and small fish about, for some of our indigenous water birds like grebes and kingfishers to eat - but more of this cormorant-induced downward spiral later.

I well remember, back in the 1990s, making one of my Go Fishing TV programmes with long time buddy, Bob Church, at Rutland, at a time when this very problem was starting to emerge. At least three-quarters of the 1½ -2lbs rainbows we caught had signs of being grabbed by cormorants, there were horrendous beak marks, and we had trouble presenting fish without scars to the cameras. It was not long after that, Anglian Water changed their stocking policies toward introducing noticeably larger trout, to help bury the cormorant problem under the carpet. Excuse me, but am I missing something here? Why not simply shoot the bloody things?

Unfortunately, as I have personally witnessed over the past three decades, by following the sequence of events that have occurred in an 8-acre lake at the bottom of my garden – it's not my lake I hasten to add - there is a rather more sinister element to the cormorant phenomenon; certainly more than most realise, especially the 'twitching head-in-the-sand fraternity'.

Old pal, Bob Church, and me following a day's filming on Rutland Reservoir back in the 1990s for my long-running Anglia TV series Go Fishing, where most of the trout we caught had been badly marked by cormorants.

With powerful binoculars on the window sill of our kitchen, which overlooks the lake lengthways, my wife Jo and I have seen the lake's prolific stocks of quality roach and rudd, once both always topping during the summer months, slowly reduced virtually to nothing by the continual predation from cormorants. With little to no competition by other cyprinids, save for a handful of big, and old carp, the lake's tench population has obviously benefited, as indeed many have in still waters countrywide. With the entire larder of aquatic insect life to themselves, those tench have, in fact, grown to be enormous, heavier by at least one third. The pike, however, just like their prey food, have diminished, save for a few which seem to eke a living from the eels that enter the lake from the adjacent River Wensum, and I'm

Even this young cormorant had managed to swallow and partly digest eight ounces of roach from my lakes before I shot it at nine o'clock in the morning. As an adult bird it could account for a staggering quarter of a ton of fish annually. That's the equivalent of nearly 3000, six-inch roach.

sad to say, by predating upon far more young waterbirds than pike living in a balanced fishery. This sinister downward spiral is entirely due to cormorant predation.

I wonder how many bird lovers realise what cormorants have been responsible for, because now, when the joy of spring emerges, I am afraid that new clutches of mallards, coots, and moorhens do not last very long. Even young goslings fall foul of the pike, which have little else to eat. As for great crested grebes - I used to love their head-nodding, courting antics - I have not seen a pair on the lake for several years. I'm not surprised, because what would they eat? There are no young shoal fish. The same goes particularly, for kingfishers with no fry to eat, and to a much lesser extent herons, because the latter at least have a far more catholic taste in food, polishing off frogs, toads and newts, voles and mice, young ducklings even, plus the odd lizard and slow worm that crosses their path.

Yes, I'm afraid the lovely, private, and secluded lake, something my eyes see every day of my life, is living proof at the bottom of my garden, and a prime example of what the Black Death is capable of creating. It cannot be put down to fishing pressure here. There are seven cormorants roosting in the tall birch trees between lake and river as I type this.

The River Wensum runs beside this lake. It once held huge shoals of quality roach, plus a few monsters, and was the envy of other river anglers all over England back in the 1970s and '80s. Over the years, it has suffered the same fate and been virtually wiped out by the Black Death. Yet, and here is the anomaly which proves beyond doubt that cormorants are largely to blame for the demise of our silver shoal fish, over on the other side of my house, not 100 yards away, and fed by the same water of the Wensum water table, is my own little, two-lake fishery. Both rudd and roach are prolific, despite the fact that they share the two small lakes, which are joined beneath a bridge and cover less than three acres in total, with wels catfish and a prolific stock of king carp and grass carp to over 20lbs. Why? Why is my little, heavily-stocked fishery full of self-perpetuating roach and rudd, yet the close by 8-acre lake and River Wensum are barren by comparison? Well, it's certainly not rocket science, is it? In the lake and river on one side of the house the cormorants are rarely shot, whereas they are blasted whenever they try to land on my own little fishery.

I wonder when the proverbial penny will drop for the bird-loving fraternity. The knock-on effect of severe cormorant predation upon our indigenous silver shoal fish affects the lives of so many indigenous birds, too. The RSPB, for instance, have sanctioned the culling in the UK of the north-American, blue-beaked, ruddy duck for a number of years now. Why? Because it dares to interbreed with the Spanish white-headed duck. Where? In Britain? Oh no! In Spain, would you believe? Yet, the same organisation keeps its head in the sand continually, by allowing 18,000 cormorants to chomp their way annually through 52 million small, silver shoal species; fish that were once the backbone of our river fishing and the inheritance of our children. Small wonder the majority of freshwater anglers, even though we are bird watchers and bird lovers by nature, have trouble relating to pompous organisations who seem not to be bothered that large concentrations of fry, and small silver shoal fish simply do not now exist in enough numbers, thanks to cormorants, to feed kingfishers and the great crested grebe. It beggars belief, it really does.

If you come across otter prints in the mud along at your local fishery, be it a famed specimen barbel and chub river hot spot, or a stillwater carp haven, start worrying.

OTTERS

Yes, I mentioned earlier that I had more to say about the otter. I dread to think how much money, time and effort this furry, cuddly, big-fish munching, wanton, indiscriminate, killing-machine of a predator, which most stillwater fishery owners, think of as the devil incarnate – and rightly so - has cost my little two-lake fishery, and most of the well-stocked stillwater fisheries around me. During this last decade, I've lost sleep, carp and catfish averaging at least 15lbs apiece.

This is a fishery, incidentally, that I first designed on paper some 25 years ago when the land was just birch scrub and habitat to little other than lichens and super-thin trees all reaching for the sky. I cleared the entire three-acre area by hand with a bow saw; attended and organised the excavation by dragline;

created feature islands and pleasing contours and then lovingly landscaped its many curves, bays and promontories, by planting over 400 trees, which now provide nesting habitats to countless birds. I planted numerous lily roots of cultivated, coloured, and common yellow varieties, before introducing various carp, many of which were mere inches long at the point of stocking.

Therefore, it is particularly galling, 25 years on, to have all that loving work and a life-long dream compromised, and continually destroyed. During the 1990s, Blair's government, urged on by a minority of do-gooders, most of whom in all probability will never clap eyes upon an otter due to their nocturnal habits, decided to ensure that these animals were introduced along many of our river systems. The rivers were already dangerously low in most fish populations, remember, and with the lowest runs of eels, the otter's favourite food, ever recorded. Someone really did their homework on this one, didn't they?

Yes, I have reason enough to want the otter included in this chapter as an aggressive alien, because our river systems are nowhere near so fish and animal-packed, due to cormorants, as they were when otters last existed in the UK, long before their eventual decline in the 1950s. Indeed, it's now not at all difficult to understand why otter hounds were bred, and why otters were considered vermin, and as such hunted by country folk since time immemorial. There were certainly no otters locally in the area when I built my lake, so no one can use the excuse that the otters were there first.

So this member of the mustelid family, which includes wolverines, skunks, polecats, weasels and stoats, may as well be an alien

A classic otter kill. During the night, a near-20lbs common carp has been dragged half way out of the water on one of the islands in my lakes. A pound or so of throat and stomach has been removed, and the rest of the fish abandoned. Wanton? Otters personify the word.

species as far as I'm concerned. It's certainly alien and disastrous to the beautiful environment I have created. The last thing our fish-starved, mainly through cormorant decimation, river systems needed at this present time, is an infusion of predatory otters. Along with mink, and once again we have the good old 'do-gooders' to thank for their release from fur farms into the wild, they constitute one predator too many. Plus there's a risk of contacting Weil's disease, (Leptospirosis) which is a potentially life-threatening infection carried in rat's urine, unless treatment is sought early on, and as a secondary host in the urine of mink, hedgehogs, and I don't doubt, otters.

Is not the otter, apart from its cuddly, misguided Tarka label, not unlike one giant predatory, waterside rat? For heaven's sake do not touch a dead mink or otter without gloved hands, because the disease can easily infect through scratches, cuts, and abrasions. As usual, the do-gooders, who ironically have little chance of ever seeing an otter in the wild unless they stay up all night with expensive, military-style night glasses (and how many idiots do?) have swung the predatory balance completely off the scale within our fragile river systems, with numerous, unscrupulous introductions of otters during these past two decades.

It's not catastrophic enough having cormorants virtually wiping out the middle and lower end of what should be a healthy pyramid of fish, with millions of fry at the bottom, gradually leading up to a few big fish at the top. We are now suffering otters wiping out the largest, and most desirably sized fish of an upside-down pyramid at surprising speed. Do I sound angry? You bet I am. I'm sick to the teeth of being shat upon as a responsible angler. There are close on two million of us who, via our licences, syndicates, clubs and

What was a stunningly coloured, metallic carp before falling foul of 'Tarka'. Note how the tip of its tail has been bitten off; something otters do initially in order to immobilize their prey. This particular fish was one I stocked when just four inches long.

trusts, plus the creation of beautiful and scenic water playgrounds, do more for the wildlife of waterborne and waterside creatures by far than any other faction of society in the UK today; and don't tell me otherwise.

Are these faceless do-gooders planning on reintroducing wolves or bears once the rivers have been completely ruined? At the time of writing, while our upper rivers and many stillwater fisheries are being raped by cormorants and now otters, the do-gooders are at it again. They are introducing beavers into Scotland, and in my local East Anglia, along the Suffolk coastline, they want to introduce the huge, white-tailed, fish-eating sea eagle, which has a wingspan of eight feet. What a great idea! Let's introduce another

These two fresh and bloody scales, which I found one morning 80 yards from the lakes, proved that an otter had been active the previous night. A fox, leaving only these two scales, belonging to at least a double-figure carp, as evidence, had obviously carried off the carcass.

Foxes become aware of otters raping a stillwater carp fishery, and quickly carry the corpse away when the otter has finished. A few scales, as shown in this photo, may be the only evidence you will see, so look carefully.

fish-eating, predatory bird to where we have all but cleared out the stocks of small fish from the sea. Are we eventually to suffer the indignity of old dears having their Jack Russells or Scottie dogs grabbed when walking them along the beach, when the eagles can't find any food? Why do you think cormorants roost and choose to feed inland? Are we to experience local farmers missing numerous young lambs they can ill afford, simply to placate the illogical minds of the do-gooding fraternity?

Incidentally, this particular eagle is exceptionally common in north Norway, where I have spent many wonderful hours photographing and feeding them small fish while cod fishing among the Norwegian fiords, so I do know the score with this particular creature. We are talking about a pristine, wilderness, fish-packed environment there, though, where the eagles live in harmony with people and all other wildlife, because there is more than enough of everything to go round. However, northern Norway is hardly the upper Wensum, or anywhere within the British Isles that is trying to support getting on for 60 million people, is it?

Our country's massive and important leisure industry incorporates two million anglers, who inject over three billion pounds into the economy, and are obliged to pay for a licence, unlike all the others enjoying the waterways and our countryside, such as ramblers, cyclists, canoeists and twitchers. The fact that a relatively small faction of society can influence, and even ruin, the enjoyment for so many others makes me wild.

I'm typing this less than half an hour after taking my usual early-morning stroll with the dogs - and don't believe that old adage, 'otters keep away from where dogs have been', it's a fallacy - around our two-lake carp fishery, the creation of which has consumed over one third of my life. Despite erecting an otter fence, which cost me more than the first house I purchased, along the 'river-only' side of our lakes, from which otters visit because there is little left in the Wensum to eat, I have come across yet more evidence of their chomping my carp. However, there was no carcass dragged up on to the marginal shallows, and until I walked up the steep incline along the western end to the top path, I was relieved, through careful observation of the lake's margins through powerful binoculars, to see that apparently the otters had not been for over a week. I was wrong. Among the leaves in the middle of the path, 80 yards from the lake, were two large and bloody, fresh, scales (I sniffed them) from what could only have been a double-figure carp. How did they get there?

Why don't they just eat eight-ounce roach? There are enough of them in my lakes. This is why I label them wanton, indiscriminate killers! Well, the order of events following an otter eating a small amount of flesh from the large carp they seem to prefer, dragged halfway out of the water, is for a fox to sniff it out, usually the next evening, although sometimes within minutes of the otter leaving the kill, and to drag it away. Although foxes will take off with carcasses so rotten your nostrils hurt, unless fishery managers, owners and club secretaries check the margins of their fisheries meticulously each morning, they might never suspect the work of otters. Sometimes, however, great piles of scales depict the obvious. Yes, I guess I've become a bit of a Poirot over the years.

If most of the stock are leather or only partly-scaled mirror carp, or catfish, then there will be little evidence to see, but what happens eventually is that foxes get used to otters providing them with free carcasses from well-stocked carp fisheries during the colder months of the year, when the river larder is at its most bare. They are out patrolling the same lakeside routes and I follow their paw prints in the snow. The foxes look for them purposefully and cart them away from carp lakes and pits, long before dawn breaks.

So, the evidence of a partly-eaten carp is not actually seen, and all you can hope for is a few scales among the leaves as evidence; which is exactly why I was nearly fooled this morning. How far will a fox drag or carry a partly eaten otter kill? Well, a good friend of mine owns a local golf course, beside which runs a superb, winding stretch of the River Wensum, further downstream between Taverham and Ringland. He has mentioned to me on several occasions, that he has found big, partly-eaten chub to over 6lbs, dumped inexplicably, right in the middle of the fairways; sometimes half a mile from the river. His early morning golfers had obviously scared off Mr Fox.

Perhaps the saddest facet of the otter in its role as a wanton, indiscriminate killer, to fishery owners in particular, is like that of the fox, which goes through a chicken run and damages or kills many of them in its fervour, when it only needs one to eat. In well-stocked fisheries, such as my own for instance, the otter will often maul, maim, and play with several large carp before one is killed, then partly eaten, and left. If that is not the meaning of the word 'wanton', I don't know what is. At least with chickens the cost of replacing them is nothing compared to replacing just one big carp. So in my book, otters are actually worse news than foxes.

Those carp or other large fish that are lucky and manage to slip away having just parts of their fins bitten off - to immobilise their prey, otters often chew off a large part of the tail - can and often do live to take your bait another

A prime time for getting out there to look for otter prints is when a couple of inches of snow cover the banks. These came from beside a favourite Wensum millpool during the most severe 2009-2010 winter, when the pool was badly 'ottered'.

day by regenerating their missing fin parts. This is something I like to point out to my guests when they catch such a carp from my own carp fishery. A lighter, thinner, edging of the fin tissue, the regenerated part, can be distinguished easily from the ragged original fin. Many of the chub I catch from the River Wensum and Waveney in these troubled times can be distinguished in the same way as having been rather lucky otter escapees. Sadly, it is something I find myself constantly noticing and thus looking for these days.

Then there are the fish that are not so lucky, having been bitten and played about with so badly, that should they get away, simply sink to the bottom where they slowly die, gas-up and float to the surface as 'stinkers' a couple of weeks later. The majority of these, should they drift into the bankside, most fishery owners never see, because along comes Mr Fox, having sniffed them out, to carry them away. Believe me, foxes will drag anything away no matter how decomposed it is. So, do not make the mistake of assuming that all dead carp that float to the surface or beneath ice, have died through natural causes. This is the case with some diseased fish, whose condition has lain dormant all winter, due to low water temperatures and subsequently the fish's low metabolic rate, but kills the fish when temperatures rise in the early spring. This is a natural phenomenon, and completely different to otter maiming.

Incidentally, here's something fellow 'otter-sufferers' like me might like to try. Like most good things in our household, it is the brainchild of my wife, Jo, bless her, who suggested, as otters do not seem to like hunting when humans are around, that we give the impression of people talking, together with lights shining out over the lakes. So I rigged up an old but powerful radio outside the cedarwood summer house, to which we had fortunately already run electricity, situated halfway between the two lakes. So that from dusk till dawn, lights are shining out, while the radio blares away all night with Talk Sport. From nearly 100 yards away, you can hear the drone of inane chatter from grown men about whether there's enough room on David Beckham's body for another tattoo, or whether Wayne Rooney prefers porridge or a fried egg in the morning. It's all enough to make the likes of John Charles and Bobby Moore turn over in their graves. Sorry, it's that angry old man in me again.

We have suffered just one otter kill - they obviously can't stand it either - while all this is going on. Otters seem to hunt carp and catfish in our stillwaters at the coldest part of the winter, from December through until March, when the river larder is particularly bare. It's been over a month, now, of chatter and lights around the two lakes so even taking the cost of electricity or batteries for two to three months, I doubt it would accumulate to

The badly ravaged tail from an escapee 6lbs bream caught from a local millpool. However, in time, even fin tissue as bad as this will be regenerated, providing the bream does not meet Mr Otter again.

even the cost of replacing just one big carp. It's certainly worth trying.

Even with fisheries not close to the road, and where the owner or club/syndicate members do not live close by, I'm sure that for the sake of their fishing they could arrange a rota system. For just a few months of the year, someone has the job of turning on the radio and the lights at dusk and putting them off again at dawn. It will certainly get someone about to monitor daily at least what happens around the lake during the coldest part of the winter. It may not even work on other fisheries, but anything's worth trying if it helps avoid the carnage by otters to fish you have looked after for 20 years, lying there with their stomachs open. It makes you feel like crying.

Sadly, some carp-based fisheries are targeted by otters all year through, and the owners certainly have my sympathy, whereas my own small fishery is worst hit at the coldest time of the year, from December through till March. I guess when the nearby River Wensum starts fining down after winter flooding and becomes easier to hunt in; when all kinds of furred and feathered riverside creatures start to come out of the winter doldrums to reproduce, otters will then direct their attention to amphibians and particularly water birds and their new-laid eggs or newly-hatched young. Oh yes, these are all gobbled up by this marauding killing machine; sadly, do-gooders really do not have a clue.

What recompense does the good old Environment Agency offer to the hundreds, possibly thousands, of fishery owners who have suffered through first cormorants and now otters destroying their stocks and life's work? A paltry £100,000 for the erection of otter fences to fisheries with public access. That's not to each fishery for the enormous amount of money it costs to replace a stock of say 30-50, 10-30lbs carp, (at a conservative estimate anywhere between £10-£30,000) plus the price of erecting a suitable fence. That £100,000 represents the total amount available throughout the entire country! That's it – the lot. This is just about enough to benefit a handful of fisheries in total. Really makes you feel as though your licence money is being well spent, and that the EA is fighting on your behalf, doesn't it? No, it bloody doesn't. It's almost laughable, except that it genuinely makes me want to cry.

Make no bones about it, and I would dearly, honestly, love to be proved wrong, most of the middle order shoal fish such as dace, roach, skimmer bream, and rudd have already been decimated by the Black Death, so in quality fishing, albeit now in adult specimen fish only, much of the upper river fishing, as we have come to love and to know it in this country, has but a few years left before it's all completely eaten out.

Following a total demise of upper rivers, man-made and man-managed, stillwater carp fisheries won't be far behind as otters move further afield for their food, as indeed they are already doing. The consequences we are now facing are truly horrendous and mind-boggling. We are fast approaching an angling Armageddon unless something drastic is done about cormorants and otters.

Ironically, I attended a most important and what I truly believe will go down as a most historic meeting on Thursday 11th March 2010 in Newbury, Berkshire, hosted by the shadow minister for Environment, Fisheries and Wildlife, and the Member of Parliament for Newbury, Richard Benyon MP, which amid all the present gloom, really gave me hope.

Steve Partner and photographer, Lloyd Rogers, from Angling Times were present to record the dialogue offered by Martin Bowler, Chris Logsdon, Tim Norman and I, about how cormorants and otters have just about cleared out the larder of so many of our freshwater fisheries - of our angling future, no less. I believe the new Conservative coalition government, formed at the general election on May 6th 2010, will finally start to put the wishes and dreams of Britain's two million anglers into action. I certainly do hope so.

Incidentally, because of the severity of the predatory problems facing freshwater fishing in the UK, Martin Bowler and I have been working behind the scenes, with political intent, now for almost a year. Together with Ruth Lockwood of ECHO, Korda Tackle guru, Danny Fairbrass, and broadcaster Keith Arthur and others, including the Angling Trust, we hope that we can stem the tide of destruction. For those who wonder whether I am actually Martin's uncle or not, let me set the record straight here once and for all. When the mood takes him, when we are together at functions and suchlike, he jokingly refers to me as 'Uncle John' because his granddad, the late Joe Bowler, who first took me trotting, was in fact my uncle, which actually makes us second cousins.

This has become rather confused over the years by the fact that because my kids, which are the same age, called Martin's dad, John, 'Uncle John', when they were young, while John's four kids, including Martin, called me Uncle John. If you are not confused now you certainly should be. Anyway, I have always thought of Martin as more of a son than a second cousin or nephew, and I'm immensely proud of his angling achievements, which have prospered without the slightest help from me. In fact, he has helped me enormously along the way by laying on superb perch, rudd and barbel locations for my Anglia TV Go Fishing programmes.

A unique meeting indeed. Angling gurus, the angling press and a politician get together prior to the 2010 election. Left to right: Me, Tim Norman, Martin Bowler, Richard Benyon, Conservative MP for Newbury, Steve Partner of Angling Times and Chris Logsdon.

I was immensely proud to be invited along, and to be part of his and Hugh Miles's 'Catching the Impossible' TV series, and actually catching a badly needed big pike for the camera from Oulton Broad. In fact, he still calls me a jammy old sod - but I have digressed here.

Personally, I would like to go back to a government department dedicated, as the National River Authority was when the Conservatives were last in power, and do away with the Environment Agency, whose mandate for fishing covers less than 10 per cent of its work anyway. Flood defences, sewerage and drainage are not angling directives, so let's have a 'National Rivers and Lakes Authority' - not a bad title eh? - that truly understands and is fully dedicated to the importance of water being the precious, and finite resource that it is, and to all those creatures living within it.

Let's have an authority that truly understands, respects and values the importance of angling as a giant of a leisure sport, or fieldsports industry, call it what you will, and just how important and valuable our impact is upon society in general. Angling doesn't generate fishing hooligans, for instance, or yobs that terrorise housing estates. Neither is it grossly in debt as are most football clubs at the top. Our contribution to the national wealth is worth billions. We are two million placid, caring people and environmentalists of the very highest order. So why are we anglers not consulted upon all the issues that directly affect us and our sport? I continue to live in hope and my fingers are crossed, for the end of Blairism and the nanny state.

CAPTURE THE FISH – CAPTURE THE MOMENT

I've said on many occasions over the years, if I was some way from home when I suddenly realised I'd forgotten my bait, I'd probably carry on driving to my destination and then gather some natural baits in the form of caddis grubs, worms, slugs, or pop into a shop and buy a loaf of bread on the way there. Whereas, if I'd left my cameras at home, God forbid, I would feel compelled to return for them, whatever the distance. Now, while this may seem strange to some, it perhaps illustrates how important photography is to my fishing, and indeed has been through over half a century.

I guess it all started in the early 1950s really. I was born in 1943, when Dad parted with his old wartime Box Brownie so I could capture whatever I was catching from the River Lea and local park lakes, which were my nearest fishing spots to our flat in Enfield, North London, at that time. This was then replaced with a variety of cheapies, all taking black and white, 127 negative film, of course, before I bought my first 35mm camera, from Boots, called an Halina.

This little, Italian made I believe, all metal camera actually produced some passable results, especially with colour transparency film. By this time I was around 15 years old and taking fishing photography seriously, with

a growing collection of slides and a projector. I even went on, a year later, to give my club, The Enfield Town Angling Society, yearly film shows of both my own and the club's exploits. I dumped the Halina however when I tried Ilfachrome colour transparency film and found that due to the film's thick emulsion, it became shredded when simply winding on. In retrospect, I think the back plate in the Halina, used for controlling film portage, was just too fierce. Obviously, its manufacturers had not tried all films before putting it on the market. My favourite colour transparency film in those days was Agfacolor.

Over 50 years ago, I took this colour transparency shot of the enchanting, evocative and diminutive River Rib in Hertfordshire, using an all metal, 35mm Halina camera. You could say that was when the photographer in Wilson was born.

No automatic, electronic wind-on in those days, remember, nor automatic focus or exposure. You had to calibrate suitable shutter speed with the correct F-stop (aperture) by using a hand-held light meter; and for those who have grown up with modern, 'point-and-shoot' digital masterpieces, if all this seems like steam radio, you could not be closer to the truth.

Obtaining great fishing pics 50 years ago was indeed an

Yes, this was flash photography back in the dark ages (no pun intended) with nothing automatic or dedicated. A simple reflector-type flashgun and removable, one-shot flash bulbs.

art, and one that you had to work really hard at. So much depended upon various light conditions, the quality of your camera, film speed – that's the speed at which the film accepted light during the shutter opening and closing, rated in speeds from 25 ASA up to 1000 ASA - and whether or not you could go through the soul-destroying function of adding 'fill-in' or 'full flash'. It was a case of disposable flash bulbs in those days, which lasted but one shot, and the spent bulb was removed from the flashgun, before inserting another for the next shot.

Things improved greatly with the appearance of battery-operated, electronic flash units, but in the early days these were not dedicated to any particular camera, and you had to calibrate all sorts of combinations of shutter speed, film speed, and F-stops to obtain desirable results. I dread to think of the wasted hours and money I could then ill-afford, spent trying to capture good, poor-light photos of big roach, for instance, due to the flash 'over-cooking' those highly reflective scales of the roach, which invariably started to feed only when the light was going. I then went through several basic

35mm, split-image cameras with built-in range finders, mostly German, with excellent lenses, before purchasing my first single-lens reflex camera.

It was by now the late 1960s, incidentally, and the camera was a Minolta SR 7, which, because I could look through the actual lens, and see whether the subject was in sharp focus or not, took me to a new level of photography. It had neither a functional exposure mode, nor pop-up, built-in flash, like most of today's excellent and inexpensive, middle of the road 35mm SLRs, but the guy who sold it to me, second-hand, included a 135mm telephoto lens to clinch the deal, which also took me on to a new level of appreciation. I could blur-out the background so that the subject, someone with a fish, stood out magnificently; 135mm telephoto lenses were at the time, and probably still are, considered the lens for child portrait photography.

Before pressing the shutter, always think about how you see the photo in your mind's eye. Would the subject matter be best displayed in a horizontal (landscape) format as in the smaller pic opposite? Or in this larger, portrait pic, where ducks grace the foreground?

Of course, good photography, be it fishing or any other subject matter, is about first seeing and imagining what you wish to capture in your mind's eye, before even taking the camera out of its case. The actual framing of the photo is all-important, whether you see the subject best taken lengthways, (landscape) or in an upright frame (portrait), and this will depend on the subject matter. For instance, if you simply want to capture someone holding the fish they have just caught, then get in and completely fill the frame. Forget all the clutter around them. I see so many so-called trophy photos, which also include all the angler's tackle items spread haphazardly around the swim, or the rod cutting across the back of the angler's chair, or worse still, positioned upwards so it looks as though it's sticking out the back of his head.

Sure, you can sometimes crop out all the unwanted bits afterwards, but this reduces picture size and will show in lack of clarity

This landscape framed pic certainly gives a better idea of the location being fished, which is Hellesdon Mill Pool on the River Wensum near Norwich, but is it what you 'see' in your mind? Photography poses many alternatives.

when you come to enlarge the image. It may then appear nowhere near as sharp. So think seriously about every photo opportunity, and get it right straight away. Put the subject bang in the middle of the frame and then come as close as you dare, remembering to keep the horizon level. Try framing the subject from varying heights; at eye level, from bending down, or kneeling, and above all, keep the camera steady as you press the shutter part way down to focus, before pressing all the way.

Are you looking for a wide, purely scenic shot, for instance? Or perhaps the photo includes someone playing a fish, (where the wide-angle lens, due to its depth of field ensures everything is in focus) and where things like rod movement and jumping fish, or fish crashing on the surface, need to be taken into account. For the latter shot, a fast shutter speed is vital in order to 'freeze' the action. Fortunately, most modern cameras, even point-and-shoot models, have 'sports' or action modes to facilitate this. Coming into photography the hard way, so to speak, angling photographers of my generation will know full well when to increase the ISO number, that's the equivalent of what we used to call ASA or film speed. This enables the camera to capture action shots by increasing shutter speed combined with a high F-number in order to freeze all movement within a fair depth of field, something which is really only worthwhile in good light conditions, incidentally; most important, this.

TROPHY SHOTS

Even while playing a big fish that you will obviously want a trophy shot of, think about an attractive background that is nicely and evenly lit, not full of contrasting shadows, where a trophy shot can best be taken, preferably with water in the frame. It will look so much better. Choose somewhere, which in addition to your prize fish will also give an idea of the type of location from where it was caught, and actually tell a story; a beautiful river, a tranquil lake, a busy canal or whatever. One photo has the opportunity of saying so many things.

With user-friendly sized fish like roach, perch, chub, tench, bream, trout or bass, it's usually possible to show your specimen, plus where it was caught, with the fish in one hand and the rod and reel in the other, and on exactly what tackle. Alternatively, the modern carping trend of photographing a whopper being held against the background of a ploughed field, barbed wire fence or patch of vegetation so no one can possibly work out where the fish was caught, is rather sterile to say the least.

Unless the light and conditions are absolutely horrific at the time of capture, torrential rain, for instance, don't be tempted to sack your fish up for photographing later. Think about a trophy shot immediately after capture. Following a hard fight, the fish will be completely knackered and perfect for holding up to the camera; unlikely to jump around and wipe its protective slime all over you or fall and injure itself. In fact, there is no better time for taking a photo than immediately after capture. It will be less hassle for you and far less stress for the fish, compared to leaving it in a tube or sack for an hour whereby it will have regained its strength and then be almost impossible to hold still. Simply leave it in the water, in the landing net, in the margins while getting the camera ready, and return it immediately after the photo session.

A species that is particularly difficult to photograph, because it always seems to find the strength to jump out of your arms, is the Asiatic grass carp. My advice here is to play the fish to a standstill and then hold it upside-down in your arms until the person taking the photo is ready. This has the result of immobilising all fish, incidentally, try it and see. Then quickly, turn it up the right way and fire off a shot or two.

By comparing the drawings of holding and photographing trophy fish using a wide-angle lens, you will see that holding the fish out a little to the right or the left, B, provides a pleasing format for a landscape shot, as opposed to A, merely holding the fish straight out in front of you. Always be choosy in showing its most photogenic side, without lost scales or blemishes, and without a blade of grass or a leaf stuck on its chin and spoiling the set-up.

HOLDING FISH FOR
TROPHY SHOTS

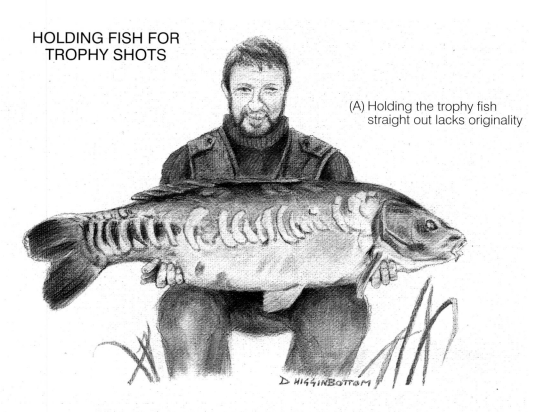

(A) Holding the trophy fish
straight out lacks originality

(B) Hold fish a little to the left or
right – showing its most
photogenic side

A trophy shot is capable of saying so many things. Take this lovely bream I'm displaying, caught from a River Wensum weir pool, for instance. It was caught while trotting with a float, hence the centrepin reel.

In photograph C, however, by standing, the photographer is too much above the subject. In D, the camera is possibly too straight on and results in a rather basic shot. Whereas in E, with the cameraman kneeling down so the camera lens is closest to, and almost below, the fish, the trophy will be shown to its largest, most beautiful size, with the smiling captor behind, still in focus. Sometimes it helps if the captor moves his head slightly forward with this shot, and smiling behind your fish, as opposed to giving a grim expression as though you wished you'd never caught the thing in the first place, goes without saying. Try taking four different shots of the same angler and fish, from four different heights: standing upright, bending at the hip, kneeling, and then literally lying on the ground. The results will amaze you.

Yes, wide-angle lenses, with their massive and most forgiving, enormous depth of field are a real boon to taking 'wow' trophy shots; as are built-in 'pop-up' flash units. I must admit to using the pop-up flash on my 35mm digital, Nikon D200 most of the time. It's as though it was built for the inclement and contrasting light problems of our sport. Even during the brightness of a summer's day, rarely is it that most photos won't be improved by a little fill-in flash. It helps enormously in flattening out those horrible shadows created by the peak of a cap or hat, or shadows cast from bankside foliage and trees, for which your own eyes have automatically, already compensated but the camera lens cannot. It needs to be helped along.

For most fishing situations, I tend to keep the flash permanently on, even with my little point-and-shoot digital camera which is a Panasonic Lumix DMC-TZ7, a model I purchased when starting to write this book.

(C) In order to obtain a good trophy shot I'm purposely standing too far above the subject matter, which, in this shot, is brother Dave holding a colourful red tail catfish, caught from the Monsters Lake near Bangkok in Thailand. There is just too much background information.

(D) By bending down and getting lower, this is perhaps passable as a nice trophy shot, but again, the background information is competing with the fish for recognition.

(E) Now, by kneeling low down, slightly below the fish to take the shot, its mouth and whiskers become more visible and pronounced, as does its sheer bulk. You can still see it was caught from a lake, but the fish's statistics are more pronounced.

Left to right, husband and wife team John and Jenny Alton from Shrewsbury, help Canadian guide Tony Nootebos to hoist Jenny's 170lbs white sturgeon for a trophy shot. A pic I captured on her Panasonic Lumix, ultra-wide angle TZ7. It's such a fabulous little 'point-and-shoot', I bought one myself.

I'd been out for two weeks to the Fraser River in Canada's British Columbia, as I do annually, escorting a party of Brits sturgeon and salmon fishing out from Harrison Hot Springs. I happened to mention to one of the guests, Jenny Alton, from Shrewsbury, that to photograph her 170lb sturgeon, which guide, Tony Nootebos, had dutifully heaved into the boat - all seven feet of it! - and was helping to support it with Jenny and husband John, I would have to hang out the end of the boat to capture its full length on her little point-and-shoot. She replied, "No you won't, John. It's got a wide-angle lens."

I was flabbergasted, and so impressed that I purchased one within a week of arriving back home. Until then, point-and-shoot cameras were not produced with wide-angle lenses. The front cover of this book was in fact taken with my TZ7. It has a massive, three-inch, unbelievably crisp, LCD.monitor screen, and its 10,000,000 pixels performance, coupled to the 25mm ultra-wide-angle lens, produces truly amazing results. Like many of today's point-and-shoots, it also has a motion picture (HD video) mode with zoom functions available even during recording. That's not what I purchased it for, though, and besides I already have a professional video camera. Its ultra-wide-angle lens was what I wanted.

The Lumix TZ7's 'auto-intelligent' mode automatically adjusts the optimum focus and brightness based on the movement of the subject via 'AF'. Tracking when taking stills, I truly wonder at times why I lug around a heavy camera bag full of Nikon gear to the tune of several thousand pounds. In truth, on many short fishing sessions, or where I have a long walk ahead, I now do not, and rely totally upon my Lumix TZ7. I suppose I'm a masochist at heart, though, and of course I love the variety of shots from lenses of varying focal lengths, so a telephoto lens is always in my bag along with the 12-24mm wide-angle that I tend to keep on the D200 because I use it more often when making long trips.

For anyone who enjoys, and does as much boat fishing as I do, a wide-angle lens is vital. Incidentally, don't encourage scratches to appear on your LCD screen by leaving it unprotected. Companies such as DuraSec (www.durasec.com) produce precise-fitting, wafer-thin, ultra-clear screen protectors, cut to fit most cameras.

While talking about camera protection, waterproof gear specialists Overboard (www.overboard.com) produce some excellent waterproof cases for both cell phones and compact cameras. Their small camera case, ideal for digital compacts with zoom lenses, (stock No OB1052BLK) has transparent sides which allows you to take pictures in and under water, while at the same time keeping your camera safe from mud, grit, sand, water splash and anything else you don't want on, or in, it. It operates by simply sliding the locking switches outward to open the case, and then sliding them back to seal the unit once the camera is inside. It has a screw-thread, removable, rubberised outside lens housing, incorporating a glass front for optimum results and comes supplied with a neck lanyard, so you can keep your camera safe while 'rock fishing' in the ocean, for instance, yet it's immediately accessible and usable the second you need it. This great piece of kit, perhaps most importantly of all, also floats.

Unfortunately, the end of my Lumix TZ7, when extended and ready for use, comes way short of the front of the lens housing, resulting in only the middle of the frame being seen in a circular format. The remainder is black, being obscured by the end of the lens housing.

It's handy to have a waterproof case for your little point-and-shoot if you wish to take shots like this. Friends shark fishing off the rocks along Namibia's famous Skeleton Coast in south-west Africa.

So to take a frame without this, I need to unscrew the housing cap, which solves the problem but of course leaves the camera open to water splash. The Overboard case however does fit my little Exilim Casio digital camera without any masking. The main reason I purchased the waterproof case initially, was simply to keep the camera dry when boat, surf, or rock fishing, so it earns its keep nevertheless.

Unfortunately, no camera can possibly do everything. Even the Lumix TZ7, when it comes to self-timer photography, is rather limited. I can only take one frame at a time when in the 'self-timer' mode, and this has to be reset after each frame; not exactly great when much of your fishing is on your own. Camera manufacturers please note. On the other hand, my previous point-and-shoot, a now ancient Exilim, Casio of just 4 mega-pixels, has a great self-timing function. It can fire off up to three frames at ten-second intervals, which usually means that by the time I pick the fish up and hold it nicely towards the camera, the first shot is invariably wasted. The next two, however, are usually well usable, many having appeared in my books over the last few years. So there we are. Choose carefully when selecting a new camera, always opting for functions geared specifically to your personal needs.

Incidentally, whenever you need to take a picture of yourself with a trophy fish, select a nice location that is well, and evenly, illuminated. Push a telescopic bank stick into the ground and extend to roughly the point above which you intend to hold your fish. Then set the camera up a few feet away, in wide-angle mode to ensure maximum depth of field, on a tripod, monopod, or simply another bank stick into which a camera screw thread adaptor that accepts the thread in the base of your camera has been screwed. With

the camera set in manual mode, focus sharply on the top of the extended bank stick.

Prepare for the shot by kneeling behind the stick pretending you are holding a fish just above the bank stick and even rattle off a few shots to see if all is within the frame. When it is, lower the top of the bank stick, to below the bottom of the frame, press the shutter, and trust you will be smiling and holding the fish exactly side-on to the lens, and just above the bank stick at the sharp focus point when the camera fires.

Cameras, which can fire off three shots at 10-second intervals give you the best results by far. Some cameras really do make life easier. The DSLR Lumix DMC G1, for example, is probably the best all-round angling bet for someone who does not already own an SLR. With a choice of interchangeable lenses and weighing up to 55% less than conventional systems, it makes self-photography so incredibly simple by having an LCD screen which pulls out to the side and revolves to the front. This screen actually rotates 180 degrees horizontally, and 270 degrees vertically, so that you can visually confirm that everything you want in the shot is within the frame before pressing the shutter/time delay button. So, smiling to order is simplicity itself.

Available for all Digital DSLR cameras, except Olympus, is an incredibly innovative and clever piece of kit produced by Zigview (www.zigview.co.uk Tel: 0118 979 0713) which consists of a separate 3-inch LCD screen connected to several yards of cable which plugs into your SLR camera, allowing you to set up a self-take photo, trophy or even an action shot by the same means. You simply arrange the shot with the LCD screen at your feet, out of view, and when happy with the shot, you press the shutter/time delay on the display panel. There are various time delay options, from a quarter of a second up to one hour, and you can preset how many shots you wish the camera to take. There are various dedicated models for different cameras, but don't make the mistake I did by ringing up either Canon or Nikon for advice; they will simply say there is no such accessory available.

ACTION PHOTOGRAPHY

While your big fish is waiting patiently in the net in the margins for you to set up a trophy shot, it just happens to be in the perfect position for re-enacting an action pose, with little extra stress upon the fish. Whatever your camera, simply hold your rod in your right hand, if that's how you played the fish, while gripping halfway along each side of the landing net frame in each hand, then lift steadily upwards as though you are about to hoist the fish ashore on to the unhooking mat, water dripping, and all.

You can look pleased with yourself or even give the camera a smile, but try not to mask your face with your elbow or landing net pole, depending on how you feel at the time. Standing sideways on to the camera or by having the photographer come down to the water's edge, the best light option will dictate which, creates great atmosphere, particularly if the cameraman bends or kneels down almost to water level, and the fish in the net is held slightly closer to the camera. The wide-angle lens is, again, of paramount importance here for depth of field alone.

To create another great action shot, an 'action trophy still' really, the captor needs to be able to wade crutch-deep into the river or lake from where the big fish was caught, so barring those rare UK heatwaves, far more opportunities arise to those who fish abroad

and target big fish in tropical freshwater. This really is a big fish photo opportunity for any monster that can just about be held comfortably, supported by both arms in front of the body - say whoppers weighing between 60-100lbs. Anything larger is difficult for the average man to deal with, believe me. So go on, choose a scenic location and give it a try.

The secret, once comfortably holding your prize fish - you're standing crutch-deep remember - is to bend at the knees until the fish's belly and fins dip beneath the surface, and then quickly stand upright, remembering to keep smiling at the camera. As you do this, water will cascade from the fish and if 'frozen' will give the shot unbelievably great action, providing the cameraman is also in the water, with the camera held mere inches above the surface and quite close, using a wide-angle lens for maximum depth of field. An example is this memorable 92lb Indian mahseer that I'm just about managing to hold, caught by Andy Davison's camera back in the 1980s. Yes, I know only too well, that's nearly 30 years back - just look at the colour of my hair!

Using a continuous, high-speed shutter, sometimes referred to as motor drive, where between 5-7 frames per second are fired off, as the fish is hoisted up each at somewhere between 700th to 1000th of a second, depending upon the available light and how far the ISO speed is increased, produces some really classy images. Usually, only top of the range SLR cameras will have this function. If your particular SLR cannot work its shutter at continuous high speed, you will have to make do by taking just the one shot as the fish is lifted, at exactly the right time. This is not impossible but, of course, it will still need to be taken in the middle of the sequence, with a shutter speed of somewhere between 700th to 1000th of a second. Enjoy experimenting.

To capture this fabulous action shot of me hoisting a 92lbs golden mahseer, caught from the Cauvery River in South India, for Andy Davison's camera, a fast shutter speed with the camera on motor drive, now referred to as continuous high speed shutter, was vital.

In the land of the Pharaohs, international British shooter, Matt Hance, gets help from Egypt's Lake Nasser guide, Mohammed, to haul a tiger fish clear of the surface. It had grabbed his deep-diving plug in front of the temples at Abu Simbel. Fast shutter speeds here are essential.

Earlier, I mentioned that even digital point-and-shoot cameras have either sports or action modes which increase shutter speed automatically so that fast-moving action, like a jumping fish for instance, is frozen. Well, they are some of the time at least! I say this because if you wish to get into action angling shots, then you really need an SLR with a variety of functions. Even the most expensive and function-packed, digital point-and-shoot models do not compare, especially when it comes to zoom shooting; a separate telephoto lens and quality SLR body being essential for rewarding results.

When trying to focus on a moving subject such as an acrobatic fish, a tarpon, sturgeon, Nile perch, tigerfish, sailfish, or even a pike, it is immensely important that your SLR has an auto focus dynamic-area. If used with continuous-servo AF, (continuous high speed shutter release) it will follow erratically moving subjects, which would otherwise be difficult to keep in focus. It's a useful mode with which to shoot acrobatic fish, but as I mentioned previously, in order to shoot at between 700-1000th of a second, or even faster to 'freeze' some fish, while also selecting a high F-number to ensure maximum depth of field, the ISO number will need to be increased substantially. In poor light situations this is just not on, as you'll raise the ISO so high, that noticeable noise - called 'grain' in the old days when shooting with film - will impair the results.

So as a rule of thumb, only bother with high-speed action photography in reasonably good light. Don't bother if it's dull and overcast. In such conditions, I simply put the camera down and get on with my fishing.

SUNSETS AND SUNRISES

One of the great things about fishing is that it often gets you there out in the open, at exactly the time when Mother Nature decides to be at her most bountiful and artistic. In certain situations, sunrise and sunsets in particular, this angler happily misses out on perhaps another fish, just when they are about to throw caution to the wind and start biting aggressively, in order to capture beautiful events. Trouble is, the automatic-exposure mode of your camera, most cameras, in fact, can be easily caught out when trying to capture sunrises and sunsets, because it detects more light around than there actually is. Again, your eyes have adjusted to the situation, while the camera hasn't.

At such times, my advice is to add at least one stop, that's opening up the lens one photographic stop, to accept more light during shutter function, by putting the camera into 'program' or 'normal picture' mode, and using the exposure compensation to add at least +1. The exposure compensation facility usually offers up to -2 or +2 in either 1/3 or 1/2 EV divisions. So it's well worth playing about with various settings always on the + side - you want to give the shot more light, remember, during the shutter function, until your sunrise/sunset shots look good.

Digital photography is not going to cost you a fortune in film stock, as it did yours truly over the years; but then I did learn mountains of useful stuff along the way. Being able to experiment has certainly always worked for me, as I hope this selection of photos proves. Incidentally, if creating a black, silhouette effect of an angler in the foreground, where the sky is beautifully coloured, you can actually accentuate the density of colour in the sunset by using the exposure compensation

The Zambezi River that bisects much of Zimbabwe from Zambia, is arguably the most photographic sunset location on our planet.

Captured by the camera of pike guru, Jason Davies, during a magnificent sunrise, here I am playing a big fish along the Cut-off channel in Norfolk, highlighted by a little fill-in flash.

facility to come down a stop to -1. Again, experimenting will give you the knowledge and skills you need.

To me, and I've been lucky enough to fish the world over now for many years, the most evocative, inspirational and easily the most breathtakingly beautiful sunsets I have ever seen, in shades of red, orange and purple, have been on Lake Kariba, also called the Kariba Dam. This separates Zambia in the north from Zimbabwe in the south, once named North and South Rhodesia, respectively. It is, of course, none other than Africa's Zambezi River, dammed for 170 miles, where, after flooding in the 1950s, it created one of the planet's largest man-made lakes. Few of the hardwood trees were felled and it is these, now leafless, forms, called 'the sticks' by the locals, protruding high above the tranquil surface of the lake almost in petrified form like preying monsters, which help to create the most wonderful foreground montage to the mother of all sunsets.

By the same token, helped by being in the right place at the right time, I have experienced some truly wonderful British sunrises and sunsets. Occasionally, throughout my local River Wensum valley, for instance, which is interspersed with hundreds of island-studded gravel pits, some marvellous opportunities arise, yet usually for a few moments only. You simply have to be ready when it happens, forgetting all thoughts of fishing by opening up a stop here and a stop there, half a stop - sometimes even two stops - to capture those rare few seconds of what Mother Nature has to offer. When you come to think about it, it's not so different from fishing itself, is it? If you are not there to capitalise on

certain fish feeding at a certain time, then you won't enjoy success, will you?

One more tip I'd like to pass on when endeavouring to capture sunsets is to look for any kind of foreground objects that will give extra character and texture, such as trees for instance. In the tropics, palm trees kind of say it all, whereas birds, boats, or the silhouette of a lone angler in the margins or along the shore, all add to the beauty of the sun rising or setting while telling their own story. Boats, both at anchor and moving along, also really help to make the shot come alive, as does the casting angler, even as a silhouette when framed close to where the sun's reflection hits the surface. A little thought, the right equipment, and a willingness to experiment and learn your photographic trade, will not only improve your photos – it will dramatically increase your angling enjoyment.

An evocative sunrise along the Wensum Valley in the village of Elsing, at Three Bridges Farm lakes, not far from my home. Fortunately, I was there at 4.30 on a summer morning to capture it.

THE CYPRINID SPECIES

CARP

As you will discover in the following roach chapter, I adore float fishing for all species, and I'd say that 90 per cent of my carp fishing has revolved around either float, or floater, fishing. I've just got to have a float in there somewhere. Why? Because I learned from a very young age, by guesting - I'll use my old mate Rod Hutchinson's terminology here - the local council park lake, that the simple float is by far the most accurate indicator of a bite. I guess I was in my early teens then.

Indeed, I caught hundreds of common carp – okay, they were all small, between 2-6lbs - on breadflake and on lobworms presented beneath a few inches of peacock quill, with a single shot on the bottom, 10-12 inches above the hook. Here I am, over 50 years later, doing exactly the same thing for very much larger carp, and in far off places too, so it works wherever you are, accounting for exotic tropical species like red tail catfish, pacu, the mighty arapaima and even those giant, black, Siamese carp in Thailand.

Viewers of angling on TV may well remember my brother Dave, during my Discovery Dream Fishing TV series, eventually landing that massive 170lb arapaima, hooked on nothing more than a peacock quill float rig and a chunk of chicken. What wonderful television it made! A couple of years later, and I can still feel the awesome, uncontrollable power of that 72lbs caho - Siamese black carp - my largest carp ever, that I hooked during the filming of my next series, John Wilson's Fishing World made for the Discovery Shed channel in 2009. On one of my System pike rods, 40lb test braid, and a peacock waggler float, it fought for an incredible 50 minutes until brother Dave finally slipped the net under it. Think now, how many times have you played a fish longer than half an hour? What an unbelievable fish! Talk about not losing touch with your roots.

Isn't that what it's all about; catching fish on simple, effective, methods? There is no magical boilie presentation, and there never will be, of course, as some carp gurus would have us believe. Nor are there hundreds of different, effective ways of presenting a boilie. Do you really believe that carp are that cute? If you do, then shut this book immediately, because 'My Way' is not for you. You will have gathered by now that everything I do is based on common sense and watercraft, which is why I think carp are most easily caught on the bottom using simple float tackle, or off the top on floating baits. Quite frankly, I do not believe that carp are any smarter than any other species. Some of them are just bigger, that's all.

Filmed for the Discovery Shed Channel by cameraman, Paul Luenberger, and watched by brother Dave, here I am connected to a caho – a black Siamese carp - which fought for an incredible 50 minutes at Cha-am, day ticket Fish Park near Hua Hin in Thailand.

What an incredible creature! Black Siamese carp are filter feeders, with huge mouths and deep, thick-set, fully scaled bodies and large fins. I certainly needed the help from brother Dave to display this magnificent 72lb monster.

THE LIFT METHOD

I explain my affection for float fishing using a length of plain peacock quill set over depth, and even expound the virtues of a flat float when river fishing and stret-pegging - a devastatingly effective carp rig, incidentally - in Chapter Four, with my favourite species, roach, and at various other times throughout this book. After all, and I must have repeated this hundreds of times over the years, what could be more natural than an unpainted, white, bird quill lying flat on the lake's surface?

Now, you may find it a trifle strange that in most situations I prefer to fish a flat float for

carp when lift-float fishing, because you are not going to see the float ever lift as such. Although when it suddenly starts drifting as though someone has cut the line between shot and float, that to me is as good as a lift bite, so I strike immediately. However, let's start with how to rig up my lift float for carp.

Firstly, four to six inches of unpainted peacock quill is set a foot or so over depth, fixed bottom-end only to the line with two, yes two, strong, silicone rubber float bands set side by side. You need not only to stop the quill from sliding down the line on the strike, but because when one band breaks from the line cutting through it, your float will still be connected. Please do not be tempted to use a float with a bottom ring so you can lock it with a shot on either side, as though waggler fishing for bream, because when a carp goes belting off into lilies and the shots get held up, bang, the line will snap immediately. With a band-held quill, either the float will go sliding way up the line when it catches around the nearest pad or stalk, or quite simply the quill will come out, which is when you realise you would rather lose a few inches of peacock quill than a sizeable carp.

At the business end below the float, depending on actual bait size, a strong, size 10 or 8 hair-rigged hook is tied on and 6-8 inches above this, a single swan shot is gently pinched onto the 8-12lbs reel line. (see diagram) This, too, I expect to come off easily should it snag among weed or lilies. Incidentally, the baits I present regularly on this rig include: various particles, maize, soft dog and cat treats, plus 10-15mm boilies and pellets.

I have caught more carp using float tackle than by any other method; note the peacock quill float. Simplicity personified.

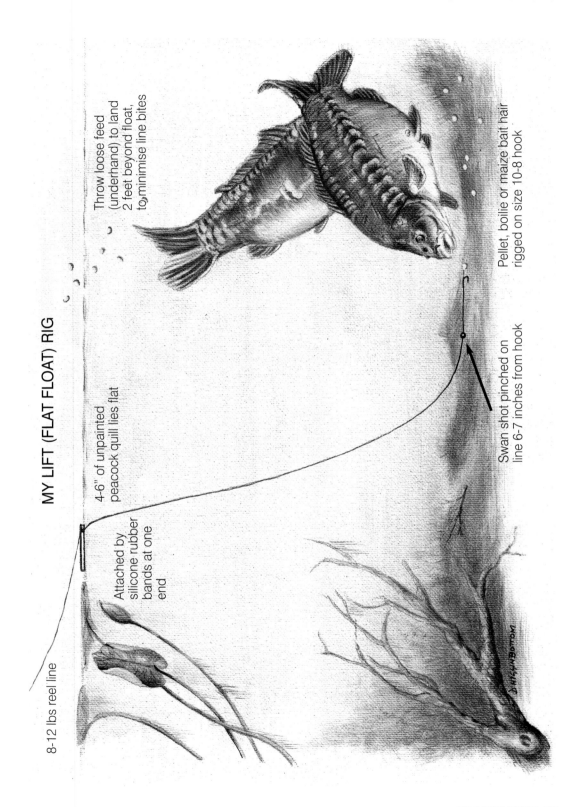

MY LIFT (FLAT FLOAT) RIG

Throw loose feed (underhand) to land 2 feet beyond float, to minimise line bites

4-6" of unpainted peacock quill lies flat

Attached by silicone rubber bands at one end

8-12 lbs reel line

Pellet, boilie or maize bait hair rigged on size 10-8 hook

Swan shot pinched on line 6-7 inches from hook

Having encouraged carp into an area fairly close in, say no more than two rod lengths out, by loose feeding hempseed or small, high oil content, attractor pellets, plus a few samples of the chosen hook bait, to get them grubbing about all within a small area, the secret to presenting this rig is not to cast straight on top of the feeding fish. Far better, as I do, is to flick the float rig, using a low trajectory sideways cast, way past the feeding area. The second it lands gently on the surface, and you've only a single swan shot to consider, remember, with the rod tip held up high and the bait no more than a few inches beneath the surface, slowly wind to the perimeter of the baited area. Then, in one smooth movement allow the bait and shot down to the bottom on a controlled but not over- tight line. This ensures that the bait will be furthest away from you nailed to the lakebed by the single large shot, with the float lying flat slightly closer. Do not allow the rig to hit bottom and then wind it into position. You'll either foul hook or spook any carp that the rig touches, or at best drag the bare hook into bottom detritus.

When free-baiting once the rig has settled, cup the loose feed in one hand, with your fingers and thumb close together, and throw accurately using a gentle underhand swing, so it comes to land in a relatively small patch, around two feet beyond the float. With practice, great accuracy can be achieved by underhand throwing. Now all this is of paramount importance, because if, for instance, the loose feed lands around the float or, worse still, your side of it, line bites will result. You get line bites anyway when close-range float fishing for carp, but you don't need to encourage them. This is the main reason I prefer to fish the float flat. Occasionally, it will sway, twitch, or tilt upwards a little, sometimes quite quickly if a carp feels the line, but usually, it will only

cock and disappear beneath the surface all in one movement, to a real bite. As I mentioned earlier, also remember to strike immediately if the float suddenly starts to drift away as though the line below it has been cut. This is your top indication of a lift bite, when a carp has sucked up the bait and lifted the shot off the bottom.

Should you try to fish, supposedly more sensitively, by winding down to cock the float with just a quarter of an inch showing above the surface, as in the true lift style, you will observe all kinds of float movement, from taps and twitches, to the tip going completely under. In other words, indications that, were you fishing for roach, you would have no hesitation in striking, but beware, due to line bites and pecks from smaller species, you will be striking into thin air most of the time, possibly foul hooking carp and disturbing the swim by casting too regularly. So be patient.

For this fascinating and most demanding technique, I never put the rod down, preferring to hold it steady in readiness throughout for a firm, upward strike, my forefinger hooked around the line in front of the bail arm, for times when I'm day-dreaming or bird-watching; unless I am centrepin fishing, by far the best reel for this lovely method, in which case the drum slips easily beneath my gentle thumb pressure should I not see the float disappear.

Let's assume you are using a fixed spool reel, though. The most comfortable way by far to keep the rod steady, which is vital when fishing with the line tight to the flat float without it continually twitching or being dragged, and this obviously applies when using the same method for tench or bream, is to first ensure you have two fingers, eachside around the stem of the reel.

To get this hefty mirror carp to accept a big lobworm hook bait presented in a tiny gap in beds of dense weed while punt fishing, float fishing was the only technique possible.

This puts the tip of your forefinger directly opposite the spool for imparting instant pressure should a fish immediately head for a snag. Your wrist should be comfortably arched and your entire forearm on top of the handle, not beside it. I know this is quite basic advice, and something that feels a little unnatural initially, but when teaching people how to hold the rod when a fast upward strike is required, as with the lift method, I've noticed most seem to want to hold the rod with their forearm rather loose beside the rod handle. This results in a weak, half-hearted strike and the end of the rod under their armpit.

So get used to having your arm on top, and resting the handle on your right thigh, assuming you are right-handed, with the rear of the reel touching your knee. This is done most effectively when sitting comfortably on an upright stool, not a low-type chair. Now with the rod handle balanced horizontally along your thigh, you will find that you can actually relax your grip around the reel stem, because it is your forearm that is doing most of the balancing. In this way, you can fish for hour upon hour without arm ache, yet make a fast, hard strike in an instant. When carp are not charging away with the bait and hooking themselves, as on a bolt rig, merely moving slowly away with the bait, you'll find that a fast, hard strike is usually required to set the hook firmly. In fact, I choose to hold the rod with my forearm on top of the handle for all techniques that demand a fast response to that float, or floater, disappearing. I tend to use rod rests only when stret-pegging in flowing water. I'm happy to lure fish, fly fish or long-trot all day long without putting the rod down, so why not with other methods if an instant strike is going to result in more fish on the bank; as indeed it does, on so many occasions. Think about it.

To keep carp feeding and to offset their fear once a fish has been hooked, I immediately throw in a few handfuls of loose feed. It takes some presence of mind during the excitement of playing a fish, but is always worth doing. Much depends on swim depth, of course, and in really shallow water of, say, four feet and less, you cannot expect fish to stay feeding with so much commotion going on. By being quiet on the bank and keeping low down and well back, the inbuilt curiosity of fish can have them back and feeding confidently again literally within minutes of one being netted. As for the actual netting, large, spoon-shaped, barbel-type landing nets with a deep mesh are not only lighter, but also much better than the standard over-sized, triangular carp net that tackle dealers like to sell for the job. For any kind of close-in stalking through undergrowth-type carp fishing, my advice is to stick to the manoeuvrability of a large, spoon-shaped net.

FLOATER FISHING

I think I get wound up and frustrated by carp more when floater fishing than at any other time. I'm sure most of us do. Apart from freelining large baits in clear water where individual fish can actually be observed sucking them in, repeatedly watching carp come up to, nudge, and even appear to slurp down but refuse at the last second, even small floaters such as Chum Mixer biscuits, sometimes makes you want to tear your hair out. I guess this is because you actually get to see the sheer size of the carp you have just missed. It also makes you realise just how discerning and particular even confidently feeding carp can be when it suits them. Just how many fish in the past, when you have surmised they have ventured nowhere near your baits, must have sidled up to inspect your bottom baits presented on bolt rigs and totally refused them, without so much as a flicker on the line, or a bleep from the buzzer.

Floater fishing for carp slurping off the top is always pure joy and usually a lesson in how they approach the hook bait floater. If they approach from head-on, the line is not felt, whereas coming in from either side, the line could be touched by their lips and barbules, and the floater ejected.

It's all a wonderful learning curve, and floater fishing is so instructive, because you can see it all happening, which is why I floater fish whenever the situation arises. The size of carp to be caught is almost academic; although like everyone else, I like to feel the power of a big fish whenever possible. At least with floater fishing, and this, to me, is the technique's greatest asset, you have the wonderful opportunity of estimating the size of what you might soon catch and match line strength and hook size accordingly, once fish are up on the top and feeding confidently. Although due to the obvious refusal of larger floaters presented on larger hooks and thicker line, by cute, over-fished-for carp, you are often in a situation of compromise. That's why it's all so much fun and yet so agonisingly frustrating.

Many of the habitat-rich lakes that I fish demand that, while I may wish to put a floater out 40 yards into clear water to cruising fish, later on in the session there may be the occasional fish that mooches in close to the bank to mop up uneaten floaters that have drifted in. Then, I will want to dunk my floater quickly, on a completely free line, straight down to a fish slurping in baits with gay abandon among the marginal greenery, seemingly oblivious to my presence. A word of warning here; don't be tempted merely to lower your floater down on the controller rig. More often than not, the weight of the dangling, controller in mid-air will affect your strike, and pull the floater out of the carp's chops. Tackling-down however, by removing the floating controller, stop knot, bead and hook, and tying the hook back on again all takes agonising minutes, when the 'slam-dunk' feeding carp could depart any second. However, how I actually rig up a controller negates all this worry, believe me.

MY VERSATILE FLOATER RIG

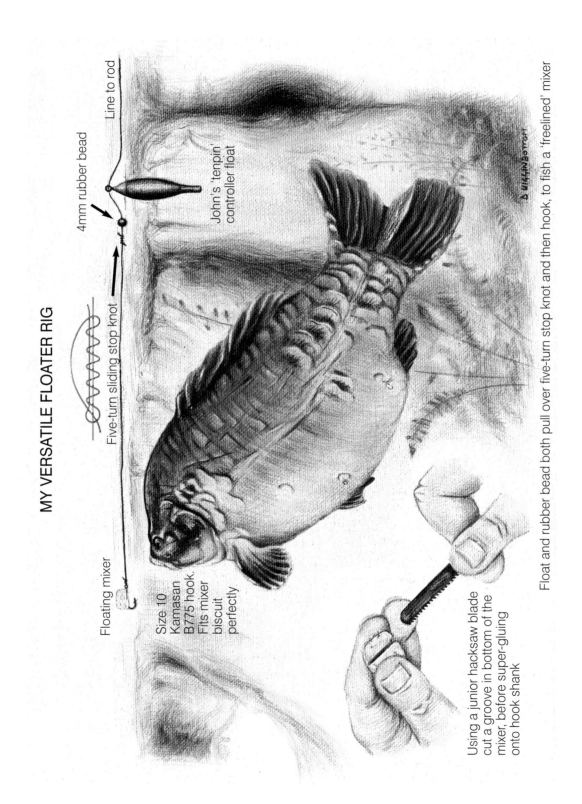

Line to rod

4mm rubber bead

John's 'tenpin'
controller float

Five-turn sliding stop knot

Floating mixer

Size 10
Kamasan
B775 hook.
Fits mixer
biscuit
perfectly

Using a junior hacksaw blade
cut a groove in bottom of the
mixer, before super-gluing
onto hook shank

Float and rubber bead both pull over five-turn stop knot and then hook, to fish a 'freelined' mixer

D WILKINSON '07

I start by threading the line through the top ring of my JW 'Tenpin' controller - this is a size 8 swivel - then thread on a 4mm rubber bead, followed by a five-turn stop knot of reel line, around 4 feet from the end of the line, and then tie on the size 10 hook. I use a pearl black Kamazan B775, which has a 10-degree reverse, short, curved shank and an ultra-sharp point. It is exceptionally strong, and best of all, is no longer than the width of a mixer biscuit, which is most important in my book.

Now, and here comes the incredibly easy, yet devastatingly effective, part, to de-rig you simply pull both float and rubber bead - it must be rubber of course - first over the nylon stop knot and then over the eye of the hook. This is why you need a controller like my 'Tenpin', with a large enough ring to pass over the hook - and hey-presto you are freelining within a jiffy. It's so gloriously simple. Try it and see.

Now for bait attachment, and despite the numerous variants which I have tried and tested over the years from hair-rigging, to silicone bait bands. I still cannot improve on the simple glue-on method of first cutting a shallow groove in one side of the bait, before adding a drop of Superglue to the hook shank, and holding them together for a few seconds. Unlike bait bands, that sometimes, during a long, hard cast slip down and affect presentation, the glued-on floater sits perfectly on top of the hook shank with the bend and point perfectly placed beneath for a positive hook-up.

This immaculately scaled and proportioned common carp came to a freelined floater presented mere feet from the bank among dense marginal shrubbery at my own two-lake fishery in Norfolk.

Once fish respond to loose floaters, and are slurping them down confidently, having catapulted them upwind to cover maximum area, I try to restrain myself from casting 'blind' until the size of fish or a particular specimen that I'm after comes into view. Repeated casting often makes feeding fish restless. Then I make a long cast way past the feeding group and wind slowly back so that the fish I'm seeking must intercept the floater head-on. Most important this, because then I stand the very best chance of it being slurped down with a firm hook hold to follow.

Fish that approach the floater from either side of the attached line could, and do, feel it on their lips or against their barbules and subsequently spook off. Many do, in those agitated swirls where for a split-second you think the floater has disappeared, and maybe even struck what seemed to be a genuine bite. I'll even pull a floater slowly away from a fish I don't wish to hook, or one that will spook if it attempts to take it because it's approaching from the side; unbelievably, they will sometimes follow quite aggressively. Surface spirals caused by the tails of other feeding carp do tend to swirl the odd floater away sometimes and I think confidently feeding carp are merely responding to this when they give chase.

TENCH

Much that I have already said about the lift method, and about how to hold the rod perfectly steady for an instant strike when carp fishing, applies equally to tench. For a more sensitive presentation, though, I use a slimmer length of peacock quill, between 3-5 inches long, again held by two silicone bands close together, and a shorter distance, 2-4 inches, between a single AA shot and the hook; usually a size 14-10.

This is because the mouth of the tench is different from that of the carp, which is underslung, with upturned lips. Just like crucian carp, the tench has no option but to literally stand on its head if it wishes to inhale a bait resting hard on the bottom. This is, indeed, its downfall and why the lift method is so devastatingly effective. When the tench sucks up the bait while standing on its head and prepares to right itself, during this time not only is the float lifting in a gloriously unmissable bite, but the buoyancy in the peacock quill is actually supporting the single shot, until it lies completely flat. This is when the tench then feels its weight and prepares to eject the bait, so the slightly over depth float is wound down cocked, so that a mere quarter of an inch of the tip is showing, and the strike made fast and hard, to pick up loose line, while the float is lifting. In fact, from the very second you see it starting to lift. See diagram.

Some wait for the float to cock again and slide under, just like in the Mr Crabtree cartoons, but as all modern tench anglers know full well, in many instances, this does not always go according to plan because sometimes when tench feel the shot, they blow the bait out instantly. Of course, all bites do not develop as lifts. It all depends on whether the tench is actually moving and in which direction it is heading, toward or away from you, when it inhales the bait. So a proportion will be positive dips of the float, or belt-off bites where, one minute the float is there, and the next you are playing a tench, which has felt resistance from the rig and panicked off without spitting the bait out, almost hooking itself. Occasionally, it's possible to induce shock, or bolt, bites by using, say, three 3SSG shots on the line instead of the single AA, but in my experience, these tactics do not work on all waters.

JOHN'S LIFT FLOAT RIG

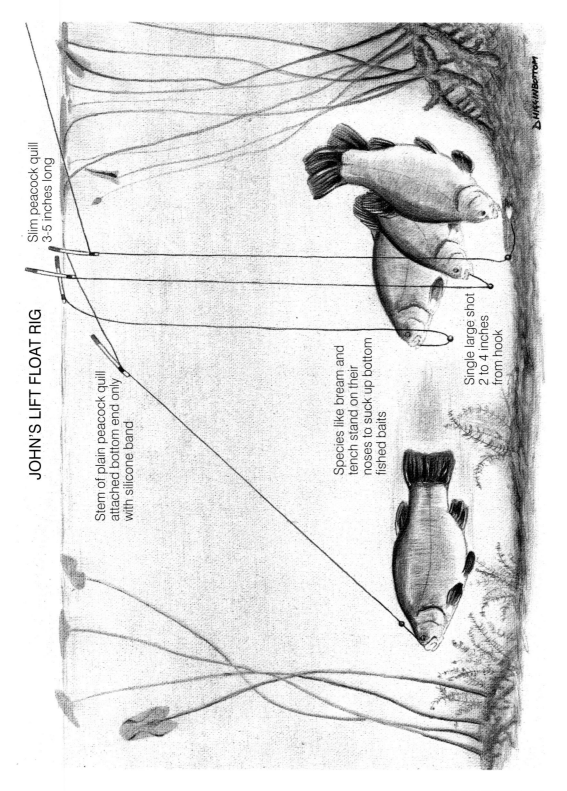

Slim peacock quill
3-5 inches long

Stem of plain peacock quill
attached bottom end and only
with silicone band

Species like bream and
tench stand on their
noses to suck up bottom
fished baits

Single large shot
2 to 4 inches
from hook

This dark, superbly proportioned tench succumbed to early morning lift-float and centrepin reel tactics from the wonderful Capability Brown designed estate lakes at Stowe in Buckinghamshire. It was the first of many.

Incidentally, as I have mentioned with carp, do not be tempted, when lift float fishing for tench, to use a peacock waggler and lock it either side of the bottom ring with shots. The line will fracture should a fish get snagged in weeds or lilies when the shots restrict the float from sliding up the line, and you do not want shots anywhere else on the line, except for that single AA a few inches above the hook. They visually reduce the effectiveness of the lift bite.

Although sometimes I'll present maggots or casters on the lift, I prefer to use mostly larger offerings like sweetcorn, maize, cockles, chick peas, breadflake, a crust/flake cocktail, 10-12mm boilies or pellets. I think tench are more likely to move away, having taken them, to look for others and consequently give a more positive bite, as opposed to chomping on the spot and then inhaling other small baits close by. I am forever adjusting the distance between shot and hook. There are sessions when, unless you find the right distance, bites simply do not happen, or do not develop into strikeable registrations.

When using boilies or pellets, a ruse that I like to adopt is to Superglue the bait to a short, quarter-inch section of 4-5mm wide, elastic band, trimming it back with scissors to leave just enough tab to nick the hook through. Now, why this little trick should work better than that same pellet or boilie on a hair rig, or glued directly on to the hook shank, I am not exactly sure, but it does. Could be simply that being highly buoyant, the section of rubber band makes the pellet behave more naturally. Try it and see. It works with chub, barbel, carp and bream, too.

MOVING BAIT GENTLY ALONG BOTTOM, WHEN FISHING THE LIFT FLOAT

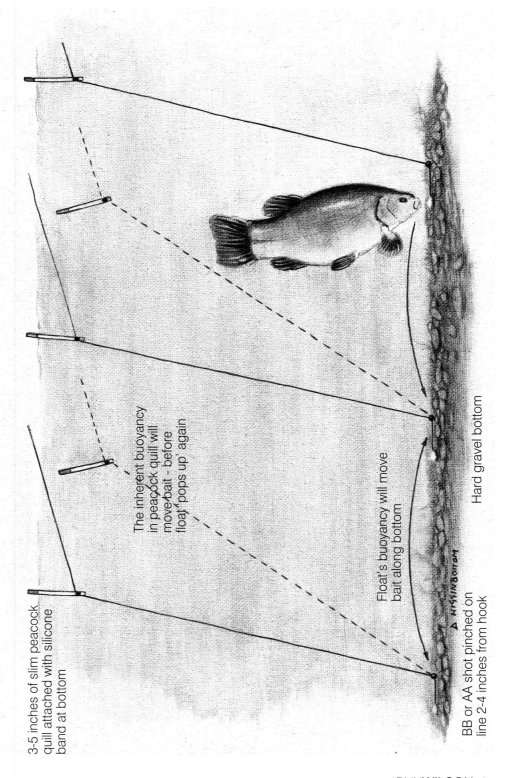

3-5 inches of slim peacock quill attached with silicone band at bottom

The inherent buoyancy in peacock quill will move bait – before float 'pops up' again

Float's buoyancy will move bait along bottom

Hard gravel bottom

HIGGINSBOTTOM

BB or AA shot pinched on line 2-4 inches from hook

When tench are in a particularly finicky mood, I like to wind the cocked float tip gently down to the merest 'blimp' in the surface film, and hit the slightest lift or dip. When bites are not forthcoming on hard bottoms, sometimes I also like to move the bait just a few inches along the bottom, (see diagram) which can induce an instant bite should a tench be sitting there looking at the bait and doesn't fancy it getting away. I know a lump of bread flake or pellet should not move, but no one tells that to the tench I catch.

With a centrepin reel, obligatory and magical for tench on the lift, in my opinion, this movement amounts purely to gentle, forward thumb movement upon the drum. Once the float is wound a couple of inches below the surface, its inherent buoyancy is then enough to drag the bait along, before the float pops up and I tighten up to it again. The event takes seconds and works best with minimal shot on the line. Without moving another muscle in my body, I can make the float disappear, or lift an inch, simply by my thumb movement, which is why, for any close-range float fishing, the centrepin is without equal.

Of course, because any pressure you impart to the reel's drum during the fight is felt through that ultra-sensitive skin on the ball of your thumb, potential break-offs due to too harsh a clutch setting, as with a fixed spool reel, are unheard of. It's as though tench were invented for fights on the centrepin reel. You can instantly give mere inches, feet, or yards of line at the blink of an eye, to stop a small hook pulling, or a light breaking strain line from parting, all through super-sensitive thumb pressure. Conversely, you can put on all the brakes when a biggie heads for a snag. There is no other reel in fishing so deliciously designed for enjoyment than the centrepin, and if you don't use one, you should. (see 'Long-trotting for roach', Chapter Four, for

casting tips.) Coupled to a 12-13 foot heavy float or basic Avon-style rod, matched with lines in the 4-7lbs range, there can be no more efficient or pleasurable tench or bream outfit than a centrepin combo.

I also love presenting big lobworms to tench beneath a length of peacock quill fished cocked, but with a distance of between 10-12 inches from shot to hook. I go out of my way when bites are slow, to keep moving the worm. I think tench expect animal baits to move anyway, so I deliberately use a longer, more buoyant length of quill than I really need, still with the AA shot, in order that, whenever I wind down to submerge the float, its buoyancy immediately raises the worm from the lakebed in a most tantalizing manner. A bite can happen at any moment. I love ledgering big lobs too, and often inject a little air into the head end to raise it enticingly above any bottom weed. Freelining big baits like lobs, whole mussels or a dollop of pellet paste can prove unbelievably exciting, and produces the most powerful and confident of runs. I guess my second-favourite technique next to the lift, though, is feeder fishing, using a pair of matching Avon ledger rod outfits, with 6lbs test mono on small fixed spool reels.

FEEDER FISHING

Way back in the mid-1970s, a big tench weighed 5lbs and a whopper needed to make just 7lbs. I say 'just', because for several reasons tench of this size are now everyday catches, whereas in 1976 the British record stood at 9lbs 1oz. Some of my local Norfolk Broads and especially East Anglian ancient estate lakes at that time, nearly all designed by Capability Brown, were so incredibly rich in organic sediment; full of bloodworms, plus mountains of huge swan mussels, and were the absolute top locations to concentrate upon.

This magnificent tench brace came while mid-range feeder fishing on one of my local common lakes in the village of Lenwade, Norfolk, while filming series 16 of my Anglia TV programmes. This lake, actually a gravel pit, is barely 20 years old.

It seems strange that many of today's monstrous, double-figure tench are caught from gravel pit fisheries that did not actually exist when I was feeder fishing back in the 1970/80s. Take a four-acre pit in my local village of Lenwade, for instance, one of the renowned Common Lakes complex, situated just eleven miles west of Norwich, where in 2002 I made one of my programmes in series 16 of Anglia TV's Go Fishing, catching several lovely tench to over 7lbs for the cameras.

Since its excavation, completed in 1985, this particular pit has since produced grass carp to nearly 40lbs and numerous tench into double figures, was but 20 years old at the time. It's quite phenomenal, isn't it? I can state this with such accuracy because one of my own lakes was due to be excavated once this particular pit was finished, and I couldn't wait for the dragline and giant Massey Ferguson front loader to move on to my property, only a mile away, and start work. Moreover, when my own pit was completed six months later, and I started planting trees around the perimeter, I had a dozen or so weeping willows (*Salix x chrysocoma*) left over. These I planted on the island of the Common Lakes pit; but I have digressed somewhat here so back to feeder fishing.

Feeder fishing, often at distances between 30 and 70 yards, was essential on most of the estate lakes I fished - and still do fish, incidentally – in those early days, because their margins had silted up so badly. They were too shallow for float fishing close in, except at the deepest dam end, and in cross-section, most were like a saucer, with the deeper, tench-occupied areas running down the middle. So feeder fishing using clear Perspex, open-ended feeders was the order of the day, and still is. Once a carpet of bait, either maggots, casters, chopped worm or sweetcorn, had been deposited on the silty bottom, with a plug of dampened breadcrumb groundbait at each end, those tench did not take long in finding it.

Hitting bites at range in shallow water, however, proved difficult with the sloppy, fibreglass ledger rods of the day. By the 1980s, the inherent stiffness and quick return of carbon fibre revolutionised distance ledgering, to the extent that anyone buying a middle of the road, carbon ledger rod today, just doesn't know how fortunate he is. How I should love to put the clock back 40 years and use modern tackle for the tench I used to fish for then. If only, eh?

By scuba-diving many of my local lakes, sometimes while friends were actually fishing, believe it or not, and seeing beneath the surface how various rigs worked, I soon came out in favour of the incredibly simple, fixed paternoster, ledger/feeder rig. This is

constructed by using a length of reel line as the feeder link, joined to the reel line using a four-turn water knot – and 40 years later, I still prefer to fish the same way. It's so easy to fish lighter, by using the, say, 6lbs reel line as the feeder link and tying on two feet of 3-5lbs test (see diagram) which then becomes the hook length.

We are not talking bolt or shock rigs here, just simple ledger tactics. For bite registration, with or without the aid of electronic buzzers as the front rod rest, I prefer to use simple clip-on bobbin indicators. With the rod pointed at the bait, these bobbins are fixed on to the line between butt ring and buzzer/rod rest, and retained on lines of non-stretch, heavy Dacron or fly line, which does not twang back as you strike, like heavy

When feeder fishing at medium to long range, 40-80 yards, constant observation with binoculars will invariably put extra fish in your net. So when you see patches of feeding bubbles erupting, even if they are nowhere near your hook baits, get a bait over them post-haste.

JOHN'S FIXED PATERNOSTER FEEDER RIG

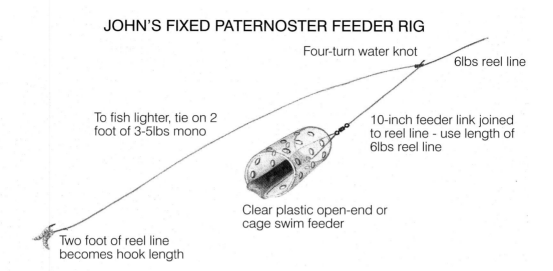

Four-turn water knot

6lbs reel line

To fish lighter, tie on 2 foot of 3-5lbs mono

10-inch feeder link joined to reel line - use length of 6lbs reel line

Clear plastic open-end or cage swim feeder

Two foot of reel line becomes hook length

gauge monofilament, and attached via a snap swivel to the front rod rest. In fact, I have a split ring whipped on to my front rod rests immediately below the screw thread to accept the snap swivel. To counteract subsurface drift or strong winds, a swan shot or two are pinched on to the retaining line immediately below the bobbin.

In flat calm conditions, when tench may be super-finicky, and the bobbins are not registering hittable bites, I keep my eyes concentrated in front of the rod tops and on the line where it enters the surface. With both rod tops pointing directly at each bait, I can strike the slightest twitch long before it may, or may not, develop further. Sudden drop-back bites where the bobbin falls down suddenly, because the tench has swum towards you, are common when feeder fishing, and must be struck instantly, walking backwards quickly in order to pick up the amount of slack line that results.

When feeder ledgering very shallow estate lakes, make a point of setting up the two rods - assuming you will use two - low to the ground and this is of paramount importance.

Remember always to strike sideways, with the rod tip held low. To pull the line through the water, as opposed to striking upwards against a mountain of surface tension that can reduce striking proficiency by at least 50 per cent. Before I cottoned on to this logical fact, I missed out on so many fish back in those pioneering days of stillwater feeder fishing for tench back in the 1970s, but everything is a learning curve.

For the same reason, when ledgering in long, shallow waters like estate lakes, remember to strike in the opposite direction to the wind and surface tow. Down below, close to the bottom where your line is lying, the water will actually be moving in the opposite direction. Think about it. The wind sends surface layers of water down to the dam end, where, instead of piling high up on the bank, just like a competition swimmer performing a roll-turn, all that water is forced down close to the bottom where it flows backwards in the opposite direction. Yes, there is certainly more to the art of feeder ledgering in estate lakes than would first seem apparent,and trying to understand it all will put more fish into your net, be they tench or bream.

BREAM

Most of what I've written about tench, in both the lift method and feeder fishing, can be applied to bream fishing. Indeed, good hauls including both species are often made from estate lakes and gravel pit fisheries, because both species tend to frequent the same areas, so it is often difficult to separate them. A classic situation that springs to mind here is the beautiful, rhododendron-clad estate lake at famous Blenheim Palace, in Oxfordshire, where on numerous occasions I have enjoyed wonderful day-ticket sport on the float while punt fishing, accounting for equal numbers of tench and bream in the same session, so don't ask me what I was fishing for.

However, where the species can be separated, my favourite float fishing technique for deep-water bream, say, 13-14 feet or deeper, is slider float fishing. Why? Because once you have mastered the peculiarities of a slider float to overcome

depths greater than the length of a 13-14 foot float rod, a sporting reel line breaking strain of just 5lbs is all that's required, compared to reel lines of 9-12lbs demanded by bolt-rig ledgering. A big bream hooked on slider float tackle is an entirely different beast to one cranked in on carp gear, believe me. Most anglers look upon bream in a different light once they have caught them using a slider float, or from the swirling waters of a weir pool while trotting.

So, whether you are out in an anchored punt over deep water, or plan to attack a deep hole or gully from the bank of a gravel pit, say, or deep-water reservoir, what are the pointers to look for when fishing the slider float? Well, to start with, do not select a loaded antennae-type float, or any other partly-weighted float.

Here's proof of the slider float's effectiveness. I'm fast into a double-figure bream from a 13-foot deep swim way out into the centre of the lake. Presentation at relatively close range, using just a 5lb reel line, provides wonderful battles from an anchored boat.

JOHN'S SLIDER FLOAT RIG

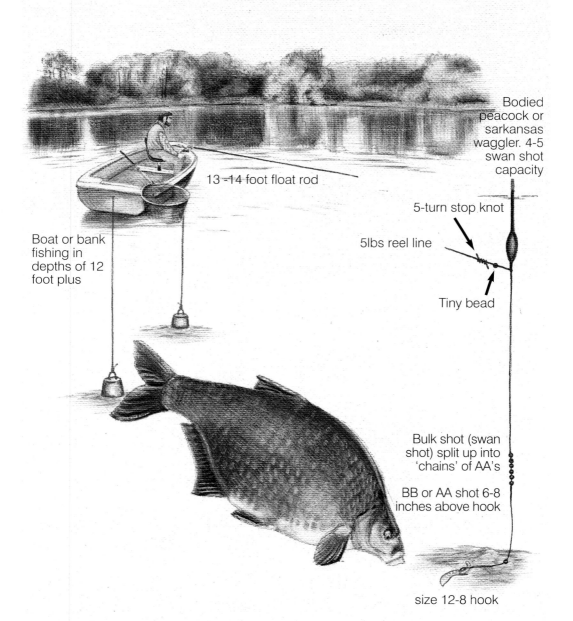

Bodied peacock or sarkansas waggler. 4-5 swan shot capacity

13 -14 foot float rod

5-turn stop knot

5lbs reel line

Tiny bead

Boat or bank fishing in depths of 12 foot plus

Bulk shot (swan shot) split up into 'chains' of AA's

BB or AA shot 6-8 inches above hook

size 12-8 hook

Brother Dave, now living in Thailand, with a beautiful early morning, near two-tone big bream, caught slider float fishing in a deep Norfolk gravel pit. Note the spawning tubercles all over its snout and shoulders denoting it's a male.

What you need is a plain-bodied, peacock or sarkansas waggler with a neat bottom ring that requires at least 4-5 swan shot to cock it. Now I know that this sounds like overkill, but to withstand the problems of both wind and surface drift, you need a fair amount of weight down the line. My basic rig (see diagram) consists of a 4-5 swan shot, split up into a chain of AA shot, bodied slider, stopped a little over depth by a tiny bead and five-turn stop knot, made from a few inches of the reel line.

At the hook end, a size 12-8 presenting a lobworm tail, breadflake, sweetcorn or a bunch of maggots, is tied directly to the 5lbs reel line with a BB or an AA shot 6-8 inches above. About 20 inches above this, I pinch on the bulk-shot, and two feet further up the line I pinch on a small shot against which the slider float rests prior to casting. A tip here is to cast a few yards beyond the baited swim, and immediately the rig hits the surface, after dunking the rod tip to ensure all the line is sunk between float and rod tip, quickly wind in those few yards. The bail arm is of course left open for the reel line to flow unimpaired through the float's bottom ring. Watch the coils coming off so that when the bait and shot touch bottom, and the float cocks, tighten up to ensure there is minimal bow in the line.

The float should actually cock in two distinct stages; the tip going down to where the bulk shot takes it, and then shortly afterwards a little more, to where the BB or AA sinks it further. Most important this, because whenever a bream hoovers up the bait from the bottom and rights itself, invariably the bottom shot is supported and so the float tip lifts momentarily (try striking these bites) prior to it totally submerging seconds later. Remember to strike sideways, low to the water, to pull the line through the water as opposed to upwards against water pressure, while winding frantically to pick up the huge right-angle of line created between rod tip, float and bait.

When fishing at fair distances, I simply concentrate on winding like a madman for a couple of seconds when the float goes, and then heave the rod back sideways, while continuing to wind. This can often prove to be more effective for setting the hook, and with so much line out there is no chance of snapping up.

When bank fishing, it's wise to keep the rod tip a couple of inches below the surface at all times, to alleviate surface and wind drift, with the rod set on two rests. When fishing at relatively close range from a punt or boat, though, when for much of the session I will be holding the rod anyway, I like to keep most of the line on the surface with the rod tip held low, in readiness of a strike which I then make hard and upwards while winding frantically. When a big, slab-sided bream is contacted on slider float tackle, a most pleasurable and

exciting encounter will follow. Big bream especially, really show their mettle when hooked on relatively light float gear and will make repeated runs, so adjust the reel's drag accordingly and don't be in a hurry to see them in the net.

WEIR POOL BREAM

My only ever double-figure bream in running water, though I have lost count of those from pits, meres and estate lakes, came from a weir pool in my local River Wensum while filming an episode of my Anglia TV series Go Fishing. It could not have come at a better time - right on cue, as they say, although to be truthful, I was actually hoping for a barbel at the time.

Good friend, John Smith, not only owns a River Wensum weir pool, he catches some stunning bream from its swirling waters, too, mostly using quiver tipping tactics and large baits.

I think it's fair to say that many weir pool bream go totally unfished for, I guess because many anglers do not envisage bream occupying such fast and turbulent water. The fact is, bream, and particularly large river bream, love the turbulence overhead and the reduced currents below provided by deep weir pools, and the way in which a regular food supply is delivered to them where they hold station just above bottom in the deepest part of the pool. The secret in catching them, summer and winter alike, is making up a firm, bread-mash groundbait, and following in with a large piece of breadflake covering a size 10 or 8 hook, presented on a simple fixed paternoster ledger rig, incorporating between 2-4 SSG swan shots on the link, depending upon current strength. In summer, in addition to breadflake, sweetcorn or sweetcorn/redworm cocktails are often the killing baits.

My personal plan is to ledger the deepest part of the pool using just enough shots to hold bottom, because I know full well those bream will be producing drop-back bites when they hoover up the bait and drop back with the flow. So I watch the rod's quiver tip like a hawk. Having the rod positioned high on two rests to alleviate any drag from current pressure is essential here. The very second I see the tip nod and spring back, and many of these bites move the tip no more than an inch, I strike instantly, hard and upward, lifting the rod as high as I can to pick up any slack line.

More often than not, the fish will only be felt at the very top of the striking arc, so it pays to wind down quickly upon feeling any resistance. It is indeed a sad fact that those not familiar with the technique and the peculiarities of weir pool bream, are bound to miss infinitely more than they hook. Connecting with drop-back bites is almost an art form in itself, and well worth studying, so hold the rod throughout and be ready for an instant strike. Bites that come to rods supported on rests several feet away are nearly always missed; remember that.

CHUB

I haven't really got a favourite way of catching chub and I guess that's because I employ so many techniques and baits throughout the river season. I love to work floating plugs on my little American bait-casting outfit (see the 'Throwing Lures...' chapter), and it's always a thrill to see a fat chub attack them on the surface during the summer months. I also adore those same predatory instincts of chub that appear from nowhere among the weeds or from beneath overhanging branches to engulf in their cavernous mouths, a super-buoyant, deer-hair mouse, popped and jerked against the flow using a tiny fixed spool, ultra-light spinning outfit.

I also love to stalk those same, often ultra-shy clearwater, river chub, creepy-crawly, Indian-style, by watching them come shooting out of their holt beneath a raft of weed caught around overhanging branches. Chub in such swims are an absolute 'cert' to suck in a fat slug or lobworm, simply freelined downstream on nothing but a size 4 hook. It's 'hold-on' fishing at its very, very best, and if you have the stealth and cunning to creep silently to within feet of a summer chub, then you have the credentials for catching any fish in any water around the world. Certainly, I know of no fish more sensitive to bankside movement, vibrations or shadows cast upon the water.

I also enjoy the delight of wandering along diminutive, overgrown streams, and offering an upstream nymph, or better still a mayfly, using a little 4-weight floating line/brook rod outfit, and seeing those great rubbery lips noisily slurp it in from the surface film. This is the beauty of chub; their catholic taste in food allows for so many avenues of approach.

*Freelining large baits such as a fat slug or big
lobworm, which proved the downfall of this chunky
River Waveney chub from a run beneath a floating
reed raft, has no equal during the summer months
when, in clear water, individual specimens can be
seen and immediately targeted.*

This plump, 6lb-plus chub came to long-trotting tactics from the fast waters of Berkshire's marvellous River Kennet at picturesque Aldermaston Mill. A day ticket location that provided great autumn action during the filming of my TV series Go Fishing.

Long-trotting during the milder winter spells, once the river has fined down after flooding and the bottom is nicely scoured clean of weed and willow moss, takes some beating in terms of sheer pleasure. Working my way slowly downstream from swim to swim, carrying the absolute minimum of tackle, I fish the same as I do when long-trotting for big roach, as explained in the roach chapter. The reel line on my centrepin is raised to around 4lbs test, with a size 10 or 8 tied directly, presenting a lump of fresh white breadflake, and I opt for the buoyancy of chubber-type floats carrying up to 5 swan shot, or more. The wide, red tip permits me to explore distances of 50 yards or more downstream, without losing sight of the float, and a good chub, hooked that far away in a fast current, can take several begrudging minutes before it allows itself to be

encouraged upstream towards the net. Again, just as with roach fishing, small balls of mashed bread introduced regularly help those chub to stay interested, and moving up and down the swim.

Winter chub, especially in mild weather when rivers are running fairly clear, can also be caught trotting down small livebaits using a 'perch-strength' outfit of say 6lbs mono with a size 4 hook tied direct. Up the line, set a foot or so shallower than the swim, is a ¾-inch diameter pilot float plugged to the line with two inches of thin diameter peacock quill. Ideal baits are small, 3-4 inch dace or bleak hooked gently, once only, through both nostrils, kept down close to the bottom by a couple of swan shot pinched on 20 inches above the hook.

Search all those obvious chub haunts, especially deep runs beneath overhanging trees. Bites are usually quite savage, with the pilot float trotting happily away, and the bait twitching beneath, then suddenly zooming under, and are best responded to by winding firmly but gently down to the fish and bending the rod back slowly while still winding. A quick wind-down and hard strike usually results in the chub ejecting the bait post-haste. Numerous modest-sized pike (jacks) will also happen along on these small live baits however, plus the occasional good perch or zander, so with a monofilament line tied directly to the hook without any wire, the occasional bite-off will occur, despite instantly tightening-up. A large single hook is no cause for concern, though, and it's surprising just how many pike are, indeed, cleanly hooked, neatly in the scissors, and subsequently landed.

I also love stret-pegging for chub (see diagram in roach chapter) in slacks and lay-bys when the river is well up and coloured. The top bait is then a whole lobworm on a size 6 hook, with a handful of broken lobs thrown in several feet upstream for attraction. In fierce currents, lower some lob fragments close to the bait with the aid of a bait-dropper.

The most effective winter technique by far, at least on all of my East Anglian rivers like the upper Bure, Yare, Waveney, Wissey and Wensum, and I suspect on similar, clear-flowing rivers all over England, is quivertip ledgering in conjunction with regular helpings of mashed bread. This I extol the virtues of and give guidance on how to make, in the roach chapter, incidentally. It is so devastatingly effective. Walk a stretch of river from the bottom (downstream end) up, and introduce a few balls of mash into all the potential chub-holding swims, like deep bends, rubbish rafts, side stream entrances, over-shoot pools and the like. If you do this while walking upriver, before actually commencing fishing at the most upstream run, before working your way methodically downstream again, you will always have a bend in your rod.

Summer magic for Martin Bowler and me, with this lovely brace of River Wensum chub, caught, as several more were that morning, by stalking along the clear-flowing and weedy river at Ringland, freelining lobworms.

Gorging on free nosh without becoming suspicious puts Mr Chub into a very catchable mood. Offering a thumbnail-sized piece of fresh, white breadflake from the inside of a new loaf, pressed on to a size 10 or 8 hook and simple fixed paternoster, swan-shot ledger, into swims already baited and rested for various lengths of time, could keep you catching all day through, with the very real potential of an instant fish from every swim. It just needs a little forethought is all.

Fellow angling writer, Bruce Vaughan, and I have been chubbing together for close on 40 years. He makes the best bread mash, always from stale bread, and always the night before a session. What's the point in getting freezing cold hands at the start of a winter session?

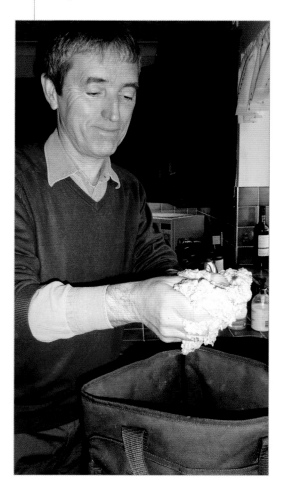

Actually, adopting this ruse has provided me with bumper hauls of 22 and 23 chub respectively, all between 3½ and 5½ lbs, in a single session from my local River Wensum.

Only when the river is in spate and full of mucky, freezing snow water, do I change tactics slightly. Sometimes, a 'smelly' bait has greater pulling power, so I'll bait with a juicy lobworm, or put my faith in smelly cheese paste, but still loose feed small amounts of golf ball-sized bread mash, containing either worm or cheese fragments. Do remember, as I have already recommended in the roach chapter, to use old bread when making mash. It not only sinks better than new bread, it actually sinks much faster.

Another consideration when quiver tipping small rivers for chub, is to sit comfortably, well back from the water's edge and angle the rod tip up a little, pointing downstream at around 45 degrees to the bank. Surprisingly, you will connect with more bites as a result, because quite simply, more line is picked up on the strike, yet you will still be able to distinguish those light taps and knocks on the tip. Angle the rod tip straight out at right angles from the bank (90 degrees) and you'll miss most registrations.

In addition, and regardless of the elements, more bites will result in chub on the bank by using just a front rod rest to angle the line above spiralling currents along the margins, with the butt resting upon your thigh. Your hand can then be positioned loosely in a totally relaxed manner around the reel stem in readiness of an instant strike. If it's in your pocket you will miss a much larger proportion of bites, believe me. That two-second lapse between bite and strike may not seem long, but it is. It's too long! Try holding on to your rod as I have described for an entire session, and experience the difference.

MY FIXED PATERNOSTER LEDGER RIG

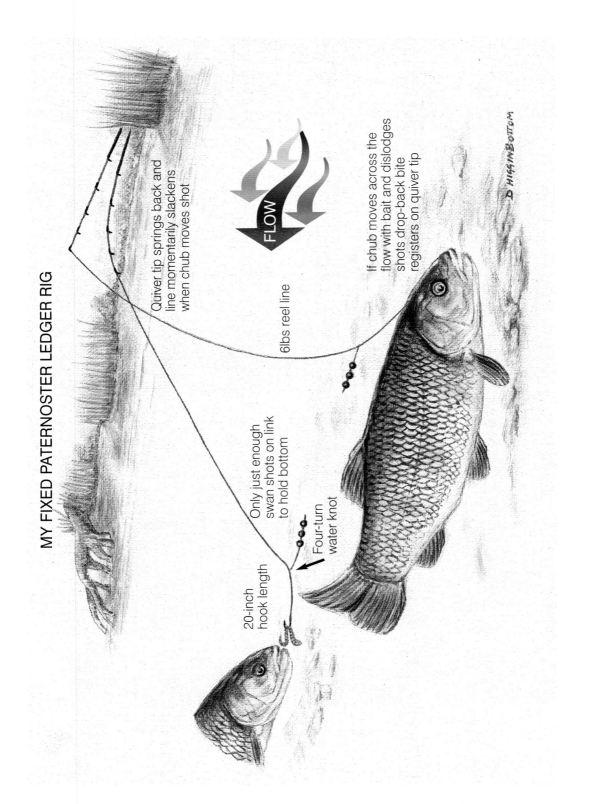

Quiver tip springs back and line momentarily slackens when chub moves shot

FLOW

6lbs reel line

If chub moves across the flow with bait and dislodges shots drop-back bite registers on quiver tip

D HIGGINBOTTOM

Only just enough swan shots on link to hold bottom

Four-turn water knot

20-inch hook length

Part of a truly memorable catch made during an afternoon winter session along my local River Wensum, way back in the 1980s. Just look at the colour of my hair! A succession of tiny, drop-back bites resulted in over 20 specimen roach to nearly 3lbs, plus several big chub. I thought I'd died and gone to heaven.

Juggling the amount of swan shots on the ledger link (see diagram) so that the bait only just holds bottom (and this applies also to quivertipping for roach), is the formula for instigating those gentle drop-back bites caused by a chub or roach moving across the current, or upstream toward the rod with the bait. You could be cajoled into thinking that the shots are merely resettling in a fast flow, but these gentle, seemingly innocuous registrations occur quite commonly when the bait has been cast downstream and across, resulting, if you hit any drop-back bites quickly enough, in many a bonus fish in the net. So keep your eyes fixed upon the quiver tip and react to any peculiar registration. Try for instance, to position the very end of the white-painted tip against a dark background, like a shadow on the surface or against the bark of a tree trunk on the opposite bank, so that each and every tap and rustle is shown clearly.

One memorable afternoon, at a time when large shoals of specimen-sized roach were prolific, I once had an enormous haul of pound-plus roach, including a couple of monsters approaching 3lbs, plus several good chub, from a deep glide in the River Wensum near Norwich. The quiver tip merely easing back an inch every so often accounted for all but one or two of the unmissable downstream yanks. Had I far more shots on the link than was actually required, I doubt most of those tiny registrations would have occurred, and I would never have enjoyed such wonderful sport.

BARBEL

During the past decade or so, barbel have become the next most popular fish to carp – and rightly so. I even know several 'past carpers' who now fish for barbel and nothing else. Using the most effective technique for carp, bolt-rig ledgering, they have simply switched species but not tackle, and, of course, being nothing more than 'river carp', barbel respond to shock tactics with equal gusto.

Their protrusile, hoover-like mouths and super-sensitive barbules, just like the carp, are perfectly designed for sifting through the bottom strata. Barbel are, if anything, even more readily caught using ledgering shock tactics. This is due to their coned or pointed snout and the fact that they lose sight of the bait sooner than a carp does. Close your right hand around the end of your nose while bringing your left thumb slowly towards your mouth, and you will see what I mean. It disappears from sight when still several inches away from your mouth. This is why barbel move their heads agitatedly from side to side when trying to centralise the bait with their underslung, protrusile mouths, just prior to hoovering it up and doing an instant runner, pulling the rod tip round and virtually hooking themselves in the process. It is also why a sandpaper-like feeling is transmitted to the line, resulting simultaneously in the 'tiny trembling' of a super-sensitive rod tip, as they centralise the bait, because the long barbules do a 'plink plonk' against the hook link.

Of course, there are times when barbel do not necessarily bolt off immediately the bait is sucked up, as many hours of fish spotting and feeding barbel in shallow, clear flowing water will reveal, especially when picking up a bait presented on a very light link ledger. There will often be times, from sucking the bait in, to shots on the link dragging bottom, lasting several seconds before the barbel reacts. Like carp, they seem willing at times to put up with a certain amount of resistance. Indeed, I have instinctively struck barbel having watched a bunch of maggots being hoovered up and the fish turning its head to the side as they do characteristically, just before moving downstream, without so much as a tremor on a sensitive rod tip.

I remember filming stalking for barbel when making series 7 of Go Fishing back in the early 1990s on the clear-flowing River Wensum at the famous Point swim at Costessey Mill in Norfolk. Around 20 years ago this was one of my very favourite haunts, where during several earlier years I had spent much time down on the bottom among the gravel in the company of the river's barbel population while scuba-diving with my old buddy, Sid Johnson. There were no monsters in the Wensum in those pre-cormorant, pre-otter days, although far more barbel than are around today, I'm sad to say. Otters have a lot to answer for as I write this in 2010. The best barbel specimens topped out, as in many rivers of that era, at around 13lbs. The national barbel record in 1976, for instance, was 13¾ lbs from the famous Royalty Fishery on the Hampshire Avon; a catch made over a decade earlier, incidentally. I should think that even taking the country as a whole, I doubt there is now a single river where barbel have been introduced that has not produced specimens over 15lbs. It's a funny old world.

Anyway, back to the river at Costessey Mill, where for the best part of an hour prior to actually baiting my hook I fed getting on for a gallon of white maggots to a group of nice barbel in the 6-11lbs range, plus an entourage of some 20 hungry chub, all between 3-4lbs. They occupied a fast and shallow run, four feet deep, along the edge of a line of overhanging goat willows, 10 yards in length. I did this so that my good friend, and top Anglia camera man, Paul Bennett, with whom I've worked with for both Anglia and Discovery TV for a span exceeding 20 years, could capture the feeding mêleé on tape, as he indeed did through the clear water.

It made fabulous viewing because you saw the barbel's protrusile mouth working overtime in hoovering up the maggots trundling along the gravel bottom, while the chub rushed about all over the swim gorging themselves silly. When there was but a few handfuls of maggots left, I nicked a bunch on to the size 8 hook and link ledger rig, and plopped them gently into the head of the run. Within minutes, the rod hooped round into a full curvature as a nice barbel whizzed beneath the raft of willows trying to snarl me up on the roots, fair sizzling 6lbs line from the miniature fixed spool reel; or perhaps it was merely dashing into the relative darkness beneath those willows for sanctuary. Either way, I didn't actually feel or see the bite on the rod tip. I merely struck when I could see the maggots weren't there any more, just the head of a barbel turning downstream. Actually, I managed to extract two nice barbel from that snaggy overhang in less than an hour's fishing; one of around 6lbs and the other pushing double figures, so we had some great action for the program.

The point is, today most barbel anglers would approach that same swim, were it still full of barbel, which sadly it isn't, by bolt-rig ledgering, using infinitely heavier tackle. Because they would, in all probability, not be holding their rod, they would indeed need heavier tackle than I used on camera, because any hooked fish would be way under the willows and possibly nudging sunken branches and roots, the baitrunner reel facility freely giving line, before they even had a good grip of their rod. Whereas, in the programme I was striking and moving quickly downstream along the bank all in one frantic movement, in order to impart side strain immediately upon the fish, which put up incredible fights, thanks to the forgiving elastic action of my all-through Avon rod.

A nice barbel safely in the net following an exciting battle beneath the overhang of goat willows at the famous Point swim on the River Wensum at Costessey Mill, during filming for Anglia TV and series 7 of Go Fishing in 1992.

Yes, the occasional big chub also takes a liking to ledgered halibut pellets or boilies aimed at big barbel, for which I employ a small multiplier and 11-foot, 1¾lb test curve, all-through action carp rod. This River Wensum beauty pulled the scales down to 6lbs 9oz.

Mentioning this particular episode of Go Fishing makes me remember why barbel simply love to occupy dark runs beneath runs and rafts of overhanging and submerged willows, and sometimes alders. It is not only for the clean gravel - no light to grow dense weed beds, remember - or just for the soothing darkness. I found out by scuba-diving many such swims, all holding barbel, that it is also because when the surface current is deflected downward by the leading submerged branches, the flow beneath is subsequently increased to twice as fast as along the outside of the willow raft. That's why barbel love such swims. They demand a certain velocity of water to feel happy in, preferably with a canopy overhead, or the feel-safe factor of deeper

runs where the surface is swirling and turbulent, like in weir pools.

I prefer to make short, impromptu sessions close to snaggy hideouts or weir pools, using fairly substantial gear for what little barbel I do enjoy in the Wensum these days. As I have already stated, otters have chomped their way through so many of the river's specimens, including even 18 to 20lb monsters, and possibly future record fish. This is partly because, compared to the wily chub, barbel are so inherently friendly and easy to approach from a downstream direction, even by a scuba-diver, as I experienced when exploring the river in a wetsuit 30 years ago.

My tackle choice is an 11 foot, 1¾lbs test curve, Heritage carp rod, coupled to a sleek, Masterline Rovex Oberon multiplier loaded with clear, 12lbs test mono and a size 6 hair rig, fished bolt-style with a 3oz flat lead.

The running lead is cushioned by a rubber bead on either side, and lightly pinched on to the reel line, 2-3 feet above are 2-3, 3xSSG shots, which act as an all-important back-lead. Presenting 20-25 mm halibut pellets or two 15mm boilies on a long hair, I am obviously not after bags of fish because real numbers do not exist anyway, simply the occasional whopper, which I might well have to slow down before it gets its head into a snag.

Having caught specimens to within just three ounces of 17lbs, I have therefore good reason for always holding the rod comfortably with my thumb on top of the reel in readiness for a bite, and using the super-smooth drag of the multiplier for employing maximum pressure upon the fish. The fact that the line is fed evenly across and around the spool, as opposed to being transported at right angles around the bail arm before going on to the fixed spool reel, is of paramount importance to me. In addition, a small multiplier is both neat and a pure joy to use on all bolt rig set-ups, offering super-smooth casting, whatever the distance.

I also use the same outfit when obliged to fish at close range near snags for carp, in those frantic 'hit and hold' tussles. Even for float fishing at close range, it knocks the stuffing out of a fixed spool reel every time. Try it and see. You can then use that same little multiplier for tossing plugs to chub, plus rubber replicants and spoons to pike, in conjunction with a little single-handed six-foot, trigger grip, bait caster rod. (see Lure Throwing, Chapter Eight.)

Fishing for the cyprinid species offers so much variety and so many ways to enjoy our sport, that no angler's life will be long enough to fully explore them all. That shouldn't stop us trying, though!

Weighing just three ounces short of 17lbs, my largest ever barbel is, in all probability, like so many River Wensum monsters, now 'brown-bread', thanks to the heavy and wanton predation from otters along my local stretch of river.

MY FAVOURITE FISH THE ROACH

If I had been asked 30 years ago what time of day was best for the chance of big roach feeding, especially those monster 2lbs-plus specimens inhabiting the clear-flowing upper reaches of our smaller Norfolk and Suffolk rivers where I concentrated most of my winter efforts, I would have replied immediately, 'when it's around a 30th at 2.8, either at dawn or dusk.' While I realise that such an answer today would probably mean absolutely nothing at all to the vast majority of anglers, back then it was understood by most roach enthusiasts, especially my peers.

Believe it or not, a large part of my own understanding of roach behaviour came through my early photographic efforts. Nowadays, everything has changed thanks to the production and availability of auto-exposure 35mm SLR cameras and, in recent years, both 35mm SLR and 'point-and-shoot', auto-everything, digital cameras. Today, no one need worry about exposure, at what F-stop, and at what shutter speed combination the camera will need to be set relative to the speed of film being used, in order to capture that prize trophy shot, so that it is pin sharp and well illuminated. Those problems, and dare I say (tongue in cheek) being a 'sad old sod', that much of the photographic expertise, enjoyment even, has been eradicated.

It's all done for you now by modern technology, and what a wonderful advance it all is. Car owners no longer look beneath their bonnets to see if they can fix a breakdown problem, because it's all down to 'engine management', and photography is little different. Even the cheapest point-and-shoot digital camera will automatically set the ISO, the equivalent of film speed, and use fill-in flash, when needed, to illuminate dark areas or extra flash when the light is simply inadequate for the subject matter. Beware, however, in some instances they do not. Years ago, we had to mess about with all kinds of manual flash units to do the same thing, whereas it is something that is now completely taken for granted. More of all this however is in the 'photography chapter'.

However, back then, by relating to our camera settings we did get to realise when big roach would come out to play, or more to the point, bite confidently on big baits, a thumbnail-sized lump of breadflake covering a size 8 hook, for example. In certain conditions, when the light values were dipping fast and dusk was falling, roach could feed with confidence because predators were less likely to put in an appearance; and, again, just as dawn was breaking, hence our constant relation to camera settings.

My old buddy and fellow roach enthusiast, Arthur 'Nobby' Clarke and I, throughout the 1970s, played about with all manner of contraptions, such as putting a handkerchief over the flash gun or bouncing it off the inside of a white umbrella to diffuse the light, in order to photograph big roach caught in poor light, without our manual flash guns 'burning out' the highly reflective image of silver scales. We both experienced, from readings given by our hand-held light meters (SLR cameras in those days did not have built-in automatic exposure or built-in, pop-up flash), that around a 30th at 2.8 was when most of our big, clearwater roach were likely to start biting with confidence. A time coincidentally, when seeing clearly into the water just starts to become difficult for the angler. An early fish, before darkness really set in, could just about be photographed without flash using a relatively slow, 100 ASA film say, by stepping down to a really slow shutter speed (a 30th of a second) combined with the lens opened fully to 2.8.

Yes, the 1970/80 period certainly produced massive roach to river enthusiasts who presented big baits, particularly breadflake, just as the light was fading at dusk, or the following morning at dawn. This 2½ lbs plus River Wensum beauty happened along, to quivertipped flake at daybreak.

For working out camera settings and targeting big roach, whether ledgering or long-trotting, there was no better way of judging the amount of light around than with a light meter. This old-looking roach, at nearly 17 inches long, no doubt once topped 3lbs; it still pulled the spring balance down to 2½ lbs.

This magnificent haul, a baker's dozen of 1-2lbs roach came from stret-pegging a deep marginal run along a narrow Norfolk river, during the last hour of daylight in super-mild winter conditions.

If the light went any lower, then using flash was imperative. Though as I mentioned before, extremely difficult because as yet, dedicated flash units operating through sensors via metering systems which now instantly work out exactly the right amount of flash required, had yet to be invented. Compared to photographing fish nowadays, it was almost like steam radio.

Nobby and I would be constantly using our manual hand-held light meters, especially at dusk, to predetermine when roach would be likely to start feeding. More often than not, should we strike lucky, minutes later we would be setting the lenses on our cameras wide open to 2.8 and the shutter speed to around a 30th of a second. If fish came any later, then the eternal problem of flash photography would arise. Taking the shot at any slower shutter speed would inevitably result in camera shake and a blurred image, as we both found out to our cost on more than one occasion.

Yes, I often think about those old roach-rich, pre-cormorant, days when rivers were full of roach and both men and boys preferred to wet a line in running water. The fascination of running a float through, or stret-pegging with the float set extra deep so it lies flat on the surface with the bait stationary on the bottom, because big roach often prefer a static bait, particularly in really cold conditions, will always be with me as long as I live.

The memory of catching no fewer than 49 river roach over the magical 2lbs barrier during the 1974/5 winter, mostly on the float, both long-trotting and stret-pegging, and from four different Norfolk and Suffolk Rivers too, the Wensum, Yare, Waveney and Tud, will never fade. I doubt few could catch 49 river roach over 2lbs in a decade today, let alone in one calendar year, and while we are on the subject, perhaps it's worth remembering that for every 2lbs fish, there were dozens and dozens of 1-13 oz fish.

Of course, I couldn't do it today should my very life depend on it, simply because such shoals of roach no longer exist, thanks to the Black Death (cormorants) and various other negatives, none of which the Environment Agency or DEFRA ever seem to address themselves, but which both, by law of the land, are supposed to protect. Small wonder the man on the street has little confidence in those who are supposed to fight on his behalf, even though he purchases a licence in the hope of it. Tut. There I go, getting all political again.

STRET-PEGGING

Having highlighted the effectiveness of stret-pegging for catching large river roach, plus barbel, chub, dace, bream and even carp, especially from those slack and slow moving nearside bank swims, this float fishing technique, remember, presents a completely static bait perfectly to each. Let me now tell you how it is so effective in producing those glorious unmissable bites, and why.

Firstly, in nearly all rivers, deep rivers especially, the flow is always much stronger and more importantly faster at the surface. Don't worry, your bait will be situated hard on the bottom where current speed is much slower, and much to the liking of big roach, especially.

Now, you can only stret-peg happily with the float set well over depth. Accept this one fact, and you will come to love the technique as much as I do. Exactly how far over depth, and it's hardly rocket science, depends largely upon current speed.

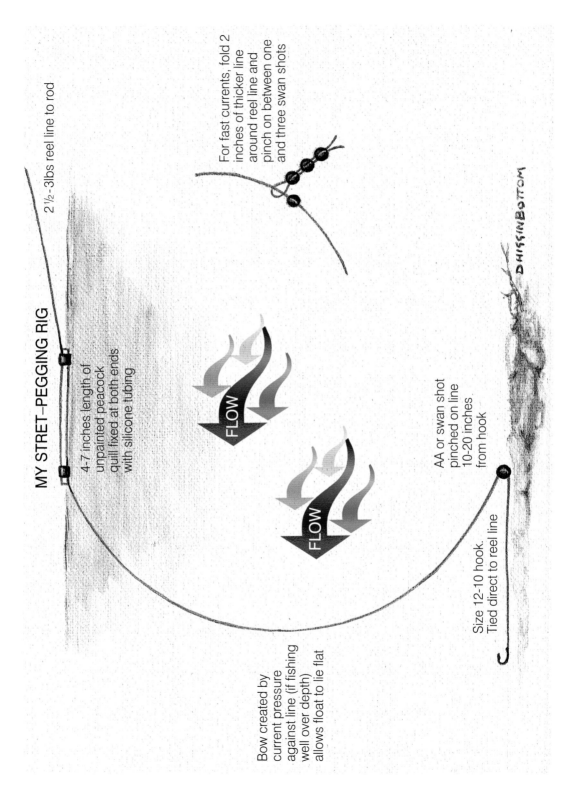

MY STRET–PEGGING RIG

2½ -3lbs reel line to rod

4-7 inches length of unpainted peacock quill fixed at both ends with silicone tubing

For fast currents, fold 2 inches of thicker line around reel line and pinch on between one and three swan shots

FLOW

FLOW

AA or swan shot pinched on line 10-20 inches from hook

Size 12-10 hook. Tied direct to reel line

Bow created by current pressure against line (if fishing well over depth) allows float to lie flat

DHISSINBOTTOM

However, do not try to fish with the float only just deeper than the swim as though float-ledgering in still water, or you will never get the hang of this basically simple technique. This is where most anglers go wrong. You simply keep sliding the float (which must be fixed to the line both top and bottom with silicone tubing) up the line, starting with it a couple of feet deeper than swim depth, so that when the bait comes to settle on the bottom directly downstream from the rod tip, the float lies perfectly flat on the surface. Fixing it at twice swim depth is nothing out of the ordinary and it still works, believe me.

If the float does not lie perfectly flat, or is constantly being half-cocked by current force, then simply slide it further up the line until it does. Casting directly downstream and allowing the terminal rig to anchor the bait hard on the bottom exactly where you want it, before allowing the float to settle and the bow in the line to form, is of paramount importance. Don't just cast out and let the rig swing round in the current. You see, (consider the diagram at this stage) the entire effectiveness of this devastating technique is due to allowing that all-important bow to form in the line between float and terminal rig.

Now, I guess this would seem rather insensitive to many float fishermen, but bites are in no way diminished, because the bow is supported by current pressure against it at all times. When a fish bites and moves off with the bait, first cocking the float and then making it slide under, current pressure still maintains that bow to some extent. This allows you to strike firmly, in order to straighten the line, before the fish feels any buoyancy in the float and thinks about ejecting the bait. By then, though, you will have hooked up. Great eh?

For gentle and slow surface currents, my favourite float is simply a 4-7 inch length of plain, unpainted, peacock quill. Now, to my mind there is nothing more natural than a bird quill lying on the surface, and I use peacock quill more than all other float-making materials. I'm even lucky enough to have a couple of peacocks roaming around my lakes and around the house, and they grow their quills all winter long in readiness for that marvellous courtship display during the spring. They then shed them throughout the summer months, when any sensible angler like me stores them for later use. Remember that around one inch of peacock quill supports a single BB shot, so two inches supports an AA shot, and four inches around a swan shot. There really is no better, more buoyant float-making material. Though if you come across some pelican feathers during foreign travel, snap them up, pronto. They make great long-trotting specials.

Back to stret-pegging, and for fishing into dusk and beyond, a chemical light source is sleeved on to the tip of the quill using silicone tubing. In currents that deviate every so often, I might use an Avon-style bodied float, but still fish it perfectly flat on the surface. I'll say this just once more at risk of repetition; the float must always be fished flat, with the rod tip angled up a little and pointing downstream at around 45 degrees. (see diagram)

By now, I'm sure you've got the message, but what about the terminal end of this float rig? Well, in really slow currents, simply pinching an AA or a swan shot on to the reel line, say, 10-12 inches above the hook, is usually sufficient. For stronger currents I simply pinch a single AA shot on to the line 10-12 inches above the hook, and above this, on to two inches of thicker line, folded around the reel line, I pinch between 1-3 swan shot. So, in effect, it becomes a mini link-ledger, running above the single shot. Ensure the loop formed is small enough not to pass over the single stop shot.

An excellent alternative to this is to replace the loop of folded line with a Drennan ring, to which a couple of inches of thicker line and sufficient shots can be added. By using 2 or 3 SSG shots on the link, virtually any current strength can be tackled. It's all so very, very simple and effective, whether using a 2-3lbs test reel line for roach, or 10lbs test with carp and barbel in mind.

One summer's evening, I caught my first ever double-figure barbel employing stret-pegging tactics from a deep, bankside run along the upper reaches of my local River Wensum. Watching, mesmerised, at that length of peacock quill sliding purposefully beneath the surface, followed immediately by the sheer power of a near-11lbs barbel trying to find sanctuary in submerged tree roots as it unexpectedly powered upstream beneath an overhanging willow, having hoovered up my three grains of sweetcorn, proved an unforgettable experience. Indeed, as so many float fishing catches have over the years.

My largest ever dace, rudd, tench, bream, pike, carp and grass carp, have all come while float fishing. I guess that boyhood fascination of watching a float has never left me. As a point of fact, I always choose to use a float wherever and whenever I can, in favour of any other bite indicator. Ironically, my largest river roach, weighing an ounce and a half less than 3lbs, came while quivertipping, but at least a couple of hundred between 2lb and 2lb-13oz have come on the float, both by long-trotting and stret-pegging.

Back in the 1970s when big river roach were common, 13-foot trotting rods were much bulkier, being wider in diameter and noticeably much heavier than they are today. This often resulted towards the end of a lengthy long-trotting session, in a large proportion of bites being missed, simply

Ironically, this beauty weighing just an ounce and a half short of that magical 3lbs barrier, my largest roach ever, did not come when I was long-trotting, but quiver tip ledgering a favourite River Wensum glide.

because your forearm could take no more. Back in the old pre-1960 days, it was even worse, trying to trot, hour after hour, using a heavy, 13-foot built cane rod to set the hook. Back then, it was also difficult to purchase a free-flowing centrepin reel fitted with a fully enclosed line guard, to ensure the line didn't flap back behind the cage in windy conditions; the nemesis of all would-be centrepin users.

Ironically, we now have the choice of numerous, superbly free-flowing aluminium centrepins, each crafted on a lathe from a block of aluminium bar stock, including a few models with fully enclosed line guards. My own John Wilson 'Heritage' centrepin, marketed by Masterline Walker Ltd, is a prime example, and the most exciting piece of gear I have ever had the privilege of designing. There are also literally dozens and dozens of incredibly light, fast-action, trotting rods constructed from super-slim, carbon fibre blanks which slice through the air with absolute ease, and have a remarkably rapid return, making for incredible striking even at range. Yet few river systems, as I write this in 2010, hold anywhere near enough shoals of big roach – any roach at all, in some cases – to take full advantage of our new angling hardware. If only, eh?

LONG-TROTTING

A lack of big roach in my local rivers does not stop me from long-trotting whenever conditions are perfect. Mild weather, combined with a coloured river fining down nicely after a flood, with no more than a foot of clear visibility, is what I'm aiming for, ideally. Invariably, I account for more chub, and even bream, than I do roach, anyway, but to feel that dogged kicking on the rod tip when I do eventually contact a big redfin, and feeling the

centrepin's drum revolving steadily beneath my thumb as I give line, makes it all very much worthwhile. My knees go to jelly, just like they always did, whenever I see the deep bodied, silvery-blue flanks and red fins of a big roach as it nears the net. I pray for the small hook not to pull out, or a pike to suddenly appear from nowhere, as they do, and make a lunge. I always feel that ardent roach anglers are exactly that, for life. I know I am. Whenever I'm asked, at tackle shows or casting exhibitions, what I would like to be doing if I had just one day's fishing left, I always answer, 'long-trotting for big roach'.

To my mind, being an explorative, searching, 'I want to know what's down there' technique, using the float to explore running water, with its never-ending variation in both current speed and depth, makes long-trotting, especially using the centrepin, arguably the most demanding, difficult and thus the most satisfying technique of all. Perhaps it's that marvellous little boy memory of watching the float tip suddenly disappearing when it shouldn't, or the fact that when it dips under exactly where you expected it should, you have obviously read your river well. For some, it's that pleasing, ultra-sensitive feeling of the drum revolving steadily beneath gentle thumb pressure, while others delight in swishing the rod back to feel the tip kicking as they look up in confirmation that a fish is on, and they haven't snagged the bottom. Me? I simply love it all. I feel at peace with the world, and with the particular river valley I happen to be searching, especially when roaming along in mild weather coupled to ideal water conditions when I can expect a bite or two to come quickly from a particular run, before moving on to the next likely swim. I've been privileged and fortunate to catch specimen roach on the trot while roaming the banks of many wonderful, southern rivers like the

Kennet, the Hampshire Avon, Dorset Stour, Frome, Test, Anton, and Itchen.

Roaming thus, means carrying the very minimum of tackle. I only take a small, lightweight stool along to where past experience has taught me that keeping a really low profile is imperative. Standing well back from the water's edge and then trotting a bait up to 40 yards down river to where I expect a group of roach to be holding, is usually precaution enough. I no longer wish to fill a keep net, so never carry one, but a lightweight, extending landing net is worth its weight in gold, particularly where thick rush or reed beds hang far out into the stream.

A small, canvas bait bucket contains my camera, waterproof trousers and of course a loaf of fresh, white bread, plus a bag of mash and a tin of maggots, should I think I might need them. Although to be truthful, wherever there are just a few big roach about, which is the case in most of the rivers I now fish, I go straight through the pain barrier of troublesome small fish by offering a bait only a sizeable roach can manage.

My standard set-up consists of a size 10 hook tied directly to a clear, 2½ lb reel line, with a thumbnail-sized piece of white breadflake folded over the hook and pinched on hard around the shank only. This then stays on well, with the hook point pulling through nicely on the strike, but at the same time, it comes off easily to a quick false strike at the end of the swim helping to loose feed it every time I retrieve.

While on the subject of baits, let's talk about mash. Now, a good and effective bread-mash, which breaks up into a million tiny particles that attract, but do not overfeed, as they drift through the swim, once all the surplus water has been squeezed out, can be made only from stale white or brown loaves. New bread turns into a sticky mess, which is why, during the winter months, I have an old keepnet hanging up in the garage, well away from the mice, full of old bread scraps drying out.

On the evening prior to a trotting or quivertipping session, the bread is soaked in the sink in tepid water (hot water makes the mash sticky), for half an hour before squeezing out the water and placing in a plastic carrier bag to go into the canvas bucket. If I have collected a large amount of dried bread, I make several batches which, all except the one I am going to use, are popped into the freezer for future sessions. Trying to make bread-mash at the waterside, by dunking in the river in the landing net and then squeezing out, is fishing time wasted at the best time of day, resulting at best in freezing cold hands.

Incidentally, here's a tip if you happen to walk from the downstream end of a fishery all the way up to the most upstream swim, before roaming back down river again. On the way up, take time to plop in a golf ball-sized helping of mash into each swim that looks 'roachy', allowing a distance of several yards from where it went in to where it might eventually have attracted and settled. Then, using a bird's feather, crossed sticks or whatever, mark where you will need to stand in order to cover the swim, then you can creep back into the same spot later on. An instant bite on your first trot through could well be the reward on your return, albeit hours later.

Polaroids and a peaked cap improve my vision, and all my essential sundries, like floats, hooks, shot, silicone bands, scissors, disgorger, forceps, catapult, scales etc., are contained in my waistcoat; this leaves just my 13½ foot trotting rod and reel.

A rarity these days along my local rivers I'm afraid, but occasionally it's comforting to catch beautifully proportioned and coloured 2lbs-plus roach such as this, when long-trotting. Sadly, the predatory pressure from cormorants and now otters has really taken its toll.

To make a long Nottingham-style cast into the middle of this River Wensum weir pool, I have gently pulled a web of line back to my left, using my thumb and next two fingers (hence the reason for having three rings close together on the rod butt) before making a sideways swing and cast. It's actually easier to do than to describe.

Now, whether you cast 'Wallis' (directly from the reel) or simply pull sufficient line off 'Nottingham' style with a centrepin, having three rings spaced fairly close together immediately above the reel allows both casts to be used. Gathering line for short casts with thumb, first and second fingers, between these three rings, as in the Nottingham style, becomes second nature, after a while and is particularly useful when using light terminal rigs with minimal shot on the line. (see photo and diagrams)

It's as well to remember that the Wallis cast was devised for the longer casts, and the fast waters of the Hampshire Avon, where you need a heavy shotting pattern comprising at least three or four swan shots, to initiate enough impetus to keep the centrepin's drum revolving in the first place.

What is more, you then need a reel line of at least 4-5lbs test that won't break as it's yanked over the thumb or fingers of your left hand to start the impetus of the Wallis cast.

If you are right-handed, both casts are made from your left by swinging the rig back and casting in a sideways, low trajectory, swing. This is the beauty of centrepin fishing, as opposed to fixed spool and closed face reels, where most anglers seem to prefer casting overhead. This creates an exaggerated loop of line in the air, which gives all the more line to control once the float touches down, simultaneously creating unnecessary shadows upon the surface, which in bright or clear water conditions could scare spooky fish. The low-trajectory, side-casting of the centrepin alleviates much of this, and, of course, immediate control of the cast is mastered simply by gentle thumb control on the rim of the reel. To my mind, there is nothing more accurate, effective, or enjoyable.

ROACH/CENTREPIN CASTING SEQUENCE, NOTTINGHAM STYLE

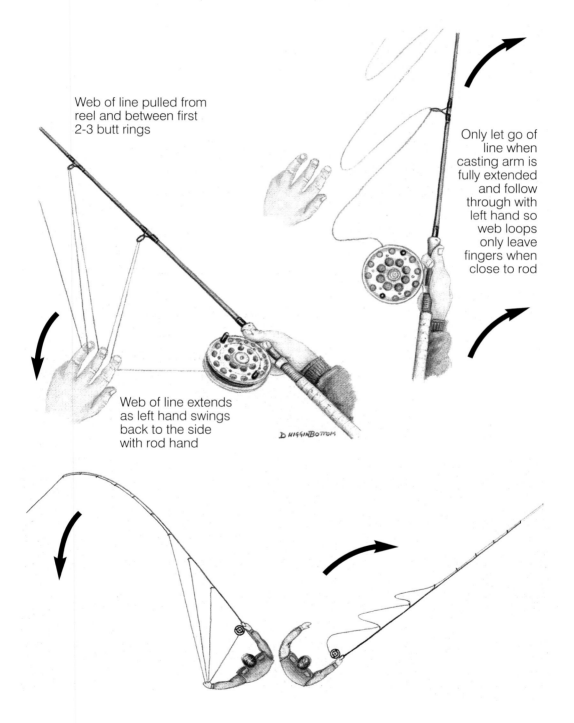

Web of line pulled from reel and between first 2-3 butt rings

Only let go of line when casting arm is fully extended and follow through with left hand so web loops only leave fingers when close to rod

Web of line extends as left hand swings back to the side with rod hand

D HIGGINBOTTOM

Now, I'm not going to fill this chapter with goodness knows how many shotting patterns and float rigs you think you'll need in order to catch roach long-trotting. In incredibly clear water that is hardly moving, where roach have all the time in the world to inspect and refuse a single maggot nicked onto a size 22 tied to a 12 ounce hook link, you really need that match-fishing hat on. That is not what I'm about, although in my earlier years an education in club fishing did teach me when to step right down, usually in clear, exceedingly cold conditions in order even to get bites, and such knowledge is always useful.

However, by choosing to present a fairly, buoyant bait like breadflake, I prefer a good shotting load to take it down quickly to just above the river bed and to keep it there throughout the trot; you certainly maximise on swim exploration. My advice always, is to use a float carrying more shot rather than less. I like Avons and chubber-style floats, always fixed firmly top and bottom by silicone bands, because they can be seen easily at distance. This ensures the bait is presented as naturally as possible and at a similar speed to all those loose pieces of mash around it. If you fish too light, the bait simply does not behave naturally, and big roach know the difference only too well.

This is why I use a line of bulk shot, usually a 'bathroom chain' of BBs or AAs which fold against the river bed should it suddenly shallow up, as opposed to swan shots which tend occasionally to become hung-up and thus create false bites. They are placed around 20-24 inches above the bait, with a small shot or two in between. This could be a couple of no 4s, or a single no 1, or even a BB. It depends totally on current strength; so don't be afraid to juggle about until a bite materialises. (see diagram)

Now, with few roach in the swim especially, you cannot afford to miss too many bites through lack of pick-up on the strike, so angle the rod tip around to follow the float as it progresses downstream, almost pointing the rod at the float, without pulling it off its line of trot. Most important this, as wily old roach, and remember they have become so large by being wily enough to avoid dangers like marauding pike, certainly won't be fooled by a lump of breadflake moving across the flow before their very eyes, through poor float control. They want it drifting directly downstream toward them, like all the other pieces, perhaps swirling up occasionally from the river bed, through current deviation. This is why, every so often, holding back on the float so the bait does lift upwards for a few seconds, before trotting through again, can promote an instant reaction and a firm bite.

As the float travels further downstream, simultaneously lower the rod tip accordingly, to encourage maximum line pick-up on the strike. You cannot, for instance, expect to set the hook, especially in deepish runs of six feet or more, by continually holding the rod up high. Learn to keep feeding just sufficient line from the reel, beneath your thumb, with the rod tip held as low as possible, unless mending line every so often. This is why long-trotting is such a skilful technique. Granny can easily pick up a carp rod with the buzzer screaming its head off, and the fish already hooked by a bolt rig and perhaps even crank in a modest-sized, or maybe even a whopping great carp. She would have trouble simply running the float through if long-trotting, though, providing she managed even to make a cast in the first place.

Simply holding the rod all day long, and continually working the tackle through, takes an enormous amount of skill and concentration and that's something that certainly cannot be done from the comfort of a bed chair. That is why I personally regard long-trotting for large, wily roach as the most demanding and most skilful technique of all, be it game, sea or freshwater disciplines.

MY ROACH TROTTING RIG

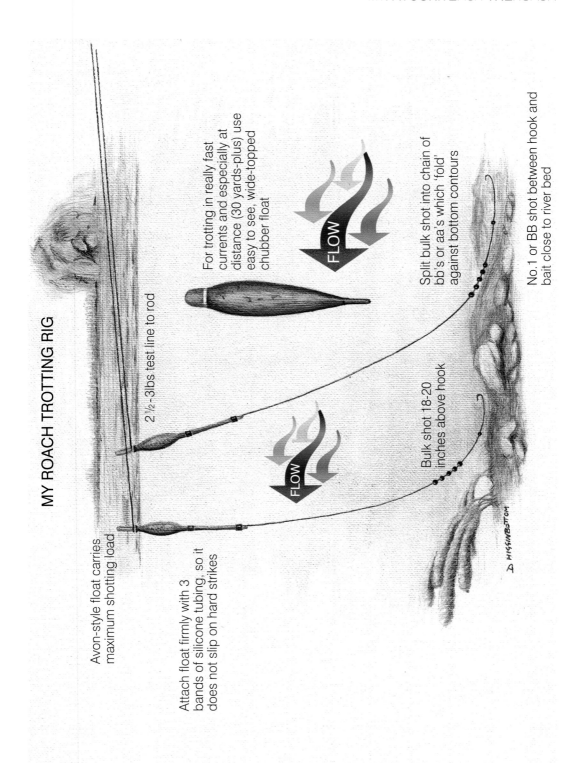

Avon-style float carries maximum shotting load

2½-3lbs test line to rod

For trotting in really fast currents and especially at distance (30 yards-plus) use easy to see, wide-topped chubber float

Attach float firmly with 3 bands of silicone tubing, so it does not slip on hard strikes

FLOW

FLOW

Bulk shot 18-20 inches above hook

Split bulk shot into chain of bb's or aa's which 'fold' against bottom contours

No.1 or BB shot between hook and bait close to river bed

HIGINBOTTOM

FISHING FOREIGN SHORES

I'll begin this chapter with my own top ten pieces of practical advice, which have been compiled over many years of fishing abroad in just about every conceivable angling situation.

10 DO'S AND DON'TS.

1: Only travel with bonded agents who have an ATOL number. Holidays and flights are then completely protected. Being stuck in a foreign country miles from nowhere should an airline or operator suddenly go bust overnight, as they do, not only results in a ruined holiday, you also have no means of returning home.

2: Ask if photos of big fish in a brochure (beware of standard library pics) are everyday or common catches. Good operators thoroughly research their locations, providing customers with an accurate idea of exactly what to expect.

3: Beware of operators who cannot answer immediately every question you ask about documents and inoculations required, expected weather, likely species, specialised clothing requirements etc., for a particular location.

4: Determine exactly what tackle outfits are required for exotic species. On escorted trips,

the right gear may be provided, or you could be expected to take your own. It's too late to find this out when you get there.

5: Beware of tour operators that say anyone can enjoy a particular location. The one to two-hour long, strength-sapping fights from large sharks caught from the shore in Namibia or South Africa for instance, would be far too strenuous for most extremely young or elderly anglers, especially those with asthma or heart problems.

6: When tour operators state that everything is included in their package price, ensure that this is so. Overpriced drinks, tackle hire or disproportionate tipping can add substantially to the cost of your holiday.

7: Going at the very best month, or months of the year in order to catch a particular size or species of fish is imperative when travelling halfway around the world to exotic locations. Don't be fobbed off with a cheap, out of season package when the fish you seek are simply not there, or not feeding due to spawning.

8: If taking your own tackle, protect rods in a durable, adjustable case or tube, and pack all sundries, especially lures, hooks and tools, in the holdall that goes in the aircraft's hold.

Norfolk anglers, Tony Wilkinson and Paul Dawson, enjoy the exotic wildlife along the fabulous Zambezi River in Africa, while using fish fillet, and drifting with the fast flow, for the high-jumping, tooth-laden tiger fish.

9: Daily sportfishing boat charter hire is the single most expensive item by far in an exotic fishing holiday. Good operators make you aware of these costs and how many anglers will be sharing a boat.

10: If you are not completely happy with certain elements of a proposed trip, do not use that operator.

Obviously, fishing abroad does not necessarily connect you with monstrous fish, although I admit it's one of the main reasons that attracts me overseas. However, if you are careful about location selection, it can and usually does at the very least, put the sun on your back at a time when things are dank, dismal and cold back in good old Blighty. I try to arrange the bulk of my foreign trips around enjoying warm weather, while being there at

the very best time for the species I am targeting. In southern India, for instance, home to the huge golden mahseer, which is still to be found within the 60-90lbs range in several wild and woolly stretches of the famous Cauvery river, south of Bangalore, it would be foolish to arrange a trip anywhere from May through to October. The annual monsoon rains turn the river into a brown, debris-packed cauldron, 20 to 30 feet higher than normal level and you may catch a few catfish, which seem to appear from nowhere when the river is highly coloured, but as for mahseer, forget it.

Far better to plan your trip while the Cauvery is slowly dropping, almost to its lowest levels, following the monsoons, because the choice, big mahseer runs, invariably situated between exposed fingers of black bedrock down the middle of the river, will then be clearly defined and nicely fishable. Any time from January until April is likely to hold promise, with the very best opportunity of a big fish happening between mid-February and mid-March.

This near-80lbs golden mahseer fought for nearly an hour in the fierce, boulder-strewn currents of South India's Cauvery River. The chances of contacting such a monster are best between mid-February and mid-March when the river is at its lowest following the monsoon rains.

It's impossible, when booking up months in advance, as I need to do when arranging my TV shoots for instance, always to guarantee sport, even when you have supposedly secured the best time frame, because Mother Nature always has a trick or two up her sleeve. Take a trip across the pond to the good old USA and Bill Clinton's home state of Arkansas (I know, it's pronounced 'Arkensaw' but can't tell you why) that the film crew and I made in June 2009. We filmed along the Mississippi Delta, on 25-mile-long Lake Chicot for my Fishing World series, commissioned by the Discovery Shed channel. It was to feature grass carp, alligator garfish, catfish and big common carp, which had all come relatively easy just one year previously when researching the area. How were we to know, that coinciding with our arrival, the state was at the start of what turned out to be the worst flooding for over 30 years?

For five or six days we simply watched the lake get muddier and muddier and higher and higher to the point that fishing was a complete waste of energy, except for small channel catfish. The introduced Asiatic, silver carp, averaging between 20-40lbs seemed to be moving and jumping everywhere, though, seemingly stimulated by the coloured and rising waters, so something was at least on the cards. Do you think I could catch one? These algae-eating filter feeders, actually introduced by the state fisheries into the area along with big head carp and grass carp for weed and algae clearance, simply ignore any bait you throw at them, and yet come jumping high into the air by the

hundred, honestly, whenever a boat passes by. They seem to be turned on by the pitch of the engine; small wonder that powerboat enthusiasts along the Mississippi and Arkansas River catchments now wear crash helmets! A boat going at 40 knots, colliding with a 30lbs silver carp leaping at 10 knots does not make good news for anyone who gets his head in the way, believe me; deaths have occurred.

As for the programme, well, what saved our bacon was the stock of big grass carp in a nearby 30-acre estate lake, situated in cotton-picking country, called the Elms, which also

Small and aggressive, bait-robbing channel catfish, one after another, were no compensation for the huge carp and garfish we were expecting to catch from Lake Chicot along the Mississippi delta in the state of Arkansas. The worst flooding for 30 years ruined everything. No wonder Wilson is not a happy bunny!

This frog-gulping, high-leaping, 4lbs largemouth bass - America's favourite freshwater species, would you believe - together with several sizeable grass carp, got me out of trouble when filming for Discovery Shed TV in America's deep south, at the Elms Lake.

The River Nile immediately downriver from magical Murchison Falls in Uganda, where the entire might of the world's longest river falls over 100 feet through the rocks into a wide gorge, is without question the most evocative and mesmeric spot to fish on this planet. Playing a Nile perch within its dangerous waters is merely the icing on the cake.

held a prolific head of largemouth bass in the 3-5lbs range, all readily catchable on a little baitcasting outfit. Seeing them come crashing out of the surface to inhale a floating rubber frog was truly magical fishing. In fact, without those grassies and bass, we would have suffered egg on our faces, big time.

So, once again I cannot reiterate enough the importance of booking up exactly the right window of opportunity. Even then, you need to keep your fingers crossed. Should you plan a visit along Africa's magnificent Zambezi River, for instance, to engage in battle with the awesome, tooth-laden tiger fish or the enigmatic vundu catfish, then do so sometime between the end of August and the first week of October. After that, the rains could come at any time and it all goes pear-shaped. In other catchments, the mighty Nile watershed for instance, at magical locations such as Murchison Falls, November through until April, maybe as late as July, is when you need to be there. Your dependable tour operator should be able to furnish you with these exact details, though, so don't settle for less.

Surrounded by shrubbery at Cha-am Fish Park near Hua Hin in Thailand, I'm enjoying the phenomenal fight of a stillwater catfish. They live in water temperatures of between 80-90°F, where their metabolic rate goes almost off the scale. Freelining, float fishing, or ledgering; all methods work here.

THAILAND

In recent years, because my brother Dave married a Thai woman and settled in the city of Hua Hin on the east coast, I have enjoyed several fishing holidays targeting the big fish of Thailand's spectacular commercial freshwater fisheries. With an array of huge, hard-fighting species of both Thai and South American origin, introduced into relatively small lakes of between three and 20 acres, the subsequent sport is little short of phenomenal. Some would say that the fishing is just too easy, but then I would counter by saying, who said it has to be hard, anyway? We all, do we not, make our own challenges?

Here is an article I wrote for Angling Times in January 2010, about fishing in Thailand, prompted by their features editor, Steve Partner.

'I always find Steve Partner's Comment spreads most enlightening, because he cuts right to the chase, whatever the controversy, in his role of devil's advocate. I particularly liked his 'There's just no Challenge' piece back in November's AT, which pondered the question whether big fish of a lifetime caught abroad in exotic locations with the help of a guide actually have any credibility, or even any merit at all. This subject is so vast and complicated, there's possibly a book here, but as I'm lucky enough to travel regularly, catching whoppers, while escorting groups of Brits all bent on doing the same, Steve's reasoning and remarks were most interesting because they applied exactly to what I have been doing for almost the last 20 years, helping others to catch big fish. Honestly, I've never considered the guiding aspect in anything but a positive way. Not that I ever try to psychoanalyse my own thoughts on foreign adventure, anyway. I just love it all, especially when producing monsters from oceans, rivers, or lakes I have never seen before. In many ways, it's the ultimate challenge.

If I enjoy a particular location and species, like Canada's monster lake trout, giant white sturgeon or five species of Pacific salmon, Africa's huge Nile perch, tiger fish and catfish or India's marvellous mahseer, then I want to return again and again. I hope I will continue to do so until I become too old and decrepit, or find that certain destinations simply fail to please any more because the fishery has simply deteriorated through commercial fishing or over sportfishing. I fished India's Cauvery River, for instance, targeting monster mahseer for 15 consecutive, wonderful years, until it became too popular by far.

In some countries, the political situation certainly makes travel, let alone fishing, too dangerous. Had I been asked ten years ago, for instance, what was the most stable county in Africa, I would have probably said Zimbabwe, but things change, don't they? Nowhere more so than at home, which is why so many anglers now simply try to enjoy a foreign trip or two each year instead of banging their heads against the brick wall of do-gooders and declining locations back home.

I came to live in what is now my home county of Norfolk, 40 years ago, because among great Broadland fishing with tench, bream and pike, the roach fishing - still my first love - was nothing short of spectacular, with really big roach, too. However, three decades of the Black Death has ruined all

that, without a word from the good old Environment Agency, who still take our licence money, and whose mandatory job it is to protect inland waterways. What a laugh - although it makes me want to cry!

Now, otters are munching their way through the paltry concentrations of sizeable chub and barbel, too much of a mouthful for cormorants, that are left. The future for upper river fishing in my neck of the woods looks bleak indeed, so small wonder anglers are going abroad to fish in increasing numbers.'

On another tack, I guess I could pop along to a local commercial water, springing up like mushrooms all over East Anglia, and sit shoulder-to-shoulder with many others all bent on filling their keep nets with pasties, but I don't find that in any way appealing. I much prefer to get away from it all with my own fishing, which is why, right now, I'm sitting beside one of Thailand's increasing number of commercial big-fish waters.

Yes! Call me a hypocrite if you like, but the attractive lake before me, just like all the rest, has been stocked with both Thai and South American heavyweights from Mekong pussies to arapaima, with a whole host of beautifully marked and coloured species in between. All of them give the most exciting and absurdly powerful fights (water temperature is around 90 degrees here, remember) with stamina that is quite incredible. If you want your string pulled, this is the place.

Someone about the stamp of my 15-year-old granddaughter and just as pretty, has just delivered a couple of ice-cold beers (it's tough out here) and from the menu I've ordered a bowl of Tom Yung Goong, a hot and tangy prawn soup with that unforgettable

Between powerful encounters with Mekong and red tail catfish, I'm enjoying a sumptuous lunch freshly prepared at Cha-am Fish Park near Hua Hin. Along with a couple of ice-cold beers, it has been delivered on a tray straight to my swim.

infusion of lemon grass, followed by a plate of tempura batter fried prawns that comes with two different chilli dips.

In addition to the spicy food, I love the opportunity of photographing at close hand big and exquisitely colourful fish as they crash dive near the net. I love the continual chatter of breathtakingly coloured birds, and the amazing diversity of luxurious plants, which seem to grow everywhere with the proliferation of weeds. Sure, there's unbelievable clatter, third-world poverty, far too many people living in close proximity to each other with all the associated noise - but not where I'm fishing, and that's the point. I am personally, getting away from it all.

This is my sixth trip to Thailand but this time, brother Dave, who lives here in Hua Hin,

invited me out to open officially a new three-acre fun fishery that he has helped to develop, called Greenfield Valley Specimen Lake. There is also a similar-sized match lake, and an eight-acre whopper lake presently under construction. It is all very pretty with attractive villas close by, plus a bar and a superb restaurant.

Email: reservation@huahingreenfield.com, or contact Eddie on 081 447 0298, 02 936 6540, or Jules on 089 458 2612, 086 782 6545.

Now, I'm well aware that catching a stocked monster out here can in no way ever match the skill factor of say hooking and subsequently landing a huge mahseer, having risked life and limb amongst swirling currents covering the black bedrock of a mountainous Indian river, but no one says it has to, do they? I wonder how many of those who visit carp fisheries in France and trout anglers who seek the whoppers from day ticket fisheries in the UK, view this?

Local guide Eddie, who also hails from the UK, scoops up a medium-sized arapaima that I hooked on a piece of chicken - which works wonderfully in most Thai fisheries - from the Greenfield Valley specimen lake near Hua Hin. Day ticket action at its best.

Brother Dave cradles a modest sized Mekong catfish I hooked on freelined bread paste at the renowned Cha-am Fish Park near Hua Hin. Without question the most phenomenally powerful freshwater fish anywhere in the world. Just look at its huge tail and anal fin.

Fishing here is no different from life itself. You simply decide upon, and make your own challenges. It's one and the same. This permits me to feel exuberant with exhaustion as another big red tail or Mekong pussy rips line from a tightly set clutch on my multiplier, knowing I'm in for a good 30 minutes of acceptable pain.

Actually, at the start of my trip, Dave and I enjoyed a string of red tail, and tiger catfish to 60lbs, plus some hefty pacu, many of these on the fly, from the Monsters Lake on the outskirts of Bangkok, close to the bridge over the River Kwai, of motion picture fame. We then returned for some Mekong agony, and I'd recommend anyone to try playing one themselves for half an hour, at the local Cha-am fish park. Honestly, until you've played a 50-70lbs Mekong catfish, by far the planet's most awesome, stamina-packed

freshwater species, on a 50lbs test braided line and uptide rod combo, you cannot appreciate the power of these phenomenal creatures.

Believe me, I've yet to hear a visitor complain the fight was anywhere near belittled by the fact he had help from a guide. Yet, I personally still have trembling knees when a big River Wensum roach, truly like rocking horse droppings now, decides to make one final dive before I get to see its silvery-blue back and red fins in the mesh of my net, and calm down.

The skill factor in long-trotting to finally hook and then land what is now a rare river creature, compared to landing even a big Mekong catfish, is probably ten-fold. Believe me, I am under no illusions, but who cares? Who's counting, even? Certainly not me. Sorry, got to go, as I can see my plate of soup and prawns being carried round the lake, and would you believe, one of my reels is screaming big time. Yes, that's fishing in Thailand.

SPAIN

Fishing in Spain is probably the closest foreign location to home, where for no great cost compared to a week in the tropics, say, anyone can get stuck into big carp and catfish, while enjoying the Rioja and tasty local food along the Rio Ebro valley, for instance. In fact, I would go further. I have been visiting the rivers Ebro, Cinca and Segre in north-eastern Spain for over 20 years now, and can state categorically, that the area around the sleepy town of Mequinenza, just a tiny part of the river system where the Ebro converges with the River Segre, is better served by well-equipped, experienced guides than anywhere else in Europe. It produces huge numbers of big carp and Wels catfish and there is literally nowhere else like it.

Left, top Rio Ebro guide, Gary Allen. Right, Catfish Conservation Group secretary and boss of Catfish Pro Tackle, Simon Clarke, and in the middle, with an ear-to-ear grin, is my long-time fishing buddy, Jinx Davey, from Bungay in Suffolk with a 115lbs Wels catfish, his first ever.

Moreover, on several occasions I have driven from my near-Norwich home to either Stansted Airport and then on to Saragossa, or to Luton and then on to Barcelona, and following a leisurely two or three-hour drive, have been putting the net beneath a 30lbs carp in the afternoon of the same day. All in less time than it would take me to drive to Wales or Scotland. So Spain certainly gets my vote.

Now, while there are some other really great carp, largemouth bass, and huge, stillwater barbel locations in Spain - even Atlantic salmon beats in rivers in the far north of the country - the Ebro/Segre story at Mequinenza is so very special and to my mind equal to how stillwater fisheries in Thailand have changed and prospered through lateral thinking. In the case of the Ebro, I guess you could even say through illegal thinking and subsequent stockings. How the Ebro system has changed since I first fished its lower reaches back in the 1980s, is truly monumental.

Guide, Gary Allen, based in Mequinenza where the rivers Segre and Ebro converge, displays an immaculate 42lbs common carp taken in the village. Gary has since landed monsters to 53lbs, while the area record is a staggering 65lbs. Call his mobile 00 34 667 455 863 for info.

Who would have thought that small numbers of Wels catfish, bleak and zander, introduced by German anglers back in the 1970s at Mequinenza, could have eventually made such an impact on its prolific stock of cyprinid species throughout the river's entire length. I know of no comparable location.

When I first fished the Ebro, for instance, it was chock-a-block with common carp of all sizes, but mostly all in single figures, plus southern barbel averaging between 2-4lbs, roach, rudd, tench, and enormous concentrations of thin-lipped mullet which infiltrated way, way upstream from the estuary. Now, as I write this in 2010, in so many areas every other carp you catch tops 25lbs, simply because Wels catfish have munched their way through so many of the smaller sizes. It's a truly unique situation, creating previously unheard of carp and cat fishing. The only similar situation I have ever experienced is in the famous Red River, in Winnipeg, Canada, where equal and phenomenal numbers of double-figure channel catfish and common carp happily co-exist, because the catfish average in size only a few pounds more than the carp.

I mentioned Thailand in the equation earlier, because although we are talking about entirely different species, it is because of that difference, that Thailand's big-fish stillwater lakes flourish. Let me explain. Before the all-predatory South American species were introduced, the indigenous Thai species stocked into angling fisheries were for the most part non-predatory. The massive Mekong catfish, swai catfish, giant black Siamese carp, esops carp etc are all algae and filter feeders. Only the giant Thai chao phray catfish and freshwater stingrays are out-and-out predators.

The Amazonian arapaima, pacu, peacock bass, alligator garfish, red tail and tiger catfish are all most effective predators which have no trouble co-existing with the non-predatory species, because small non-predatory species breed in such profusion and grow at an alarming rate in water temperatures topping 90 degrees, so there is always plenty of live food. This is why Thai angling lakes can substantiate a seemingly impossible array of different fish, all growing to monstrous proportions. In the case of the arapaima, now endangered throughout most of the Amazon region because it has simply been eaten almost to extinction, we could reach the situation when there will be more arapaima in Thailand than in Brazil. Maybe that's the case already.

Why did Thailand import South American fish in the first place, can I hear you ask? Well, the Thais are mad about keeping fish and this wonderfully unique situation was first brought about, as far as I can make out, by their fanatical interest in the tropical aquarium fish trade. As all keen tropical fish keepers know, most fish will grow at an alarming rate when you crank up the temperature, and the rest, as they say, is history.

CANADA

I've said it before, but I'll say it again; if I were a young man and knew what I know now, I would be clutching a one-way ticket to Canada and in all probability to the province of British Columbia, where the climate is not so different from ours, because I do like the seasons, spring in particular, and to watch everything grow daily. I'm not always an angry old man, you know. I still get a thrill while walking the dogs around our lakes. I love to see the yellowy-green tips of daffodils breaking through the leaves covering the pathways, or the pointed tips of green stems along the margins that will come to be the rushes of the beautiful yellow iris when it blooms at the end of May, and for me, there is not a more attractive marginal plant. Perhaps the occasion I derive most pleasure from, though, is when a certain pair of Canadian geese returns each year, as they have done now for six consecutive springs, to nest on one of the islands I made purposely for wildlife. It really does gladden my heart when I suddenly see them swimming around one spring morning looking to see where they are going to nest.

I guess I could still have experienced all this, due to our two climates being so similar, had I settled in Canada back in the late 1960s when the cruise ship I then worked on called into Vancouver, and I first became enthralled by the country's sheer size, majesty, and of course its unlimited, unspoilt, and immense fishing potential. Although I never made the 'splash', Canada has been extremely kind to this angler, and I have been fortunate enough to catch monster fish from several of its vast, wonderful provinces.

Guest, Pat Phillips, and me displaying the average size of chum salmon to be caught from the famous Fraser River and its major tributary, the Harrison River, near Chilliwack in British Columbia; on fly, on spoons, and on trotted jigs.

With the help of guide, Jean Paul Ashini, I took this lovely brook trout from the deep, clear and cold waters of Labrador's Kamistastin Lake in Canada's wilderness.

The British Isles would fit several times into the province of British Columbia, so it's hardly surprisingly that when a British carp, pike, or barbel angler tells his Canadian counterpart that we regularly recognise some of the freshwater fish we catch, through spots or deformities or scale patterns, and even give a few of them names, he receives a disbelieving smile and a funny look. After all, when one Canadian river, the Fraser, has almost as many salmon running up annually to spawn, as there are people in the UK, it's difficult to take it all in. Just like the fact that the majority of Canada's lakes are unnamed.

Yes, I've been extremely fortunate in my angling exploits when visiting this phenomenal country, having caught huge grayling to over 3lbs from the junction of the mighty Kazan and Ferguson Rivers, in the vastness of the North West Territories, which actually contain nine per cent of the world's fresh water. I've also spent two weeks in a trapper's tent beside Kamistastin Lake with the Innu Indians in Labrador to capture orange-bellied brook trout. I've had lake trout to over 30lbs in the Yukon from magical Wolf Lake, and marvelled at such an environment as the Red River in Manitoba, that I mentioned earlier, where you are quite likely to catch a 20lb common carp followed by a 30lb channel catfish on successive casts. In addition, one truly memorable morning in Manitoba, while wobbling spoons in a weedy bay on massive Lake Nueltin, I took no fewer than four pike over 20lbs, in quick succession.

I've enjoyed unbelievably exciting fly fishing for five species of Pacific salmon, plus giant white sturgeon to 350lbs from the mighty Fraser and Harrison Rivers in British Columbia. Yet a trip to the enigmatic Queen Charlotte Islands, situated off the Pacific-British Columbian coastline in the summer of 2009, while putting together the last three programmes of a brand new TV series commissioned by Discovery, really did tick all my boxes and even tops everything I've previously mentioned.

The unique fly-in Langara Lodge fishery, situated on
the most northerly of the Queen Charlotte Islands
off Canada's pacific coastline. Home to 70 guests
and the brainchild of owner, Rick Bourne, Langara
is possibly the most prolific spot on the planet for
both saltwater salmon and giant halibut.

A truly mesmerising sunset settles over Wolf Lake in Canada's Yukon Territory.

Why? Well, our base at the famous Langara Lodge, a veritable floating paradise and the brainchild of owner-operator Rick Bourne, who stops at nothing to ensure his guests have a great fishing experience, consists of two huge, three-storey floating units - giant barges really - linked with walkways, marinas, bays and a helicopter pad, just 100 yards offshore from Langara Island, the most northerly of the three main islands that form the Queen Charlottes. One unit comprises a galley and a superb restaurant, while the second has guest accommodation, a huge, comfortable lounge, a café bar, a drying room and a fish processing and packing bay.

It is all so wonderfully organised and an absolute credit to Rick's ingenuity. I have never before stayed in such a lavish and well-run angling lodge in all my travels around the world. It is even more remarkable when you think that the entire operation is in service from May until September only,

whereupon both floating units are towed all the way back to Vancouver for the winter and reinstated the following spring. For those wishing to stay on terra-firma, Rick's second venture, Langara Island Lodge nestles high up the shoreline among tall pines and bald eagle nests, with a commanding view over the Pacific and within sight of Langara's floating fishing lodge. For information about Langara Fishing Adventures, go to www.langara.com

Arriving by helicopter on to Langara's floating pad, following a two-hour flight to Masset from Vancouver, is something akin to being lowered on to a James Bond movie set, with float planes and choppers constantly coming and going on changeover days, with over 70 guests

Giant sea lions weighing up to half a ton apiece lounge among the kelp-covered rocks and watch you fish.

arriving to share the 30-strong fleet of custom-built boats, both guided and unguided. The habitat on and around the islands is truly special, almost like the islands time forgot, Jurassic Park style. That's because the last ice age actually bypassed the Queen Charlottes, leaving a uniquely abundant jungle of lichen-covered, tall fir trees where bald eagles perch. Along the shoreline you can see deer, otters and black bears, the largest in the world, incidentally, while huge sea lions weighing up to half a ton apiece honk all day to each other across the kelp-covered rocks.

Huge volcanic slabs and pinnacle rocks skirt the irregular shoreline of the islands with the clearest saltwater I've ever seen in the northern hemisphere. However, it's very cold so it's mandatory for everyone at Langara to wear the survival suits provided, and to return them to the drying room each evening so that everyone sets off in warm, dry clothes. Just 15 minutes in these icy-cold waters, remember, and it's 'goodnight nurse'.

Along with seals, sea lions, orcas and humpback whales, these incredibly fertile waters contain an unusual array of colourful bottom species, from the goldfish-coloured, yellow-eyed rockfish, to skates and salmon sharks, ling cod and what I consider the most aggressive battler of all, giant halibut. In addition, no fewer than five species of Pacific salmon are to be found migrating through and around the Queen Charlottes on their way to major river systems like the Skeena, Fraser, and Columbia. In order of size, starting with the smallest, they are pink, coho, sockeye, chum, and chinook, also called king and springs. These huge salmon have been caught on fly to over 60lbs and on bait to over 90lbs, and are around in phenomenal numbers.

Depths here vary enormously between 30 and 300 feet with tremendous tide-rips over sunken pinnacles and reefs, which are of course the areas favoured by salmon as they migrate between and around the islands close to the kelp beds. Floating kelp can prove a nuisance at times, although the salmon guides are quick to steer the lines (up to four 'mooching' rods can be worked on each boat) away from snags in order not to hang up and spoil their critical bait presentation of a cut-plugged herring, which everyone uses for salmon trolling.

The popular Canadian angling term 'power-mooching' is perhaps best explained as follows: the guide carefully sets the slowly-turning herring, mounted on a pennel rig of two size 4/0 single hooks, fixed five inches apart, having been cut off at an angle behind the gills (hence the terminology 'plug') so it revolves somewhere between 12 and 30 feet down, with the aid of an 8oz banana lead. This is fixed on the 25lbs test reel line, 10 feet above the herring, with two, two-inch lengths of bathtub style swivelled chain, to alleviate line twist. There are masses of jellyfish in these seas, which sometimes tend to catch up around the chain swivel; so most guides use two sets of chain swivels for this reason.

Once working at the desired depth, the 10½ foot rod is angled out, set in a quick-strike rod rest, and the guide uses the steering wheel plus little spurts from the engine to vary the bait's movement. It can be incredibly exciting fishing, knowing you could lock up any minute with a chinook of up to 50lbs or more. So you stand there like a gunslinger, eyes going from one rod tip to another, and you have to be quick. Sometimes a hit will come when the engine is slipped into neutral, so the bait drops, and sometimes a slamming hit happens when the herring spurts forward into life. You then grab the rod from the rest and immediately point the tip at the munching salmon and wind like mad to fully tighten the mono reel line and actually feel the fish before following up with a heavy strike.

On 25lb mono, there is little chance of snapping up with the silky-smooth drag on large centrepin reels, but the barbless hooks, mandatory in British Columbia, fall out all too easily if you fail to wind in quickly when a salmon turns around and swims toward the boat. This is something that cost me a very big fish indeed, certainly well in excess of 40lbs. Its first run scorched off over 100 yards of line against a firm drag setting, but following its second run, I simply failed to keep the line tight enough. This prompted a rather old-fashioned look from my guide, Nick Hui, when the monster shook the hooks out.

You can actually see them shaking their heads violently, through the crystal clear water 20 feet down during the fight. It's such exciting and quite unique salmon fishing. As we were filming at the time I could certainly have done with a happy conclusion to such a monstrous salmon, especially as these chinooks are so breathtakingly striking, like the proverbial bar of silver, and incredibly thickset and deep in the body. However, as I went on to enjoy a succession of chinook beauties weighing into the high-20s, plus hordes of double-figure cohos, I was more than pleased with what we managed to get 'in the can' as they say.

Other guests landed several monster chinook salmon over 40lbs during our four-day stay at Langara Lodge, the best going 48½lbs to Scott Burn of Ontario. However, I was also after securing a big halibut and

making a rockfish program, in addition to salmon, so I could only give the salmon a certain amount of time before we switched tactics to bottom fishing in deeper water down to 350 feet for a massive halibut and numerous colourful rockfish.

Unfortunately, there is no rock or beach fishing around these unique islands, more appropriately referred to as Haida Gwaii, meaning 'Islands of the people' in the native language. They are home to one of the planet's oldest and richest native cultures, as signified by the totem poles along the shoreline. This is all overlooked by the galley and restaurant. All drinks with meals are complimentary at Langara, where the menu, which changes daily, reads like something from a Gordon Ramsay restaurant. Truly, I defy anyone fishing here not to put on half a stone during a short trip; the food is that sumptuous.

The second lodge contains all the guest accommodation, plus a huge, comfortable lounge, filled with wonderfully preserved, cased and uncased specimens, of all the Pacific species you are likely to catch, plus a café and pastry bar, open 24/7, and a fish processing and packaging plant. Most Langara regulars return home with a box or two of frozen, filleted salmon and halibut. It's all very much part of the deal and the North American culture. Would you believe, the options in prepared salmon, for instance, includes lox-style, smoked salmon, hot smoked salmon, candied salmon, canned salmon, smoked canned salmon, salmon steaks and plain filleted salmon. I tell you it's another world.

Now, the problem with bottom fishing in the Queen Charlottes, and I admit it is a nice problem, is that while I would have loved to have used a 20lbs class outfit to really get

Experienced Langara guide, Nick Hui, has my chinook salmon of close on 30lbs safely in the net following an incredible scrap while trolling, power-mooching style, through the incredibly clear water of the Pacific Ocean. Note the super-smooth centrepin reel.

the best from all the colourful and arm-wrenching rockfish which seem to cover the sea bed, in the 10-30lbs size range, fishing that light is just not on. That's because at any second you can lump into a sizeable halibut, and by 'sizeable' we are talking at least 30-70lbs, and it's just as likely to be a monster between 100-200lbs. Certainly, they are around in prolific enough numbers, and have been caught at Langara to 300lbs. Most of these aren't going to see the light of day on a 20lb outfit, though, because they fight so incredibly hard. They are surprisingly powerful, believe me! I really wanted to capture a big halibut on camera so I stuck with the outfit my guide Nick provided, which consisted of 100lbs test braid on a lever drag reel, and an 80lbs class, seven-foot rod.

Incidentally, the last time I fished with such an outfit back home was off the south coast, many years back when out with Mel Russ of Sea Angler magazine and my old mate, skipper Brian Joslin, who still operates out of Rye in Sussex, trying to put a conger program together for my long-running TV series Go Fishing. This, in a force 5-6, would you believe! It was actually so long ago, braid had yet to reveal its magical properties upon the British sea angling world, so we used 50lb mono on an 80lb class rod for sheer lifting power, which big conger fishing demands to stop them from going back down into the wreck, which some unfortunately did. Halibut do share a striking similarity with big eels, in that they too decide instinctively to power-dive when they have been pumped way off bottom, high up in the water column, and suddenly see light above. Fortunately, wrecks are not a problem for halibut in the Queen Charlottes but barnacle-encrusted rocky reefs and high pinnacles are, so I was glad I went for the heavy outfit.

Yellow-eyed rockfish are among the most colourful species, fresh or salt, that I have caught anywhere in the world. This brace held by guide, Nick Hui, actually grabbed a hook each, on the three-hooked halibut bait - a whole coho salmon head - shown opposite, down in 300 feet of water.

Anyway, even the big rockfish plus a sizeable skate and medium-sized halibut fought no less on such a heavy combo, and anchoring in depths between 250-350 feet, the large diameter reel was a real boon, even though it's always tiring bringing fish up from over 300 feet down. With a 2lb ball lead, required to keep a hookbait consisting of the whole head of a double-figure coho salmon down on the bottom, on a huge fixed wire boom and a five-foot 150lb test mono trace, when the tide really got going, any lighter outfit would have been plain stupid and exceedingly hard work.

Three size 8/0 hooks mounted on a 150lbs test mono trace and worked into a fresh coho salmon head, is the standard halibut bait at Langara Lodge. Miraculously, even modest sized halibut in the 30 to 40lbs bracket manage to gobble them up.

You may think that my guide's hook rig was interesting, comprising as it did of three, yes three, 8/0 hooks rigged five inches apart, each being nicked firmly into the coho's head; obviously, they don't like taking any prisoners in British Columbia. Yet a 20lbs skate, 18lbs yellow-eyed rockfish, and halibut in the 30-40lbs bracket (babies) all managed to engulf a whole coho head. Incidentally, the yellow-eyed rockfish is far from being accurately described by its name. Yes, it has huge yellow eyes with black pupils, but its body colour of goldfish-red is absolutely stunning, and by far its most identifiable feature. Many of these rockfish and ling cod, another interesting species, came to a 24-ounce shad/jig, which I worked up and down just above bottom while waiting for one of the two salmon heads to be grabbed.

Mentioning skipper, Brian Joslin, has made me think that the last time he and I got together I fluked a rather rare catch (for the south coast at least) in the form of a 17lb coal

fish and a 28lb cod from his boat off Rye, on that truly memorable trip, if my memory serves me correctly. At the time, Brian asked if I could put him and a bunch of friends on to somewhere special that I had been on my travels. Immediately, I suggested the mighty Fraser River in Canada's British Columbia for salmon and especially the phenomenal sturgeon fishing. When he reported back, having made the trip, he and his group had landed dozens and dozens of 100lbs-plus beauties up to nearly 300lbs. Well, Brian, here's another hot recommendation...

The Queen Charlotte Islands are perhaps even one notch better, and for several reasons. Not only have you five species of Pacific salmon, still feeding in the sea on the herring mountain, but also the immensely powerful Pacific halibut, plus skate and sharks and a huge assortment of other big and colourful bottom dwellers. There is nowhere so prolific for halibut than around the Queen Charlottes, and we are talking specimens here in the 100-300lbs bracket as being likely catches, with the species topping out at around 500lbs. Of course, Alaska has more or less the same thing, but it's simply further north up the Pacific coastline. Really, if you've been up to Western Scotland and felt the heavyweight power of a big skate, had 40-50lb cod in Norway, and landed 100lb-plus blue sharks off Milford Haven, a big, magnificent halibut off the beautiful Queen Charlotte Islands is a tempting and very real option. In fact, I'm tempted to say you owe it to yourself.

So how did I fare with these big flatfish, having less than four days filming to put both a half-hour salmon and halibut program me together? Well, for starters, we were fortunate in that, following a week of strong north-westerly winds putting enormous swells on the Pacific, everything quietened down, permitting us to try for halibut on our second day. Immediately, I was surprised to find that any kind of chumming, like a carrot sack full of fish bits tied around the anchor chain is actually illegal in Canadian waters. Therefore, you must simply rely upon presenting a big, juicy, blood-packed bait down on the bottom on each of the rods and trust there is sufficient scent trail to bring fish up to them (hence, the whole coho heads), and believe me it works. So prolific are these clear seas that within 15 minutes of the baits hitting bottom, the rods start knocking.

During the filming, we managed to get a mile off shore (yes, just a mile) on two consecutive days and experienced big fish running off with the baits both times during our four-hourly sessions. Why only four hours? Well, I was salmon fishing in the morning and again in the afternoon following our halibut session. That's the beauty of fishing around these islands. Nowhere, for

either salmon or deep-sea action, is any further away than a 15-minute boat ride.

I would have dearly loved to see the first leviathan I hooked into, after cutting my teeth on a small halibut and several chunky rockfish. This thing powered off, 250 feet down, away from the boat diagonally, across the tide, screaming line from the reel against a firmly set drag, just like a tope, only it felt the size of a barn door on steroids. Over 20 minutes later it was halfway up and I felt that I now had some sort of control. Wrong! The monster suddenly came off and boy was I sick. Upon reeling in, the lowest 8/0 hook tied on the 150lb mono was missing, but there was simply no time to lose, or to even wonder why. On went another blood-dripping coho head and fresh trace and I was back in the game.

The sheer amount of fish here is mind-boggling. Within half an hour, I'd hooked up again and although noticeably far, far smaller than the monster I'd lost, it provided me with an exciting, arm-wrenching, gut-busting battle. Characteristically, halibut shake their heads every so often, but being a flatfish, instead of side-to-side as with an 'upright' fish, the rod tip is wrenched up and down. It's so strange, but think about it for a moment. Then they suddenly power-dive, and you have no option but to yield line or get pulled overboard. Within 20 minutes I had it up to the boat, a six-foot long, two-foot wide, eight-inch thick beauty of around 150lbs, and was I over the moon. Wilson had caught his big halibut, but more importantly it was all nicely captured on tape by cameraman Paul Leuenberger, warts and all. Yes! The grunts, the pain and the ecstasy; and if I can find a suitable excuse to get me back again (you know my number, Rick) out to Langara Lodge, I'll drop everything and be there like a shot.

This six-foot long, 150lbs halibut really pulled my string, with heavy, gut-busting dives and lunges for over 20 minutes, on a powerful rod and 100lbs test braid. Just look at the size of that tail!

SOUTH AFRICA

Prior to February 2010, when I escorted a group of eight Brits to South Africa and the Western Cape for a sharking safari on behalf of Tailor Made Holidays, the last time I fished in Capetown was in 1968 when working on board the P&O cruise ship, SS Oronsay, during my merchant navy days. The changes that have taken place in this beautiful country since are truly mind-blowing, so may I recommend that monumental and wonderful book, 'The Long Road to Freedom', by Nelson Mandela, to those who are a bit vague as to the history of it all. It's a fascinating document.

Picked up from the airport by guide, Robbie Janse, our party stayed 40 miles east of Capetown on the shore of massive False Bay, in picturesque Gordon's Bay, which I can honestly say, is one of the most scenically stunning, evocative and inspirational coastlines I have ever sampled in 30 years of foreign fishing. It's a veritable big fish haven during their summer period between December to March, when air temperatures can soar into the 90s Fahrenheit and sea temperatures vary between 60-70 degrees. So we were there by design, during 'prime time', which like I said in the dos and don'ts list at the start of this chapter, is of paramount importance. Moreover, the logistics of getting there were surprisingly easy. A long-haul flight from Heathrow to Capetown, via South African Airways, followed by an hour's road transfer, and one hour later we were catching from the rocks, just a five-minute drive from our accommodation. We were all extremely impressed.

Now considered extremely rare in British waters, this 60lbs thresher shark, displayed by its captor, Leon Wilson, (left) from Shropshire, with help from guide, Robbie Janse, is always a possibility, even when rock fishing, in South Africa. Its incredibly long tail identifies it easily.

Following a hectic battle through the crashing waves and some quick manoeuvres along the rocky promontory we all fished from, Leon Wilson from Shropshire landed an immaculately enamelled thresher shark of around 60lbs. This is a species rarely taken around our British Isles these days, but always a possibility from the shoreline along the Western Cape. It's distinguished from all other sharks by its incredibly long tail, which it uses to herd up baitfish, plus it has a small, neat mouth and huge black, Jaws-like eyes. I was amazed at the courage and dexterity of our two guides, Robbie Janse and Rob Kyle, who clambered fearlessly down mussel and kelp-covered rocks to pluck that shark from the surf crashing over the jagged, cliff edges.

Other likely encounters while surf and rock fishing here, incidentally, are various stingrays such as butterfly, or diamond stingrays as they are called locally, plus blue rays, leopard rays, eagle rays, bull rays and giant black rays that reach weights in excess of 400lbs. However, it is the sheer volume and diversity of sharks that attract visitors to the Western Cape; species like cow sharks, tope, spur dogs, bronze whalers, grey sharks, hammerheads, black spotted gulley sharks, huge smoothhounds, and great whites. Yes, great whites.

When our guides suggested there was every chance of hooking into a great white from the beach it was difficult to take in but one of their guests had landed a 300lb beauty only a week before. Here lies a dilemma; because deliberately setting out to catch great whites is an illegal act in South Africa, but how can you choose which sharks pick up your bait?

On only our second morning, the unthinkable happened on Macassar beach when Ken Sheath from Crawley in Sussex hooked into a sizeable great white, estimated at 400lbs plus, using a large tuna steak on a pair of size 10/0 hooks. Our guide, Robbie, saw the great fish characteristically come to the surface, as most great whites do, before sounding and heading out fast across False Bay toward the Atlantic. At this point, no one seemed worried about how far it would go because the reels Robbie uses on his 14½ foot, powerful, one-piece, carbon surf rods, are large capacity, Shimano Torium and Trinidad 30s, and Trinidad 50s; the latter, loaded with over 500 yards of 50lbs test, Whiplash braid, topped up with 350 yards of 40lbs mono. So Ken's shark had a way to go before it ran out all the line. Unfortunately, when the reel was about two-thirds empty, the shark bit through the heavy wire trace, so we never got to see it on the beach anyway. We were all as sick as parrots, but it certainly got me thinking. Where else, for heaven's sake, can you even think about hooking into great whites from the shore? South Africa certainly has a lot to offer.

How do the guides get large baits well over 100 yards out into the deeper water, you may wonder. Well, it's all down to an extremely clever device called a 'non-return slider rig'. This is a three-inch long, heavy gauge wire boom with a special coiled spring clip at one end. Once a long, 150-yard, cast has been made using just the 8oz breakaway lead, the wires of which having dug well into the sand, this is fastened over the reel line. Connected to the weighted end of the slider is a three-foot, heavy wire trace holding the pair of size 10/0 barbless hooks, and a large bait such as a bonito head, chunk of sand shark or tuna steak. Eventually, this comes to rest up against a large ring 12 inches above the weight, following much jigging of the rod tip to ensure the rig slides through the waves, all the way down the reel line from rod to lead, 150 yards out.

Top South African guide, Robbie Janse, slips the corkscrew end of a slider rig, wire trace over the reel line, before jerking it all the way down the line to the breakaway lead cast over 150 yards out. Note the large fish bait and two barbless size 10/0 hooks.

settled down and accounted for numerous bronze whalers from 60lbs pups up to 300lb-plus beauties from the beaches along False Bay, plus a couple of large diamond, or butterfly stingrays as they are known around the world. Louis Fabiano from Somerset caught the largest at around 80lbs.

The topic of conversation of every sport fisherman in South Africa is that all hooks used were barbless, and not a gaff was seen during our surfing safari. Sometimes, the guides waded into four-foot breakers in order to pull out sharks of up to eight feet long, by the tail. Believe you me; this takes a certain type of courage. Some might even call it madness, particularly in the heavy seas experienced during our stay because the next wave could literally deposit the shark right on top of you - and very nearly did on several occasions. This ain't good news, considering that most sharks, due to their supple, cartilaginous bodies, can angle back to bite their own tails, or the hand of the angler holding on to it.

There is also a three-foot section of 150lb nylon-covered wire, an up-trace, no less, immediately above the large ring, knotted to the 150lb mono rubbing leader, so that when the slider comes up to rest against the ring, a biting shark cannot go through the rubbing leader. It sounds far more complicated than it actually is, and it's so effective it's now widely used by South African shore anglers targeting big fish like rays and especially big sharks in the surf.

Following the euphoria of actually hooking into but losing that great white, our party

By far the most hectic sport we experienced was light tackle fishing from the shore of a huge lagoon, north-west of Capetown, at Varkenvlei, where sand sharks (also called guitar fish) and blue stingrays running between 5 and 15lbs almost paved the bottom. An innocuous-looking marbled, electric ray, capable of giving a nasty jolt of electricity was caught too. Clearly, there were also much larger rays and skate around, judging by the number of distinctive, black, purse-like capsules laid by female skate that we found and from which a young skate emerges 4-5 months later. At least two of our group connected with larger fish and had nearly all of their 20lbs test line run out before it parted across the rocks.

Louis Fabiano from Somerset (right) gets help from guide, Robbie Janse, to display his 80lbs butterfly stingray - called diamond rays locally - identified by its short, thick tail armed with a nasty sting. These will take fish baits intended for sharks but fall more readily to large squid.

Our two fearless guides drag an eight-foot, 300lbs, bronze, whaler shark up the beach having grabbed hold of its tail in the surf. They more than deserved our admiration.

Our most impressive catch by far came in the form of a ragged tooth shark, called 'raggies' locally, easily distinguishable by its two, large and spineless dorsal fins, came from the beach at Struisbaai, north-east of our base at Gordons Bay. The long drive, following the mountainous coastline, revealed hundreds of simply amazing, remote locations from both beach and rocky promontories, most of which are rarely fished. Along the way we saw numerous birds of prey, plus ostrich, sacred ibis, mongooses, and springboks.

No one fishes for the almost pet-like, giant black stingrays inhabiting picturesque Struisbaai harbour, because they are a local attraction, so, after hand-feeding mackerel to them, we settled down to an afternoon along an adjoining long, white and sandy beach that reminded me of the Bahamas. As the tide started to make, two large raggies were hooked and unfortunately but inexplicably

lost. Two 40lb grey sharks in quick succession then came along, before Marc Pickering from Redditch, using the head end of a freshly caught smoothhound, got stuck into a superb raggie of around 300lbs that failed to chomp through the trace wire.

This particualr shark, called 'grey nurse' in Australia, is equipped with an unbelievably wicked set of teeth, not that different in dentistry from the mako. That didn't stop our guides, Robbie and Rob (who works in the aquarium in Durban when he's not guiding), from rushing into the surf to pull it out by the tail, and up the beach. Honestly, these guides more than deserved our admiration, wading into the waves to chest height on our behalf, to make that all-important long cast into deeper water, with the tuna cutlet bait rigged to the slider around their necks before slowly coming back to shore while jigging the slider down the line. They worked their socks off to show us what South African surf fishing can offer, and I cannot recall anyone in our party saying they would not return. The fishing was that exciting and that memorable. I only wish I were 30 years younger.

Big Marc Pickering from Redditch holds the rear end of his 300lbs ragged tooth shark while Robbie Janse holds open its jaws - just look at those awesome teeth - following a great scrap from the beach at Stuisbaai. It had gobbled up the head end of a freshly-killed smoothhound.

FLY RODDING - MY WAY

This chapter is called 'fly rodding', because in most situations I am merely using the fly rod for its marvellous elastic powers of being able, eventually, to subdue even huge specimens, whether hooked on small jigs, huge flies or Chum-Mixer biscuits. I particularly love hearing that ratchet of the centrepin fly reel scream like a stuck pig as I palm the reel's drum to slow down a biggie; as opposed to the purist approach of only ever imitating some form of aquatic insect life when fly fishing. Certainly, I'm fly fishing, as such, because many of the large imitations I use are in fact 'flies', tied to replicate small fish, but then if we are perfectly honest, so are most patterns of salmon flies. Confusing subject isn't it? This is why I call it fly rodding. I much prefer to be under no illusions.

TACKLE

For catching pike, carp and even the smaller species of sea fish like bass and pollack, the absolutely perfect outfit is a powerful, 10 foot, 9-weight, tip action rod, coupled to a wide arbour, large-capacity disc drag, reel. It is also the perfect bonefish and small permit combo, should you fancy a week's tropical stalking over clear water flats in the Bahamas, Cuba or the Florida Keys. Or, make a trip across the pond to the shallow rips off the tip of Long

Island, only two hours' driving from the centre of New York, where striped bass to 40lbs and double-figure bluefish, will enthral as they rip off line, way past the backing, to give you an entirely different opinion of fishing in the USA.

Ironically, many reservoir trout fisherman will already own such an outfit and be leagues ahead. Some would say that an 8-weight outfit is heavy enough, and for many situations they would be correct. So, if that's what you fancy using, then fine. I find that a 9-weight provides just that little extra when I need it, such as punching out into and across the wind. Either way, should your rod be marked with a 'dual' rating; ie, 5/6 or 8/9, then always opt to fish the heavier line. In all probability, you will cast a little further with the lighter line, but only with at least half the line out, whereas in most situations when fly rodding, the heavier line will give you easier, smoother casting over short distances when you only have a few yards of line out. For most short-range situations, I use a line one number heavier than the rod's rating for this very reason. However, owning a variation of weight-forward fly lines to suit all occasions is of paramount importance; you will most certainly need them.

For bonefishing, carping and pike in shallow water, a good quality floating line is vital, and

Saltwater fly fishing produces some exhilarating fights with fascinating species. I caught this silver-sided trevally over a deep-water reef in the Indian Ocean off Mozambique.

it's impossible to beat the Cortland Precision 'Tropic-plus'. Although this is designed for tropical, saltwater work - bonefish and the like – thanks to its hard, durable coating, which doesn't go soft in high temperatures, and much reduced memory, it will prove invaluable for all top-water pursuits in both temperate and tropical conditions. The same line is also available with a sinking ghost - clear mono - tip for working subsurface flies just a couple of feet down through really clear water; it is also great for pike fishing.

PIKE ON THE FLY

For those wishing to target pike only using a floating line, Cortland also produce a Precision Pike Float in green/red dedicated to pike fishing, which casts even big flies like a dream. Perhaps one of the most useful lines of all is a quick-sinking 'sink-tip', particularly where bass and pike are concerned, because it will work flies well down within that productive 3 to 10-foot depth band, depending upon speed of retrieve. But never go anywhere without a Hi-D line of around 7ips, which translates to a sink rate of around seven inches per second, and I do mean this most sincerely, because I have been caught out. On so many occasions, I have been targeting big pike in deep water lakes, meres, broads and loughs, with little to show for my efforts until switching over from a standard, or even a fast-sinking sink-tip, to a Hi-D full-sinking line, which made all the difference. One occasion that springs to mind, was when out drift-fishing for pike on Ireland's Castle Hume lough in the Lower Erne system near

International fly fisher, John Horsey, and me drift a narrow arm of beautiful Castle Hume Lough in the Lower Erne system near Enniskillen, while filming pike on the fly for my Fishing World TV series made for the Discovery Shed Channel in May 2009.

Enniskillen, in the company of England International Fly Fisherman, John Horsey, during the filming of my Fishing World TV series made in 2009 for the Discovery Shed channel.

Now, fly rodding on the drift is different to most forms of drifting, both at sea and in freshwater where you work or 'drag' bottom baits, suspended baits, lures, jigs and live baits, behind or off the side of the boat as it drifts along in the wind. When fly rodding, however, you about-turn and face downwind, which not only aids casting but also allows time, while the boat is drifting, for the fly to get well down before commencing the retrieve. In strong winds, an underwater parachute, or drogue, tied at around amidships to the windward gunwale, is of

paramount importance for slowing down the boat's drift. Scrunch it up and throw it upwind so it sinks and 'bites in' quickly, then you can start the drift exactly where you want to. There will be days when, unless you employ a drogue, you will simply be travelling too fast to cover the water efficiently, and the line will be almost beneath the boat before you can start the retrieve.

By experimenting on the day, and by using different attachment points for the drogue, it's sometimes possible to work diagonally across the lake with the wind, thus passing close to known features such as drop-offs or islands. The drogue is a much underrated and underused piece of kit, and I certainly would not venture on to large, still waters without mine. Of course, when the wind calms down to a ripple, don't be slow in pulling the drogue in, or even using it in the first place. Getting the speed of drift right is half the battle.

Having tried our entire collection of fly lines, the one that produced the larger fish from deep areas, like this lovely 15-pounder, was a Hi-D full, fast-sinking line. The larger fish rarely chased our imitations up to the surface, and showed a marked preference for relatively small flies; a size 2/0 Clouser Minnow taking top honours.

CHAPTER

These colourful 3-6-inch artificials are the flies I like to use for pike, in conjunction with a 9/10 weight line and 10-foot rod outfit. Note, too, the large arbour, disc drag reel.

In my mind's eye, I can still see a monster of a fish, certainly all of 25lbs-plus, that broke all the rules by following John's artificial all the way up to the surface, where it half-heartedly nipped at the end of his fly before tantalisingly, disappearing slowly back into the depths. It was a monstrous programme-making fish if ever I saw one, but it never came again, though we drifted over the same area several times.

Most of those fish simply did not want to chase our imitations upwards through crystal clear water, except for that monster. Also noticeable during that session was my switching down to considerably smaller flies, from John's 5-6-inch glitter specials, to 3-inch Clouser Minnows. Those clear, cold water pike definitely wanted a smaller mouthful on the day. We even tried deep diving plugs and spoons, thinking we would clean up, but,no, those pike were not fooled by lures. They would take flies only, but also only within a certain depth band, and relatively small imitations to boot - but that's fly rodding. So, never be afraid to experiment by ringing the changes whenever fish do not respond.

Initially, using the drogue for a slow search, John and I worked the shallow, weedy areas, on the assumption that in May, despite freezing cold north-easterly winds, pike would be gathered near their eventual spawning grounds. All we caught were jacks until we drifted over the 10-15 feet depth bands, where to a Hi-D line only, which on the retrieve worked the fly low down on a horizontal plane, as opposed to a sink-tip which worked it diagonally and sharply upwards, we started to get into the larger pike.

When specifically targeting pike, and other toothy critters, I've found that the standard

THE RAPALA LOOP KNOT

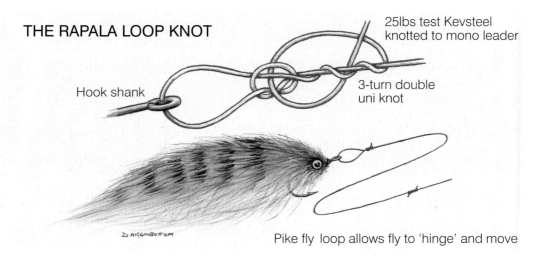

Hook shank

25lbs test Kevsteel knotted to mono leader

3-turn double uni knot

Pike fly loop allows fly to 'hinge' and move

D. HIGGINBOTTOM

Out in the Canadian wilderness in the Yukon Territory on fabulous Wolf Lake, the size of Scotland's Loch Awe. I'm putting up a super-buoyant, long-tailed, deer hair mouse which made the pike that inhabit the shallow and warm off-lake channels go absolutely wild. The line is a floating 10-weight.

pike wire that I use for most situations is insufficiently supple to allow the fly full movement. The answer is to join to the five-foot mono leader (which is a 2 ½ foot section of 20lb test, needle-knotted to the fly line, and then joined loop-to-loop with 2½ foot of 15lbs test), a 12-inch length of super-supple, 25lbs test Kevsteel using a three-turn, double grinner or uni-knot. This trace material consists of a Kevlar coating over a steel inner, and is available from any Catfish-Pro stockist. It knots so easily and is best tied to the fly using the Rapala loop-knot, (see diagram) which allows the fly to hinge sideways for maximum movement. Five feet may seem a rather short leader to those trying for pike for the first time, but using anything much longer restricts casting with large flies. The closer to the fly line your imitation, the further, and more accurately, it will cast, without any delay caused by long leaders.

Retrieving larger, sub-surface flies is really no different to smaller more imitative patterns, except that a faster retrieve is usually required in clear water. I like to vary the retrieve some, once the fly has descended to the depth required, with a mixture of steady pulls and pauses interspersed by short bursts of speed, to imitate a baitfish behaving erratically, and therefore an injured fish, and thus an easy meal.

While surface fishing for pike during the warmer months, I just love using super-buoyant patterns like bunny leeches and deer hair, or long-tailed mice along the weedy, overgrown stretches of my local River Wensum, or lily-clad gravel pits, or mysterious estate lakes designed by Capability Brown, as many in Norfolk and Suffolk were. Old boathouses, bridges and great lily patches provide productive structure and hot habitat features. They will give you unbelievably exciting top water action using a floating line, and the hits are spectacular. It's such great, explosive, tail-walking action, and the size of the pike is purely academic.

You do not need monster pike to enjoy their explosive, tail-walking antics on the fly rod. Whether from my local and weedy River Wensum, or Canada's wilderness lakes, where I caught this beautifully spotted pike, scrappy single-figure fish in the 4-8lbs category provide truly marvellous fun.

Incidentally, I connect with numbers of quality chub, too, fishing this way from my local rivers. On stretches of river so overgrown and weed-packed on the surface during the summer months, fly rodding weedless, surface patterns has often been the only usable technique.

I've experienced some truly wonderful sport over the years by hooking into hundreds of scrappy pike when enjoying Canada's far north, both in the province of Manitoba, from the warm shallows of massive Nuelton Lake, to the enigmatic expanse of Wolf Lake in The Yukon. I reckon I could count the number of doubles I've actually had, including a couple of 20s, on just two hands, but that's not all that fly rodding for pike is about. It's about laughter, great, scrappy, explosive, tail-walking battles, screaming ratchets and the love of your fly rod. Enough said.

CARP ON THE FLY ROD

Now, for some, carp on the surface opens up a whole new world of appreciation for fly rodding, culminating in truly spectacular and glorious battles wielding just a few ounces of carbon fibre. Forget that your quarry has been fooled into slurping down a Chum Mixer-type floating biscuit, and simply enjoy the long, unstoppable runs that afterwards, will make you choose your fly rod wherever and whenever you can. Simply palming the centrepin's spool, literally with the palm of your hand against the drum, even with the disc drag set tightly, in order to slow a fish down, while the ratchet screams out in agony, will bring enormous pleasure.

I prefer to Superglue my mixers on to the hook's shank. This ensures excellent presentation and the fact that they stay on even during the rigours of powerful, double-

A selection of surface, deer hair, and Bunny Leech patterns from my fly collection. Imitations that work extraordinarily well during the summer months, bringing pike out and up from the weediest haunts to play near the surface.

haul casting. Offering a mixer biscuit when fly rodding, allows you to play even big carp on relatively light tackle, and because the entire outfit bends and acts like a giant elastic band, battles will be over quicker than you ever imagined.

I like to get any loose line back on the reel quickly, so that with the disc drag set firmly, I can add any further pressure if required, by palming the reel's drum. I endeavour to keep the rod up and in a full bend throughout and so, naturally, use a super-strong eyed hook for these all-action battles. My favourite patterns are Kamasan B982 and B775, in size 10, tied directly to an 8-9 foot leader of around 8-10lbs, clear, monofilament, carefully and neatly needle-knotted on to the end of my weight-forward floating line. Using a junior hacksaw blade (bend and break a fine six-inch blade in two to create two tools) I then simply saw a shallow groove along one side of the biscuit, before adding a blob of Superglue into the groove, and then press in the hook's shank and hold steady for 8-10 seconds. It's that simple, yet so very, very effective.

Another way of attaching the biscuit should Supergluing not work out for you, is by using a small silicone bait band nicked on to the hook point and pulled gently around to halfway down the hook shank, into which the floating biscuit is secured. However, I find that powerful, double haul casting can sometimes make the biscuit work around to the bend of the hook and compromise presentation. It's always a case of personal preference, though, and just as exciting as presenting floaters to carp using standard tackle and a floating controller on a fixed spool reel and carp rod combo.

Much of the secret, as always and as with most techniques, is being stealthy and creeping quietly into a position where often only a short cast is required. Catching carp by fly rodding is not about casting continually from the shore as though you were after reservoir rainbows. Stealth and cunning are, as always, your greatest assets in ultra-close range situations, for instance where the carp are mere yards away and unaware of your presence. Don't scare them away by raising the rod to cast. Simply hold on tightly to the biscuit and catapult it out sideways using the spring in your rod tip.

TIGER FISH

Those who fish the massive Lake Nasser in Egypt with a fly rod will enjoy some magical moments, not only with the occasional Nile perch, but with numbers of the tooth-laden tiger fish. Lake Nasser is, after all, the mighty River Nile dammed at Aswan, and for 300 miles reaching all the way back south to the Sudan, so all of the Nile's fish are there for the catching.

Here I am wearing shorts in case I have to go in - and I did - playing a 20lb-plus carp in Homersfield Lake on the Norfolk/Suffolk border, during the filming of series 8 of my Anglia Television Go Fishing programme back in 1993.

Casting from the headlands of small islands out in the lake - the peaks of former mountains, no less - being particularly productive for tigers.

For the very best in fly rodding for tigers, though, it is difficult to beat the wonderful Zambezi river, both above and below the famous Victoria Falls; truly one of the world's seven wonders. Africa's fourth largest river, at over 1700 miles in length, the Zambezi offers sport with tigers on the fly virtually throughout its length, whether boat or bank fishing. This is because, for the most part, the Zambezi is a relatively shallow, clear-flowing, clean, sandy and gravel bottomed river averaging between five and 10 feet deep, consisting of a never-ending succession of sandbanks.

Pods of hippos love to hold station in the sudden drop-offs, at the end of many sandbanks in deeper water, and so do tigers in good numbers, attracted to the swarms of small baitfish, which have, in turn, been attracted by the continual excreta from hippos - so it's a case of find hippos and you'll find tiger fish.

Again, that international fly rodding outfit of a 9-weight, coupled to a sink-tip line combo, will stand you in good stead. As for flies, well, I prefer large patterns, such as Deceivers or Clouser Minnows, tied on wide gape, short shank, straight point 5/0-6/0 hooks with white, green and blue proving top colours. Unlike smaller-gape patterns and the treble hooks of lures, which all too easily become caught up in their teeth, they usually find purchase behind the awesome dentistry of the tiger fish's large teeth. If you tie your own flies, use heavy chain-eyes and tie as a Clouser Minnow, but keep the tying very short. You want the tiger fish to inhale the fly as opposed to nipping at its tail.

The awesome, razor-sharp dentistry of the tiger fish is the very last thing a bait fish sees before it gets chomped in half. Tigers provide great sport on the fly rod.

Inside the jaws of this amazing fish are ten razor-sharp canines in the roof of the mouth and eight in the bottom. Therefore, a five-inch, soft wire trace of 30lbs test, joining fly to leader, is of paramount importance. You have the option of adding the short wire trace to the five foot, 20lbs test mono leader, using the Albright knot or by utilising a small swivel; to attach the fly itself I use a twiddle stick. It is certainly not about continually changing patterns to find the most effective, so be confident in fishing the same fly, cast after cast, because tiger-fishing is all about location. If you so wish, you can always have three or four different patterns already pre-tied to a swivelled, short wire trace to make things easier. My own fly wallet contains a number of flies all pre-tied to wire traces from past tiger sessions.

The deep-bodied pacu, a South American species, is widely stocked in the 8-30lbs size range, in Thailand's stillwater day ticket fisheries, and provides great fly-rodding action with its fast, powerful runs.

a single hook-up from 7-10 hits, while those drifting fish fillets with the flow, will be satisfied with a hook-up from perhaps 5-6 hits. I would put fly fishing somewhere in between, not that any of these statistics matter, of course. What does matter is the energetic and acrobatic battle from a sizeable tiger while fly rodding. It's simply marvellous, and nothing, no other species, not even a fit hen rainbow trout in silver condition, can match the incredible speed and explosive acrobatics of the tiger fish. Along with tarpon these fish are in a league of their own.

Attacks from cape buffalo and elephant are very real possibilities, remember, so fish wherever your guide designates it safe from the bank, casting to features close beside fallen trees and overhanging branches - all those overgrown hotspots too hairy to cover from a drifting boat. You'll find tigers most willing to play ball, mostly, I guess, because they never get fished for. Experiencing up to five hits during a single short cast and retrieve, as I have done on numerous occasions, is nothing out of the ordinary. This is where using a line one size heavier than your rod's rating, as I mentioned earlier, really produces the goods. Accurately casting short, big, heavy flies takes some practice anyway, so remember to utilise only a short leader. Any more than five feet is too long and will make your fly pull unnaturally against the weight of the line, causing a delay and complete loss of accuracy.

As with all other methods of fishing, actually getting your hook to stick into a tiger, behind those wicked teeth, is the most frustrating aspect of all. Those who lure fish, using spoons, plugs and the like, will be happy with

CATFISH ON THE FLY?

Now, I have heard of the occasional angler catching wels catfish purposely from the upper river Ebro system, and from the rivers Cinca, and Segre in Spain, on large flies. However, due to heavily coloured water, it's a case of casting repeatedly into potentially good holding areas. Beneath overhanging trees, into ditch entrances, confluences, small bays and back eddies, for example, the very same spots you would cast a plug or soft rubber shad into, while drifting downstream from a small boat. Every so often you can capitalise on the situation, as up comes a catfish from nowhere and inhales the fly within seconds of it hitting the surface. There is no continual casting and retrieving as such. It is certainly a lot of work, solely dependant upon the catfish, coincidentally being close by, hearing the large fly hit the surface and making an instant attack. Naturally, it works in exactly the same way with big, splashy lures too, soft rubber replicants being particularly effective.

My good friend and Thailand's premier fishing guide, Jean-Francois Helias, displays a massive 59¼lbs red tail catfish that he caught fly fishing following a lengthy battle, using a 9-weight outfit and floating line. The successful fly was a black and white DNA Bush Pig. Jean-Francois has also caught arapaima to 154lbs on the fly.

In Thailand, however, where many of the stillwater fisheries have been purposely stocked with a variety of colourful aggressive pussies, both of Thai and South American origin, fly rodding for cats and a whole host of other spectacular species is certainly a most productive technique, and well worth trying. I experienced this just before Christmas 2009, when I visited Hua Hin to stay with my brother Dave, who helps to run a fishery there called Greenfield Valley Fishing Resort. My good friend, Jean Francois Helias, Thailand's top freshwater guide, has specialised in pussies on the fly, particularly big red tail cats, and numerous other species, for several years now, even while float-tubing would you believe, and holds several IGFA world records.

It was marvellous to team up with brother Dave again at the renowned Monsters Lake, near Bangkok, for some unusual fly rodding, once I'd taken my fill of hard battling red tail and bardok catfish on free-lined bait, chunks of fish, steak and chicken. I found action with the discus-shaped pacu wonderfully exciting using a 9-weight sink-tip outfit and a 1/0 Clouser Minnow. These muscle-packed South American battlers averaging 6-9lbs really hit the fly hard before making several runs in every direction until they started to slow down. Patterns with black or brown in the tying certainly induced more takes, due, I guess, to the principle that in the coloured lakes of Thailand, as fish are looking up into brightness a dark silhouette is more noticeable than lighter patterns. It worked for me anyway.

Pacu reach weights approaching 40lbs in Thailand, so the potential for fly rodding is simply tremendous. Brother Dave has caught them to within ounces of 30lbs, using chunks of fish, chicken and even banana, and always with a wire trace. Upon removing

the hook, the teeth are actually difficult to see, but pull back their gums using forceps and some powerful, almost human-like canine teeth are revealed, so never put your finger into a pacu's mouth. We tend to use long wire traces when targeting pacu on bait, so that when the end of the trace immediately above the hook becomes corkscrewed during the fight, we simply cut those few inches off and rejoin the hook using a twiddle stick - indeed, just as I do when live or dead bait fishing for pike.

When fly fishing for pacu, however, I simply use a six-inch trace of Kevsteel as though presenting flies to pike. With its small mouth, it rarely engulfs the fly like it does a chunk of chicken or fish anyway, so that bite-offs are never a problem, and most times the hook ends up in the scissors.

PEACOCK BASS ON THE FLY

One of the most explosive and powerful freshwater species I've ever experienced on the fly is the spectacularly coloured peacock bass in South America. Reaching weights approaching 30lbs, these bass, and there are three separate species, hit so hard that the rod is almost pulled from your grasp with sickening ferocity. I had travelled to the Rio Negro, which is just one of the mighty Amazon river's 1000-plus tributaries, and itself up to 12 miles wide in places, specifically for peacocks and I was most certainly not disappointed with their hard-hitting qualities. They attacked everything subsurface from Deceivers and Clouser Minnows, to Bunny Leeches and deer hair 'mice' patterns worked on top. Large piranhas, discus-shaped and easily averaging 2lbs, also came readily to the fly, as did several other exotic and acrobatic species like aruana and dog-chub.

Adrian Ricks, from Esher in Surrey, displays the unbelievably intricate and colourful patterns of an Amazonian butterfly bass, the smallest of the peacock basses, which provide endless action with the fly rod along Brazil's Rio Negro. The 'eye' on the tail, is a feature of all peacock bass.

In the huge shallow-water lagoons where fish were concentrated into approachable areas by boat once the floodwaters had receded - the river drops and rises over 30 feet during the rains - a floating line 9-weight outfit was just what the doctor ordered, whereas in much deeper areas a fairly heavy sink-tip line proved invaluable. As always, when targeting various species on the fly, it is a 'horses for a courses' situation. Searching through Polaroids around the shallow bays for the 3-4 feet round depressions in the bottom silt, the nests of breeding peacock bass, and then casting close by, would invariably produce instant action from the male that would come zooming out to attack the fly.

SHARKS ON THE FLY

Now, only rarely do I attempt to catch sharks purposely by fly rodding, apart from when out in the crystal-clear waters of the Florida Keys, for instance, or in the Bahamas where sharks coming up to the boat being poled or drifting over the flats is an everyday occurrence; then why not? It's all great fun watching it happen, even if the inevitable occurs and you are eventually forced to break-off. Another situation that springs to mind where a sizeable shark could find itself on the end of your 12-15 weight fly rod, coupled to possibly two full, 30 yard Hi D lines joined together in order to get the fly down, is over deep water reefs. It's here, where the exotic deep water target species of jacks and kingfish, job fish, and big king mackerel are being grabbed repeatedly by a surfeit of marauding sharks, that one could eventually grab your fly. What do you do? You hang on, that's what, and ponder the outcome. Sharks to over 100lbs have come my way, painfully I must admit, doing exactly this, providing truly memorable battles lasting over an hour.

GRAYLING ON THE FLY

Now, I do love to take grayling off the top by using buoyant sedges and mayflies during the warmer months. The Grey Wulff is a super catcher, and I just love that characteristic perfect circle on the surface these fish make when diving, having sucked in the dry fly. Most grayling I catch on the fly rod, both at home and abroad, come to leaded nymphs, gold heads and the like, or 'check nymphs'. These heavily-weighted patterns really allow you to go straight down to the river bed, particularly in deep, close-in runs beside beds of reed or sedges, where grayling are hugging the gravel bottom, very often with little more than a few feet of the actual fly line beyond the rod tip, and present your artificial at precisely the correct depth.

Casting directly upstream, or upstream and across, depending where you stand in relation to the run, and watching like a hawk as the line comes back downstream, is one way of interpreting bites. Lifting sharply into any sudden jerk of the line across the surface, as a fish intercepts the artificial close to the bottom, is all that's needed to set the hook. In super-cold and/or extremely windy conditions, a sight-bob attached to the leader, a foot or two deeper than the swim, will indicate those tricky takes. Although I only put up a sight bob when fishing is really difficult, and as an absolute last resort. I guess I think of it as float fishing, which of course it is, but it does help to present the artificial at exactly the taking depth, just above or actually bumping the bottom.

Some wonderful close-range battles result from this colourful fighting machine when conditions are perfect. I love autumn and winter sorties particularly, along southern chalk streams like the rivers Test, Dever, Upper Kennet, Anton and Itchen, holding nothing but an ultra-light 3 or 4-weight, 7 foot brook rod and floating line combo. On such tackle, any fish over 2lbs will be one hell of an adversary, fighting each and every inch to the net, in fast currents, and in my book it would take an extremely fit trout to top such a scrap.

While I adore our English chalk streams and their lovely, exquisitely coloured grayling, I have been extremely fortunate during the past two decades, to fish extensively in Canada's far north for Arctic grayling. They might well have a slight genetic difference, but to me they appear to be one and the same fish, except that Arctic grayling seem far more predatory in their manner.

Perhaps it's all simply to do with water temperature. Fishing the massive Ferguson river and lake complex, for instance, in the North West Territories, which alone contain nine per cent of the planet's fresh water - yes, the Territories are that vast - I have on more than one occasion had monstrous grayling chase large, 4-5 inch spoons intended for lake trout into the shallows. To this end, I have even taken the step of using a small spinner on my fly rod as opposed to a smaller fly pattern, which are not so difficult to cast as you might think. This does tend to sort out the better fish from big clearwater lakes, and turbulent river confluences. Hardly kosher, I know, casting a spinner on the fly rod, but who cares? Like I keep saying, it's fly rodding.

Overall, due to their aggression, Canadian grayling are also prone to inhaling outrageous patterns and sizes of flies that no English chalkstream fish would ever consider.

Here I am enjoying the acrobatic antics of Wolf
River grayling in the remoteness of Canada's Yukon
Territory, while researching for future television
programmes. I did, in fact, film my Fishing World
series here in 2009, where at any moment a bear
is more than likely to come walking along.

*Two pound-plus grayling, like this beauty, are common
catches along the pristine wilderness of the Wolf River.
Strangely, they are painted in more gold than pewter.
I have never caught grayling so uniquely coloured
anywhere else.*

Take the Wolf River in The Yukon, for instance, which starts its life by exiting massive Wolf Lake, in surface area around the size of Scotland's longest lake, the awesome Loch Awe. Tumbling fast and crystal clear over a hard, gravel bottom, this river offers arguably the world's finest grayling fishing, containing massive stocks of fish in the 1½ - 2½ range - 18-20 inch fish are common - plus a few monsters, and all attack your artificial with equal gusto.

Leaded nymphs, such as stonefly, mayfly or caddis patterns, produce well whether on the drop or down close to the polished, gravel bottom. However, what these grayling respond to most aggressively, especially when purposely cast up and across and made to skate across the current, are large, buoyant patterns made from foam rubber such as the Ugly Bug and Chernobyl Ant. A take can come at any time from casting the imitation a little upstream and immediately mending the line as it drifts downstream, to following it down the run with the rod tip, and then purposely holding hard every so often to make it skate enticingly across the surface. This brings marvellously aggressive, explosive takes and is immensely exciting and quite intoxicating sport, believe me.

Colouration, though, is what sets Wolf River grayling apart from all others I've caught both at home and abroad, including those from further north in Canada's North West Territories in the mighty Kazan and Ferguson river systems. As opposed to that classic, pewter-mauve sheen to the scales along their flanks, Wolf River fish have a most unusual and decidedly

golden sheen, with golden lines along their bellies immediately behind their pectoral fins. Such marvellous sport only happens, of course, due to so few anglers ever visiting their cold and harsh environment. It is perhaps difficult for us westerners to comprehend that the Yukon, just one of Canada's 13 provinces and territories, which is twice the size of The British Isles, has just 30,000 inhabitants, and the count of black and grizzly bears, caribou, wood buffalo and moose, actually outnumber the human population by more than five to one.

The country is so vast, so rich in flora and fauna, and such a pristine wilderness, that actually recognising a particular individual fish through scale patterns or body markings, as we now do constantly with carp, barbel, pike and tench in the UK, would simply not even enter a Canadian's mind. Actually giving that particular fish a name seems to them totally bizarre. Hell, they cannot understand why we would even wish to fish for carp in the first place!

Here are three, large, super-buoyant flies that do well on Wolf River. Left to right, are the all black, foam and rubber Ugly Bug, the more conventional Klinkhamer, and the most outrageous and super-buoyant, orange and black, Chernobyl Ant, which is fully 1½-inches long.

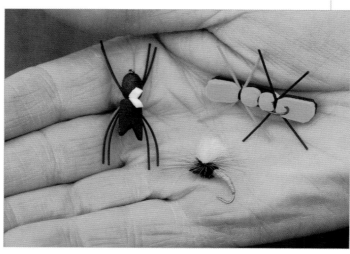

DRIFTING AROUND THE WORLD

There can be few more pleasurable ways of catching fish than by drift fishing, whether it's the pike that inhabit the larger of my local Norfolk Broads and the extensive limestone loughs in Ireland, or the high-jumping, tooth-laden tiger fish in the mighty Zambezi river, which separates Africa's Zambia in the north from Zimbabwe to the south. For these, and numerous other locations around the world, in both fresh and salt water, drift fishing is by far the most effective way of catching.

There is no better way of covering expanses of water, with an increased chance of contacting those biggies, than by drift fishing. Take the vast area of the Norwegian fjords for instance, where I am going to start this chapter, and where the world's largest cod gather for spawning in the deep, clear water off northern Norway. These fish live in the Barents Sea, and migrate south-west into the fjords during the end of the winter and early spring.

COD ON THE DRIFT

Anchoring in depths of between 50 and over 100 metres, as it is in the fjords, and, indeed, in the English Channel over wartime wrecks, is usually a waste of effort. Far better to locate ideal ground and mark fish on the sounder,

before setting up drifts to cover the area extensively. This can be pirk fishing at its very best and of course most tiring, gut-busting work, feeding heavy 8-16 ounce pirks on 50lb test braid down to the bottom from the lee side of the boat, and then physically working them up quickly for several feet in a long heave, using a 9-foot uptide-style rod, before lowering the tip quickly again so the pirk flutters toward the sea bed in that tantalizing motion of a shoal fish in trouble.

So, when at the very start of the next heave, when the tip folds over alarmingly and line starts to sizzle from the reel, you know you are into a mega cod. Should you foul hook or hook up with a small codling, or especially a coalfish, proved by that distinct juddering sensation on the rod tip, for goodness sake don't wind it up. Just leave it there for a while, while winding it up and lowering it slowly every so often. When the rod finally keels over and seems like it's connected to the bottom, wind smoothly until the hooks go home. I prefer to use giant 12/0 trebles when pirking; one, because small unwanted fish cannot usually get them into their mouths, and two, should you foul hook, or even properly hook, a small fish on one prong only, there will still be enough of the treble exposed to connect big-time with a whopping great cod. Deliberately live-baiting, as such, is illegal in Norwegian waters, but you

Here in Skervoy harbour, among the deep and bountiful fjords of north Norway, it looks remarkably like pal, Dave Lewis, is shovelling snow off the decks of our boat prior to a drifting for cod session, while Wilson takes the pics. Exactly! I'm not silly you know.

can't stop a coalfish from getting hung up on the treble of your pirk, can you?

Literally hundreds of massive cod to over 40lbs, plus big haddock, wolf fish and coalfish have come my way from both Norwegian and Danish waters, while enjoying this almost masochistic technique, plus several battles with unseen monsters that slipped the hooks. How big? Well, cod over 100lbs have been caught commercially from the Norwegian fjords, and I'm sure that it's only a matter of time before an angler boats one, and that's a fish I would dearly love to see.

Incidentally, to act as a rubbing leader and shock absorber when using a 40-50lbs test braided reel line on the drift, I use the exceedingly neat and reliable Albright knot to attach 20 feet of 80lbs test monofilament. (Details of this are in Chapter Eight, 'Throwing Lures...') The mono leader, through its inherent elasticity, acts as a buffer, should a big fish decide to make a last ditch dive when on a short line beneath the rod tip, a potentially disastrous, hook-pulling occurrence should your pirk be tied directly to braid which has no elasticity. It also allows you to swing in smaller fish by hand without the braid cutting into your flesh, so don't go drift fishing without a long, mono leader.

I have already mentioned the effectiveness of catching pike on the fly while drift fishing, (See Fly Rodding - Chapter Six) and working artificial lures can be just as rewarding. As with fly fishing, use a drogue to slow the boat's drift in order to cover maximum area, and once the drogue is working nicely, lures and wobbled dead baits of course, can be worked ahead of the boat over the lee side, just like fly fishing, or from both ends and directly behind the boat on either side of the drogue. In fact from virtually any angle.

Here among the cold, clear, and incredibly deep waters of Norway's fjords, live the world's largest cod - monsters to over 100lbs.

No wonder I've an ear-to-ear grin. Helped by top skipper, Holger Burike, I'm holding easily my largest cod ever; a monster of 40lbs, which happened along just at the right time when filming for my Fishing World TV series, among the beautiful fjords of northern Norway.

I've caught some strange critters in my time from the world's oceans, but this prehistoric-looking wolf fish, common among the cold, deep fjords of northern Norway, has got to be the ugliest, fiercest and strangest of the lot. Its wide and immensely powerful jaws are full of bone-crunching teeth and hard, crushing pads.

hippos love to congregate, or beside large fallen trees whose branches hang way out into the river creating a huge slack or an eddy below. Cast your bait, usually freshly cut fish strip or the head, presented on a wide gape size 5/0-6/0 hook, into the drop-off, and as the boat meanders downstream with the flow, quite often faster than walking pace in many stretches, pay out a little line, before tightening up and concentrating on that bow in the line between rod tip and bait, as the boat takes it downriver.

It's a great way for two mates to share a day's pike, zander, or perch fishing, while covering an enormous amount of ground, be it a massive gravel pit, mere, lake, loch, lough or reservoir. On really slow drifts, there is nothing to stop you from putting out a second, sleeper rod presenting a dead bait, or a live bait, set beneath a sliding float rig, while you are working artificials on the other.

DRIFTING FOR TIGERS AND THE GOLDEN DORADO

I mentioned tiger fish earlier on, because in freshwater they are one of the most fascinating species to target when on the drift. Take the Zambezi river for example, where throughout much of its length it has a hard, sand and gravel bottom with few snags, save for the occasional sunken, hardwood tree, compliments of the previous year's floods, and a fairly fast flow. So you simply motor to the downstream end of a sand bank, spots where

Often, a swan shot or two is required on the 30lbs wire trace just below the swivel, to keep the bait close to the bottom, and when a tiger fish bites, it does so with unparalleled speed and aggression. Sometimes, it pays to give a few yards of line before pulling firmly into the fish, and on other occasions it's worth tightening up immediately. Either way, and even on a braided reel line of 30lbs, the ensuing fight is little short of incredible, with high-leaping jumps and crashes, interspersed with unbelievably fast, searing runs. After all that, just when you are starting to count your chickens, most manage to slip the hook anyway within 10 or 20 seconds of hooking up. Anglers who actually land (and mind those teeth) one out of six tigers that pick up their bait, are doing exceptionally well, believe me. Others simply lie about the ratio of bites to fish brought to the boat.

We used a similar drifting technique along the mighty Parana river in Brazil, when targeting the South American golden dorado, a fish sharing many similarities with tiger fish. Currents are fierce and turbulent with depths varying between 30 and over 100 feet so we simply drifted along at the speed of the current, always in the fastest runs, called corridors locally.

The last occasion on which ex-schoolmaster and barbel guru, Pete Reading, and I fished together was catching barbel and chub in the Hampshire Avon for series 16 of my Anglia TV Go Fishing programmes, back in 2001. However, as the large double-figure Zambezi tiger fish he's holding proves, he's now certainly hooked on this awesome species.

We were casting our four-ounce live baits, called morinitas, presented on a strong 6/0 hook to a heavy, single strand wire trace, 30 to 40 yards back upstream. The bait would angle down through the water to eventually bump bottom over the rocks, regardless of depth.

When a dorado grabbed hold, you needed to pile on the pressure immediately to stop it getting into the river's unbelievably rocky bottom. It would then angle upwards, forcing you to recover line like a madman, and seconds later come exploding from the surface to leap high in the air, just like a tiger fish. Their teeth are not so large or as awesome looking, but they are set in jaws so strong, with such immense crushing power, that when we tried large, expensive plugs, they came back looking as though Arnie had

Yes, golden dorado, South America's highest jumping freshwater gladiator, are this beautifully coloured. I caught this stunning 20lbs fish, painted in contrasting and distinct shades of yellow, silver and black, from the mighty Parana River below magnificent Iguaçu Falls.

been playing with them using bolt croppers. Then I understood why the guide insisted on using the kind of wire used on sea booms, instead of a soft wire trace. Accidentally getting my fingers inside the jaws of big dorado, and they reach weights of 60lbs, is not something I'd particularly relish.

BACK-DRIFTING FOR PIKE

My method of drifting for tiger is similar to the one that I sometimes use for pike when searching slow-moving rivers. I use the current to drift back downstream, having first motored or rowed way upriver to start the drift, noting all the potentially good lies en route, using a silent electric motor, and or, just the oars to keep the boat side-on to the current. This enables two anglers to work two rods apiece from the rear side of the boat, the speed of the current gently working the livebaits along beneath fixed floats set a foot or so short of bottom depth. As this, of course, is constantly changing, there is always much to do and so controlling just a pair of rods each is enough, one angler tending to the oars when necessary and the other the electric motor.

With both anglers facing upstream watching for a float to go, a little oar work is often necessary to manoeuvre the boat gently over and alongside definite hot spots, like where side streams join the main flow at a confluence, or where trees overhang low to the surface, or wide bends where the water invariably deepens on the outside, so that at least a couple of the baits have the chance of passing over pike. To this end, I like to work one short and one long bait, each to cover maximum area, angling the rods out in a V shape, so each bait follows an entirely different line. As soon as one of the floats disappears, mud weights are carefully

No wonder pal, Jinx Davey, is beaming. On a dull, freezing cold day this 24lbs Lower River Waveney pike happened along to brighten everything up. The rewards of back-drifting, in order to cover maximum area of the riverbed.

lowered over each end, to strike the run and then to cover the immediate area more thoroughly, by casting around and even back up into the run from where the pike first came.

You would be surprised at just how many pike tend to be holed up in one relatively small 20-30 yard run, followed sometimes by literally hundreds of yards of seemingly nothing in the way of pike. It's a great way of spending an entire day along a particular stretch, say, between one or two miles long, plumbing all the depths accurately en route with the fish finder and really getting to know it. I've come across all kinds of odd deep holes and gullies along my local River Wensum, that previously I thought I knew intimately, while back-drifting, most of which are not visible from the bank.

VERTICAL JIGGING ON THE DRIFT

This fascinating, salt water technique is probably the most energetic and tiring of all stand-up fishing. I am certain it would also be a killing method for giant, fresh water lake trout inhabiting the deep, clearwater lakes in Canada's far north, and I shall most certainly try it when I am next there. Certainly, it is more strenuous than pirking, using an up tide rod. This was invented, and subsequently popularised, by the Japanese, who specifically target big tuna, with vertical jigs, and fixed spool reels would you believe? It's something I can't get my head around. This is, indeed, a most deadly way of catching all those big, deep water fish like jacks, trevallys, tuna and groupers, that hang around reefs between 100-400 feet deep.

At the time of writing and to my knowledge, the only UK tackle company selling suitable gear is Shimano. For a starting outfit, I would suggest a two-piece, 1.83m heavy Speedmaster V.J. AX rod, perfect for working jigs in the 160-420 gm size, coupled to a Torium 30, fast retrieve, 6.2:1 gear ratio reel loaded with 80lbs braid.

While filming my JW Fishing World series for the Discovery Shed Channel in 2009, I put this exact outfit to good use when off the island of Madagascar, working vertical jigs down close to the reefs in over 200 feet of water. I was rewarded with some beautifully marked rock cod to over 50lbs - and didn't they go! The temperature was over 100 degrees every day and I have never experienced such strength-sapping fishing, either before or since.

So much energy is used up by winding and jigging continually over deep water, that after every four or five drops, you need a breather. Honestly, it's that tiring - or could it be that I'm getting older? Either way, the secret is to get your butterfly-style pirk/jig, which is fitted with single-assist hooks, down to the bottom in a high speed vertical drop, gently thumbing the spool when required, though without slowing it down. I used both the Abyss and the Benthos speed jigs with equal effectiveness.

Once there, you pump mega-fast and wind, pump and wind, pump and wind like someone possessed, all the way up. As these pirks/jigs are specially tapered with thin backs and sides that slice easily through the water, offering minimal resistance, optimum speed is reached on the retrieve to induce a hit. When something big down there decides to attack, you need to get your fingers away from the reel and have the drag done up as tight as you dare. Even then, line gets ripped off with frightening ease, even by 30-40lbs fish, and the ensuing battle comes as close as you'll ever get to being pulled out of your boots, believe me! When working in really deep seas, and hits only seem to come from a particular depth band, then it's worth concentrating solely within that band as opposed to working the jig all the way up on every drop, which can get kind of knackering.

Unlike pirking, where the treble hook is attached to the bottom lug by a split ring, on vertical jigs, the single assist, wide gape, 4/0-7/0 hook, pre-tied to between two and four inches of heavy duty Dacron and covered by protective shrink-tubing, is attached to the lure's head-end lug using a solid ring, enabling both the heavy, 100lbs test, 20-foot rubbing leader and assist hook to work off the same ring. This gives the lure an enticing, dancing action and also alleviates any tangles. Should you suddenly be relieved of your lure, however, because a 'cuda, wahoo or shark has nipped through the mono leader just above, re-tackle with a 12-15 inch, 100lbs wire up-trace connecting the mono leader to the jig - and hang-on!

The rewards of vertical jigging; a 50lb rock cod from the clear, fertile waters off Madagascar. It grabbed my jig 200 feet down and gave a gut-busting scrap despite a powerful outfit. Note the yellow vertical jig below my gloved hand.

THROWING LURES FROM NORFOLK TO LAKE NASSER

When I first became interested in catching pike on artificial lures, which were all simply termed 'spinners' back in my early teens, most of us lads owned a cheap spinner or two, maybe even a plug or big spoon, kept in the bottom of the tackle box, to be used only if nothing was coming to live baits. To us, artificials were second-best to live baits, and dead baits had not even been popularised back then, remember. Of course, if pike were not taking the real thing, live baits, on a particular day, it stood to reason, though not always as indeed we know now, that they wouldn't be interested in artificials either. So, the rusty spinner or spoon was returned to its place in the bottom of the tackle box, until live baits failed once again.

It's a corny story, I know, but it's basically what happened in those days, when as far as choice of lures was concerned, it was either a Colorado, Kidney, or plain silver spoon, a Mepps-type spinner or a cheap Japanese jointed plug, which were just starting to be imported by a few tackle companies. There was little else. Never would any of us for instance, set off for a day's pike fishing armed with artificial lures only, as many regularly and happily do today, including myself. Hell, I set off chub fishing with just a few surface plugs and poppers, knowing I'm going to catch, which goes to show how attitudes have changed. When I think back to the occasions that could have materialised into hectic lure fishing, it almost infuriates me. There was so much we were missing out on, but at the time we didn't know any better.

I guess things started to change nationally from around the 1960s onward, when British specialist tackle shops started importing American plugs with great actions, such as Heddon's. I highlighted the wonderful actions of some of these plugs in my hour-long, John Wilson Goes Artificial Lure Fishing, video, filmed during the early 1990s. A small number of angling writers began to popularise lure fishing by accounting for some big fish, and slowly, a serious interest in the subject was born in the UK.

Later, the Pike Anglers Club, founded by the late Dr Barrie Rickards, added further momentum, as did other specialist groups like The British Lure Fishing Society, cumulating today, at the start of this second millennium, when British lure enthusiasts are arguably among the most adventuresome and knowledgeable in the world. Thanks should also go to mail order companies like Harris Sportsmail, The Friendly Fisherman, and tackle giants such as Normark, Masterline-Walker, and Rapala, who specialise in quality artificial lures.

All have made a marvellous array of artificials accessible to British anglers. In fact, the sheer diversity of lures now available to the British fresh and saltwater lure angler, from count-down plugs, to all manner of soft rubber, shad-like replicants, as I write this at the beginning of 2010, is simply staggering.

Brits certainly seem to travel the globe more than anglers in most other countries, a sad but honest reflection really, I guess, upon the demise of wild-river fishing in our overcrowded island, so they get to learn more about how different species respond to artificials in varying habitats. Much of this knowledge, as I have found over the years, can then be effectively applied to predator situations back home.

Take massive Lake Nasser in Egypt, for example, a location I know particularly well because for over a decade, on behalf of Tailor Made Holidays, and Tim Baily of The African Angler, I escorted groups of Brits to this enigmatic watershed, which is of course, none other than the River Nile dammed for 300 miles. They were all bent on getting their string pulled by giant Nile perch, and to a lesser extent the awesome tiger fish. I'm pleased to say that in the early days on the lake, most visitors did at least hook into buffalos - 100lb-plus perch - even if their hooks didn't always stay in. This tail-walking, head-shaking, gill-flaring fish is a past master at catapulting the lure clear as it jumps; a truly heart-wrenching sight. Being in the unique situation of actually observing how perch and tiger fish approach the lure in the clearwater depths has taught me so much, and this has influenced how I now like to present lures to pike, zander and perch back in the UK.

I truly think I've caught more big pike, like this scraper-20 from a Norfolk mere, on a plain big spoon than any other artificial lure. The world over, it is usually my first choice for seeing what's about.

Purely from being able to watch their reactions when shore fishing, often from a rocky plateau 20 to 30 feet above the water, I learned how sometimes, usually in bright sunshine, they would suddenly sheer off in panic at the sight of a plug's large. metal, reflective, diving vane. It was as though they associated the reflection with bad vibes. Since all perch and tiger fish are released after capture, this was possibly due to their having been caught before on the same type of lure.

A sementendu (bagras) catfish from a deep gully beside a
rock wall on Lake Nasser in Egypt, where 80 feet down it
grabbed a ten-inch long Swim'n'eel, soft, artificial lure.
Note the tackle belt around my waist; so useful for having
a variety of different lures and unhooking tools to hand
when stalking along the rocks.

This happened time and time again with Rapala CD 14s and 18s, which do have large shiny metal lips. So I tried painting the entire plug black, including the lip, and do you know, even in popular, well-fished locations, this worked unbelievably well, accounting for numbers of big perch especially, some of which I'm certain would not have hung around long enough to grab the shiny, unpainted plug. Subsequently, I also painted black all my silver Russelures, an aluminium diving plug, which also produced some nice bonus fish, both when trolling and from the shore.

Something else I learned by hours of observing, rather than catching, from elevated positions on rocks hanging out over the water, was that not all gentle taps on the retrieve come from small fish. On many occasions while trolling, when whatever is following the lure cannot be seen, I used to assume that a short, gentle tap was a small perch or tiger fish. I changed my approach when I watched one enormous perch appear from nowhere, beneath the rock I was standing on, a fish well in excess of 100lbs. It merely pursed the lure between its jaws momentarily, before immediately letting go. That continual throbbing motion of a diving plug that is transferred to the rod tip, whether you are trolling or retrieving by winding, was suddenly interrupted for the briefest of seconds as the big perch grabbed the lure, but continued immediately again as it let go.

I had witnessed the very same pause a hundred times before, and had I been trolling at the time, not in a million years would I have suspected a 100lbs-plus fish as the culprit. What a revelation! Nowadays, upon seeing any kind of pause or gentle tap on the the rod tip, I drop the lure back several feet immediately, to get the pursuer's attention before slamming the reel back into gear and

winding like mad for a few turns to give the appearance of the lure getting away. This can only really be effectively executed with a multiplier reel, which is why I use them for 95 per cent of my lure fishing. I wish I had a fiver for every good fish this ruse has produced; mostly small, I'll admit, but some very large indeed. It's a ploy that works anywhere in the world, whether I'm working spinner baits for perch back home in a deep gravel pit, or diving plugs for pike in an Irish lough.

Those who have been to the lake, or watched my 90-minute Lake Nasser Safari video which has now been extensively screened by Discovery Television throughout Europe during the past decade, can testify to the marvellous sport that existed then when purely lure fishing. There was a very real chance of hooking into a fish over 200lbs on an artificial lure, as several anglers indeed did, possibly even from the shore. Globally, that's a totally unique experience in fresh water, with the lake world record to date being a monster weighing 230lbs. Yes, we have all come a long way in the art of lure fishing, trying to fool a wild fish into believing a lump of contoured wood, plastic, rubber or metal is a living creature and thus worth chasing for a meal, but, you know, we should never get away from the basics.

As with many disciplines, successful lure fishing is all about thinking in terms of layers, or more to the point, at exactly what depth a target predator is holding, before we offer it a lure. The colder the water temperature, the fewer our chances of a hit anyway, so if we get that wrong, or use entirely the wrong one, lures per se simply will not produce. Working the correct depth band, therefore, is what presenting artificials is all about, whether the water is massive Lake Victoria in Kenya, the planet's second largest natural lake, or an irrigation canal in the Fens.

Guides Jonathan Wright (left) and Paul Goldring help me to display a near-100lbs Nile perch that I caught trolling a green Russelure along the shoreline of the Sesse Islands in the western, Ugandan sector of massive Lake Victoria.

Whatever water you throw lures into, it makes sense to have in your mind's eye, a 'layer-cake' of depth bands in which to search, relative to where at the time, you envisage predators will be lying. For instance, a pike lying close to the bottom in 15-20 feet of near-freezing water in a deep gravel pit during the middle of winter, is not going to suddenly shoot upwards to nail a spoon or plug worked anywhere near the surface. It could be interested in a count-down plug, heavy spoon, or shad counted down at around one foot per second, say, that is worked progressively through that lowest layer of water, between one to four feet immediately above the bottom. Any reasonably sized pike, assuming it lies there with its tail virtually in the silt, has only to angle upwards on its own axis and not swim an inch to intercept a likely meal.

Experienced pike anglers know full well when fish are hugging the bottom due to super-low temperatures, because every fish they catch is covered along the belly, around the pectoral fins and the gills with those tiny, double-sucker leeches that live among the bottom detritus, and the colder it is, more and more leeches will be hanging on. There are other pointers of course, like a complete lack of hits when working lures through the middle layers of water, coupled to the fact that nothing in the way of small baitfish are topping. That's because in super-cold conditions, everything hugs the bottom and moves about very little.

I'm often asked what is my favourite lure, and if I were to be pushed without any consideration of where and in which kind of water I would be fishing on a 'world-wide' scale even, I would be happy travelling virtually anywhere with just two favourites: a four to six-inch 35-40gm copper or silver spoon, and a CD count-down Rapala 14cm or 18cm plug in blue mackerel. At times, I wonder if the colour is as important as we tend to think it is. After all, most predators that eventually attack a lure are below it and looking upwards as they do, into brightness, they must surely see it initially as a dark silhouette. What is important however, with both of these particular lures, is that I can work them within a few feet of the surface, yet after counting each down to the desired depth band, retrieve them way down almost parallel and very close to the bottom. You cannot ask any more of any lure; they are so extremely versatile.

On the CD 18 blue mackerel plug, for instance, I have accounted for giant lake trout to over 25lbs while down-rigger trolling at over 100 feet in Canada's far north. I've had sailfish to 75lbs from the blue waters off Kenya's East African coast, giant Nile perch over 100lbs from Lake Nasser, and a succession of sizeable tuna, trevally, barracuda and wahoo, to name but a few from the world's oceans. I've also taken vundu catfish to 60lbs on a similar lure, a sinking Depth Raider, from the incredibly fast and swirling waters at awesome Murchison Falls on the River Nile in Uganda, so I've good reason to put my faith in big, count-down plugs.

It is perhaps worth pointing out that the treble hooks fitted as standard on these large plugs, virtually regardless of make, are perfectly adequate for species like pike. However, I would suggest you replace them with stronger hooks such as Owner trebles, or the extra-strong 4/0 and 5/0 trebles available from any Catfish-Pro stockist when targeting monsters like the Nile perch, which can all too easily straighten a prong or two as it leaps clear of the surface. I also suggest that you replace the split rings. Purchase the strongest you can find, because with the fish of a lifetime, it pays to be safe.

This illustrates what giant Nile perch are capable of doing to even a top quality lure like this Rapala Super Shad Rap, which is wired internally. The monster still threw the hooks.

Downrigger trolling for giant lake trout on Lake Nueltin in Canada's far north with Indian guide, Nap, revealed numerous problems, especially trying to set the hook by striking the line out of the down-rigger clip when working depths in excess of 100 feet.

Now, take the simple spoon, on which I've caught giant lake trout to 33lbs and more pike, weighing between 20 and 30lbs, than I care to remember, both at home and abroad. Actually, I accounted for no fewer than four, 20lb-plus pike on spoons in a single session from Canada's massive Nuelton Lake, which is the borderline between the province of Manitoba and the North West Territories. So for pike, plus the occasional big trout, perch and zander, there is no finer, more accurate way of exploring any new water, like a broad, gravel pit, estate lake, reservoir or river, than casting out and counting the spoon down at around one foot per second to ascertain not only depth, but the existence of weeds and snags.

If the spoon hits bottom after, say, 15 seconds, I'll know it's around 15 feet deep when I come to seriously work that area again, I'll start retrieving after a count of, say, 13, around 13 feet knowing the spoon should be above

Good mate and top River Ebro guide, Gary Allen, displays a beautifully proportioned and conditioned zander that I caught using a Dracko mounted, soft, rubber eel from the deep and cold, swirling waters of the junction where the River's Segre and Ebro meet, in the town of Mequinenza in north-eastern Spain.

bottom and any weed growth. While counting down, incidentally, it is not unknown for a pike to grab hold on the drop. It takes a second or two for your brain to work out exactly what's happening, because usually the line suddenly stops and simply starts shuddering, so if you are ever in any doubt, simply wind quickly down and heave hard, for the hooks to go home.

Yes, the spoon is my greatest asset when covering virgin, previously unfished ground. In a sort of 'fish as you explore' mode, sometimes it helps to draw a rough shape of a particularly large water on paper and then fill in the depths as you go around casting and fishing, for future visits. With just the one treble, spoons catch up far less than plugs, while shads, with their large, single hook protruding from the bait's back, catch up even less. However, I still think that a large spoon is a better all-round fish catcher for pike than shads in British fresh water, particularly in clear waters where the added speed of the retrieve causes a pike to follow fast in pursuit with a potential induced hook-up, as opposed to the 'up-down', jigging action, much slower retrieve of the shad and other rubber replicants. Nothing, and I do mean nothing, is written in stone, though. That's the beauty of fishing. Always expect the unexpected.

Perch and zander are much more susceptible to the jigging action of soft rubber, small-fish replicants like shads. Neither is going to give chase regularly over distances of yards like the pike, but both respond instantly to the subtle jerks and twitches, up and down movements, imparted to replicants when worked close to the bottom, and in the case of zander, virtually regardless of water clarity.

Hooked close to the bottom in 12 feet of water on a deep diving plug, Martin Bowler brings a sizeable pike up to the surface of a Norfolk mere to enjoy the explosive, top water action. That's the beauty of working lures. You tend to play most fish with a more cavalier attitude - if it comes off, so what?

TACKLE

If you are a carp angler who fancies doing a bit of lure fishing, for goodness sake obtain a lure rod for the specific job at hand, instead of merely adding a wire trace and lure to your carp outfit. Most modern carp rods have been designed with excessively long handles for distance casting and simply looking good on the rod pod. For the continual casting and retrieving demanded by lure fishing they are not only useless, but will tire you out in next to no time at all. Moreover, those from 12-13 feet in length are far too long anyway for playing a lively pike at close quarters,. You might need to change rod angle quickly to apply side strain, which means bringing the rod butt across your stomach, sometimes back and forwards several times during the fight. With an excessively long handle, this simple feat becomes almost impossible, so if you really want to get into lure throwing and gain maximum movement and enjoyment, at least ensure that you have the right tools. After all, you wouldn't distance-ledger for carp using a seven-foot lure rod, would you?

I much prefer to chin-out pike using a chain mail protective glove when lure fishing. Previous experiences, when extracting hooks and pike from the wrapped mesh of a landing net, proved detrimental to the fish's well-being. Note my six-foot, single-handed, trigger grip, Six Shooter, baitcasting rod and baby multiplier combo.

From the heavily coloured waters of the Cinca and Ebro rivers in north-eastern Spain, I have enjoyed some fabulous zander fishing using soft, rubber eels and shads, and in visibilities of less than six inches. Those huge, opaque, light-absorbing eyes of the zander give away its prowess at hunting in low light conditions, especially close to the bottom where there is much less light. This is an advantage not shared by its prey fish, small roach, rudd and bleak, which I guess is why zander fishing in the Fens is much more productive when the rivers are bank high and milky-tea brown. Those zander have a distinct advantage.

Although it would be difficult to count the number of lure rods in my tackle room, there are so many that they fall into perhaps four or five categories. So, let's run through the options for fishing both at home and abroad, starting with what is arguably the most fun item of all, the diminutive six-foot, single-handed, trigger grip, baitcasting rod. This is a tool that I simply adore using, whether boat fishing, or stalking around a small lake or throwing spoons and plugs along an overgrown river during summer and autumn. Its accurate casting of floating plugs and other top-water lures into small holes in the weeds is pure joy, be my target species perch, zander, pike or chub. Sometimes, I might have to hang on to it with two hands, should a big double-figure pike grab hold and I've taken several 20lb-plus fish over the years on these little rods, with every single scrap proving exciting.

I even use my little 'Six Shooter' baitcaster, like all my rods, marketed through Masterline Walker Ltd, when out at sea catching sand eels and mackerel for bait using teams of feathers or small Hokai lures. As fresh bait has always got to be caught, I figure that I may as well optimise on the enjoyment, and my little, single-handed baitcaster/baby multiplier combo, certainly does that.

Now, why North Americans call these lovely little wands 'baitcasters' has always confused me, because they are used solely for throwing lures using a short overhead or sideways flick. The accuracy achievable is amazing and naturally, any bait would be immediately thrown off with the velocity of the cast. Perhaps they use the collective word 'bait' to cover all artificials in the USA, but then those from across the pond do have other strange habits when it comes to lure fishing. For instance, when using baby multipliers which match perfectly with baitcasting rods, they cast with their right hand, and then swap over to holding the rod with their left, so they can wind in right-handed, something to me that has never made sense. In all other forms of fishing, you use your strongest hand and arm, for casting accuracy and playing fish, while performing the simple task of winding in with your weakest and least used, assuming you are right-handed of course. This is how I have always fished. So my advice for buying a casting multiplier, as opposed to a heavy boat model where the situation becomes reversed if you are right-handed, is to opt for a quality left-hand wind model fitted with a level wind; you will never look back.

In addition to baitcasters, where casting is all from the wrist with your hand tightly around the short, trigger grip, and your thumb resting on the control bar of the multiplier, ultra-light spinning outfits comprising a 5-7 foot rod and baby fixed spool reel, loaded with just 5-8lbs line, also have short handles with perhaps just six inches of handle between reel stem and butt cap. When targeting perch, trout, zander, mackerel and baby pike on such an outfit, using small spinners, shads and other tiny rubber replicants, I particularly love flipping out mega-buoyant deer hair mice and floating them downstream on the surface beneath overhanging trees to chub, before plopping them back. Forearm stability, as with all heavier outfits, is simply not required, it is all wrist action, and such an outfit is amazing fun to use. Try it and see.

Here's a selection from my single-handed, trigger grip, baitcasting rod and baby multiplier armoury. They each provide enjoyment-plus, but when required can subdue the largest pike. Note that for a right-handed angler like me, left-hand wind multipliers are essential.

With faithful guide, Mohammed, at my side, who has heaved more than a dozen Lake Nasser Nile perch of between 100-150lbs safely ashore or into the boat, on my behalf, I lean into a biggie from a steep, rocky promontory in a deep drop-off at Sabor.

It's wise to ensure that slightly longer rods, such as jerkbait rods intended for big pike, or light-actioned lure models in the 7-8 foot category, capable of handling everything from perch to sea trout and pike are no longer from butt cap to the middle of the reel than forearm length, which is around 14 inches.

With more powerful, perhaps longer, rods in the 9-11 foot category designed for two-hand casting for big pike, salmon, bass, pollack, tiger fish, Nile perch, and tropical salt-water predators, you need the handle no longer than that of a forearm, plus hand grip below, around 18-19 inches.

If the rod is to be used for trolling or occasional up-tiding, then 20 inches from butt cap to the middle of the reel is acceptable. Anything longer is a distinct disadvantage as I have already explained and most uncomfortable to fish with, so be sure to shop around for comfortable and well-designed lure rods. After all, when throwing artificial lures or wobbling dead baits, you might be doing it all day long, making literally hundreds and hundreds of casts. Only continually long-trotting is as demanding a technique. If, like me, you won't ever be using a fixed spool reel on such a rod, then select one with a trigger grip, screw reel fitting. It makes for extremely comfortable casting and playing, particularly of big fish.

This brings me nicely on to multipliers, because, except for the centrepin reel, there is no more effective reel for both casting and the smooth playing of any fish, particularly those whoppers. This is because the line is transported directly and evenly around the spool by the level wind and comes off exactly the same way, thus eliminating both line twist and extra friction, such as in the case of fixed spool reels, when the line goes around the bail arm under pressure. So do not be afraid of learning to use a multiplier. You will become a more accomplished, happier, and more confident angler as a result. You will also be able to play any fish, much closer to the breaking strain of the line, than with a fixed spool reel, which is why I even use my multipliers for barbel and carp in addition to pike. (See Chapter Three Cyprinid Species - Barbel.)

An excellent example of multiplier against fixed spool reels with regard to line wear, particularly monofilament, occurred on camera when I was filming a tarpon program out in the Florida Keys during an episode of my Fishing Safari series for Discovery Real Time Television with fellow angler, Chris Tarrant, and skipper John Rawle. John had fixed me up with a fixed spool outfit in order to cast a free-lined blue crab, some 30 yards (multipliers do have some limitations) to tarpon working the surface at night close to one of the road bridges. Although for drifting baits beneath floats he much prefers multipliers. I was to find out why, later.

Before long, I hooked up big time with what materialised into an incredibly strong, 160lbs monster that just kept going and going. To cut a very long and exciting story short, in less than an hour the badly grating line, which sounded like it had been sandpapered, could be heard going backwards and forwards through the rod rings and around the bail arm roller, as the big tarpon made one powerful run after another. John Rawle had put new line on the reels that evening, and just that one fight had completely broken down the new, 25lbs test monofilament. Consequently, I took rather longer than I would have liked in eventually bringing it to the boat, heart in my mouth, for fear of the line breaking, so John could shake the hook free.

For the safety of both fish and angler, you cannot drag a big tarpon into the boat for a photo. It could end up smashing the boat and tackle to bits, or be so weak upon return that the sharks would immediately get it. This is why you bring it close to the boat where it could be easily gaffed or netted, and thus landed for the skipper to touch the leader, and validate the catch, before working the hook out and allowing the tarpon to swim off strongly, which is always a lovely sight through such incredibly clear water.

The action, which included three spectacular jumps, did make great television, despite filming the entire sequence in the dark using million-candlepower spotlights connected to the battery on John's 19-foot skiff. Afterwards, John said that he only ever uses the line once when a tarpon gets hooked up on a fixed spool reel, whereas the same line on a multiplier will stand several fish before needing to be changed. Enough said.

Incidentally, when using braid on fixed spool reels, neither line twist nor deterioration is such a problem, a point worth taking into account if you must use a fixed spool reel. I, personally, would not want to match the non-stretch properties of braid against the unpredictable antics of the tarpon, which has the ability to jump while running and run while jumping. All that going on in mid-air is just too much. I rather think a greater percentage of hooks would be pulling out than with a more cushioning monofilament line.

A few words on casting and how to hold the rod when retrieving lures are warranted here. You can be using the smoothest casting reel and all the top lures money can buy, and yet miss out

With one of Lake Nasser's seven cruise ships, which take tourists from Aswan down to the temples at Abu Simbel and back, passing by, note how I'm holding the rod pointing directly at the lure which, in this case, is a large, soft rubber shad. When a fish grabs hold as I crank the reel's handle irregularly to retrieve line and give the lure motion, as opposed to moving the rod from side to side, the large, single hook goes home immediately.

on so many potential fish, if you don't keep the rod tip pointed, as near as damn it, at the artificial throughout the retrieve. To expect the hooks of large lures, especially, to pull in firmly, while holding the rod to the side, or even at an angle of 45-degrees, is not good enough. Sure, you will be able more easily to identify any bang on the rod tip and see it pull round, but while this is happening the fish can all too easily shake its head and heft the lure free, so that by the time you have wound down tight, the fish is gone.

From the minute the lure is in the air, concentrate on your actions by keeping the rod tip pointing at it, and get used to feathering it smoothly down to the surface at the end of its trajectory, so that when it touches down, its head end is facing you. This accomplishes two things; firstly, it helps prevent one of the trebles catching around the reel line which can occur easily with large-vaned, deep-diving plugs, ruining the cast, and maybe the chance of an instant hook-up. Secondly, from the very first turn of the reel's handle, any hit has the chance of being converted into a fish on the bank.

Some anglers find this discipline rather difficult, I know, because they like to hold the rod to the side and watch the rod tip for signs of a hit, but believe me, it's worth getting used to, as is simply using an exaggerated and erratic retrieve to work the lure, instead of the rod tip. You can still sense the build-up in pressure and see the tip vibrate when pointing it at the lure as a fish grabs hold. The fact is, that lure will work with exactly the same tantalizing action which is why we love 'em so much, whether you move it along with the rod tip or simply by winding. So it does

Wobbling dead baits slowly along, just above bottom, catches me an awful lot of big pike from my local Norfolk Broads. Look at the size of this 26-pounder's jaws. If it'd had a belly, it would easily have topped 30lbs.

make sense to have the tip pointing at the lure when a hit materialises, for the best possible chance of the treble going home and a firm hook-up.

A little ruse worth trying every few casts or so, is to imagine that a predator is giving chase but needs conviction to make a lunge and grab hold. Well, suddenly stop winding, and allow lures such as spoons, sinking, diving plugs or even wobbled dead baits, to flutter downward a few feet, before cranking them suddenly back into life at a much faster rate of retrieve than before. You'll be amazed by the result, but unfortunately, not every time you try it.

Nowadays, I use the low diameter and non-stretch properties of braid for virtually all of my lure fishing and much of my ledgering for pike and catfish too. I find the ensuing fight of a big fish hooked trolling, such as a monster Nile perch on Lake Nasser, for instance, rather tight and hairy during the initial stages, until the fish quietens down some. I'm sure more lightly hooked fish get to throw the hooks out than they do on monofilament, whatever the species, but then I expect that using braid and its non-stretch properties are the main reason for using it in the first place. I compensate to an extent by using rods, which though snappy, or tip-actioned for long, crisp casting, will also go into a full bend under pressure. I never use rods that lock up from above the spigot.

Another distinct benefit of trolling, using non-stretch, low-diameter braid, is that the lure will work significantly deeper than it does with much thicker monofilament. It's all down to the amount of resistance against water pressure behind the boat between rod tip and lure. The thicker the line, the shallower the lure will run. The thinner the line, the deeper it will run, regardless of the type of diving plug being used. It's nothing to do with how much line you let out behind the boat, except that the more line you have out increases water resistance and the shallower any lure will run. Which is why when I'm out trolling on large waters, I often like to have two identical outfits rigged up, one with mono and one with braid, though I may be working the same lure on each. With, say, 40-60 yards of line out behind the boat, the difference in how much further the lure might dive on low diameter braided line compared to monofilament of equivalent breaking strain, could be as much as 4-6 feet. Worth considering isn't it?

While on this comparison theme, you might think it strange that most top anglers tend to use braid of a significantly higher breaking strain than they would in monofilament; I do myself. For instance, when pike fishing on my local Norfolk Broads, and just about everywhere else in fact, I feel comfortable using a monofilament reel line of around 15lbs test. Yet, when using braid I increase this to 30lbs test. Why? Well, depending upon manufacturer, 30lbs braid in diameter is no more than the equivalent of just 10lbs monofilament, so I have all the benefits of reduced water pressure with regard to

THE ALBRIGHT KNOT

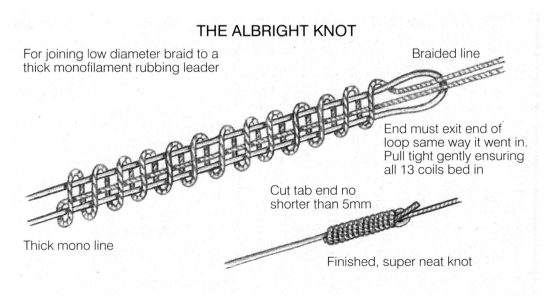

For joining low diameter braid to a thick monofilament rubbing leader

Braided line

End must exit end of loop same way it went in. Pull tight gently ensuring all 13 coils bed in

Cut tab end no shorter than 5mm

Thick mono line

Finished, super neat knot

casting and retrieving lures. That's one reason, but I think my own preference in going heavier is down to the fact that being much thinner, you only need but one nick in, say, 15lbs braid, and you could be fishing noticeably weaker. It's simply not worth taking the chance.

The curious marketing aspect about braid is that many manufacturers advertise it as 'abrasion resistant'. Compared to monofilament, this could not be further from the truth. It's okay passing through tough weed, it scythes through like a cheese cutter, and even rubbing across polished gravel and mud; but rocks? Oh no. When I'm trolling with braid in one of the Scottish lochs where my line might pass over rocks, or working a pirk close to the rough, sometimes unforgiving, bottom ground of a Norwegian fjord, or down among the rusting ironwork of a wreck, or casting from the rocky shoreline of Lake Nasser or River Nile, where when a big fish comes close in it could well dive under the very rocks I'm standing on and sever the braid, I always use a 20-foot, heavy monofilament rubbing leader. This is tied to the braid using the neat and most efficient Albright knot, which easily passes through the multiplier's level wind without fouling. (see diagram)

This is the most useful insurance policy of all and the best tip I could possibly pass on to any budding lure enthusiast. Using a mono rubbing leader also provides badly needed elasticity in the outfit when a big fish comes in close to be netted, or chinned out, and decides to panic and make one last ditch run on a short line, thus averting a possible break-off. I also like to use a clear, monofilament rubbing leader when spinning or working Toby-like spoons for spooky, clear water salmon and sea trout. Again, it creates that valuable elasticity for when a good fish

comes close in and starts to thrash about on the surface.

For the continual casting and retrieving demands of lure fishing, my preference in braid types is for a round, fairly hard one. This softens with use and is also termed 'fused' braid. Berkley Fireline original Fused, Fireline Braid and Sufix Performance Fuse are all excellent in this category. I also use Power Pro and Rovex Air Strike Braid, which are both extremely hard wearing. I do not use soft braids that fluff-out when caught by a rough fingernail.

Another valuable tip I should like to pass on, because it alleviates the problem of loosely-wound braid cutting into and between other coils, which can all too easily lead to break-offs, is to wind it on to your reel as tightly as possible, and wet! I do this at home at the kitchen sink, water shoots all over the place as the spool revolves, but I put the spool in my wife's narrow, plastic measuring jug, a quarter-filled with water, so that it remains upright. I wind the braid on using a filleting glove to hold the braid firmly between thumb and forefinger, immediately in front of the level wind, so it goes tightly on to the spool. Now, this may seem a bit of rigmarole, but it's worth every second spent, believe me. If at sea, pay out the end of the braid from the new spool while the boat is going along, and when you reach the end, tie it to your reel and wind on. Don't be tempted to put even a small lead on to the end, or you'll never be able to wind in 200-300 yards of braid.

Lure fishing truly is a global angling phenomenon, where techniques devised in the Zambesi, really can pay off in the River Thames. There's a real art to fooling predators with fake versions of their prey and doing so is certainly one of the most exciting forms of angling the whole world has ever seen.

PLAYING IN THE BIG LEAGUE

If you don't get the opportunity to play big fish on a regular basis, that sudden, frightening, uncontrollable feeling of being connected to a leviathan and unseen force like a big sturgeon, skate, catfish or sizeable shark, without question the fish of a lifetime and a personal PB, is certainly going to affect your mindset. I see it time and time again while escorting anglers whose previous PB has been a 20lbs carp or cod, say.

Quite suddenly, there they are clutching a multiplier and powerful rod combo, with the end of the rod pressing hard into their butt pad, as a 200lbs, Fraser River sturgeon heading downstream rips 150lb braid at sickening speed from a tightly-set clutch. Through sheer, adrenalin-pumping nerves, I've seen guests suddenly clamp both thumbs around the spool in order to stop the fish, or click the reel into free-spool. Afterwards they always wish they hadn't. It's every guide's nightmare, from which there is usually no return. In the angler's defence, though, when you don't play big fish regularly on heavy tackle, it's all going to be one hell of an instant learning curve. It has to be; you cannot practise on big fish, other than by landing or losing them, and neither you, your guide or the skipper wishes the latter.

If there is a formula, and I think there is, it is to try to relax, listen to what the guide has to say, and even help the boat's skipper by saying in which direction the fish is heading. Next, never take your eyes off the line between surface and rod tip and even talk to the fish if it will keep you calm. Many skippers like to have the reel's ratchet on with big fish hooked by newcomers, purely so they can assess how fast the fish is running, and how much line might be leaving the reel, but personally, the noise drives me nuts. Should the line become really low on the reel, for instance, the clutch setting may need to be reset during the battle, because it was adjusted initially to the reel being full of line. Now, when it is almost empty, far less line is given per revolution.

I think the main problem with newcomers to big fish and the playing of them on a multiplier, is to get the hang of the proper method of recovering line. This method is simple and you start by pumping when the fish stops running, in order to recover line, followed by the rod tip starting to straighten, which is when you start winding while lowering the rod slowly, still keeping it a little bent, before pumping again and repeating the process. So many anglers, again through nerves, tighten-up and almost freeze, paying little attention to what the rod top is doing.

In the deep, clear, glacial blue water of the Harrison River, a tributary of the mighty Fraser, in Canada's British Columbia, two anglers sharing a boat are both hooked up with 100lb-plus sturgeon. The guide is smiling because he knows about the pain barrier they might both eventually be going through.

You can literally see their knuckles going white while they continue trying to wind, even when a fish starts running again. This not only imparts enormous torque upon the rod, line and reel, it also beats up the angler big time, draining physical strength, and with at least a half-hour battle ahead, as is the case with a 200lb-plus sturgeon, say, you are talking serious effort. The consequences of strained arm and back muscles could well affect the remainder of their holiday, so, as I mentioned earlier, the message is one of relaxing, or at least trying to.

Posture is most important when straining against a big skate or sturgeon. Only bend forward when recovering line and while pumping, bend at the hips and lean backward to allow the spring in the rod to perform the function of bringing the fish back. For all but the largest and most powerful of fish, particularly in fresh water, I actually prefer not to use a butt pad, instead I rest the rod butt - a soft rubber butt cap is essential here - on my hip bone, occasionally swapping from one side to the other during the fight. My reason is that many butt pads are so thick, that the rod, and more importantly the reel, ends up being held several inches further out than it would be by resting the butt cap against your hip. This causes the angler to hunch over more because the reel is further away, and induces extra strain upon the back. Anglers with long arms don't suffer this problem.

As the great fish, be it skate, catfish or sturgeon, nears the boat with much of its sting now gone, you must always beware of those last ditch dives, where it suddenly has enough strength left to zoom from one side of the boat to the other, with the line potentially being scraped across the prop.

(left to right) Guides Eric, Shane and Merr, help me display my largest-ever freshwater fish, an eight and a half foot, giant white sturgeon guestimated from a length-to-weight ratio chart, to be around 350lbs. It was caught from the Harrison River near Harrison Hot Springs in British Columbia. However, in both the Harrison and Fraser rivers, monsters of three times the weight of this fish exist.

So be prepared to move quickly across the boat in order to stay with the fish's movements. When the skipper or guide finally has it under control, just ease back on the drag a little, again, in case of a last minute dive. You do not want a light hook hold to cost you the fish of a lifetime, or an expensive rod to be fractured around the engine cover of the boat.

Invariably, there will be times when you think over and over to yourself, usually in a self-accusing way, how you could have played a particular fish differently to have perhaps changed the outcome. A particular personal situation comes to mind, that occurred several years back while I was on safari on Lake Nasser. I became attached to a real monster, and my 30lb reel line, humming in the strong wind like a taut guitar string, scythed upward at an acute angle over 80 yards out from where I was perched precariously on a huge slab of rock 20 feet above the lake's surface. The great fish shot upward like a Polaris missile from 50 feet down, where it had grabbed my artificial lure, a 110g Toothy Critter Hot Tail shad.

Seconds later the surface erupted in an enormous kaleidoscope of spray as between 150 to 200lbs of Nile perch attempted to tail walk in a head-shaking, gill-flaring display before diving deep again; fortunately, the hook held. Save for several 300lb-plus white sturgeon, landed on much heavier tackle from Canada's Fraser River, this leviathan was by far the largest freshwater fish I have ever connected with. Although I've lost count of the perch exceeding that magical 100lbs that have come my way from the lake, the monster to which I was now connected, was in a different league to any of them, even my best, a 150-pounder.

After a further ten minutes of arm-wrenching battle, during which time it stayed deep down, I slowly, agonizingly, managed to pump it upward to within a couple of feet from the surface immediately below the rock face. At something like six feet in length and two feet deep, with enormously wide shoulders, its sheer bulk viewed through the clear water was simply awesome and I admit, at that stage, that I was even starting to count my chickens. Suddenly, it decided to dive down deep again, not liking the bright world above the surface, and once it reached a happy level around 30 feet down, the single hook of my rubber lure simply fell out. I didn't know whether to throw the rattle out of the pram or scream. Few lost fish have ever affected me so, either before or since. Believe it or not, I still recall that encounter in my mind's eye every so often; but that's life isn't it!

The nice thing about this bountiful lake is that when you lose a biggie, another could be just around the corner, and I did in fact finish the safari with a beauty of 120 lbs caught trolling a Reef Digger lure close to the bottom on the edge of a deep drop-off. Two other guests, Keith Potter and Steve Rutherford, also accounted for 100lbs perch, while Dave Harding and Peter Plant both boated 10lbs tiger fish, but I still cannot erase the memory of that lost monster, and probably never will. I had certainly done nothing wrong to deserve losing it.

Peculiar to giant skate fishing, and in the UK there is no more prolific area than around the beautiful sea lochs of western Scotland, is the extreme depths you might be fishing in. Out from picturesque Oban, for instance, when on Ronnie Campbell's boat Laura Dawn with my daughter, Lisa, filming for my Discovery Dream Fishing series made for Discovery TV in 2006, we anchored in depths of between 550-600 feet, the

My daughter, Lisa, and I both connected to giant skate offshore from Oban, in Scotland, aboard Ronnie Campbell's boat, Laura Dawn. See how dad's leaning back comfortably at the end of a pumping sequence, before leaning forward from the hips to recover line, while Lisa, bless her, is a bit too upright and hanging on for grim death. She got her skate, though, all 192lbs of it, up to the boat from 600 feet down.

deepest I ever bottom-fished, incidentally. Of course, with there being around 25 per cent stretch in monofilament line, winding quickly down to a bite and striking as usual is hardly likely to set the 12/0 hooks we were baiting with large mackerel and whole dogfish cocktails. So, you point the rod at the fish and simply wind and wind and wind, until you cannot possibly stretch the 50lbs line any more, and then, and only then, heave into the fish and settle down to a real tug-of-war. If the skate turns out to be, say, 150lbs-plus, as many are, you must be prepared for a long, pump-and-haul battle, once you've prised the skate from the bottom. This could take 10-20 minutes, sometimes much longer. Big stingrays fall into the same category and the

leverage these giant fish impart to a stand-up 50lbs class outfit has to be experienced to be believed.

I know the near-200lb monster that my daughter, Lisa, eventually brought to the boat, beat her up big time. Partly because she weighs but eight stone, and partly because she was straining against it for much of the time by pulling with her arms instead of allowing her back, via the rod harness, to take the strain. Like I said earlier, you should only pump using both arms when the fish either allows you to, or when it stops running, and then put that line on the reel while slowly lowering the rod. When the great fish is taking line on yet another run, keep your arms straight but relaxed and allow it to do so without straining against it.

Yes, big fish can certainly beat you up. I will never forget the look of agony on my son Lee's face when he accompanied me on an exploratory trip to the 1000 mile long

Skeleton Coast in Namibia, and he got stuck into a 200lb shark from the shore. Like all the rest that power due west from where you hook them, this fish went 70-80 yards out, straight over the reef and so incredibly far out into the Atlantic Ocean, you think it's never going to stop. Indeed, the real big ones of 400lbs plus, simply don't. Being a 16-stone body-builder, Lee naturally assumed he would be able to contain a fish no heavier than himself, simply by arm-pumping pressure alone, but when he turned round to say, 'Do you want a go, Dad?' after just 15 minutes on the shark, I knew he was in trouble.

Apparently, the lactic acid in his arms had made them lock up, and I did eventually help him with that first fish by showing him the rudiments of pumping Namibia-style. This involves walking steadily, 30-50 yards back up the beach, almost into the desert behind, in order to gain line whenever the shark allowed, and then running back down into the surf again winding like a madman to recover it all. Trying to regain line simply by pumping while standing still on the beach as you would when in a boat, is not possible using a 14-foot surf rod, except with small fish up to 50-70lbs or so. Arms are not strong enough, but your back is, and this is what it's all about.

Playing big fish is yet another technique we can add to our angling skills locker, and while hooking into a monster can be intimidating for those new to the experience, there's a pure excitement about it that simply can't be found anywhere else. Once you've fought a fish that's far stronger than you are, you'll know why so many of us find the sheer, adrenalin-fuelled thrill of it so addictive.

Along the golden sands of Namibia's 1000 mile Skeleton Coast, my son Lee, using a one-piece, 14-foot, South African surf stick, battles with a 200lb bronze whaler shark nearly 300 yards out beyond the breakers. He's never had such a good workout, before or since.

IN PURSUIT OF PIKE

Much of my local pike fishing these days is enjoyed in the company of a friend, on occasion even two, sharing a boat somewhere on my local Norfolk and Suffolk Broads and their tidal rivers, the Yare, Bure or my favourite, the Waveney. It is the ultimate 'getting away from it all' pastime, where very occasionally we spot a rare bittern, but regularly enjoy seeing marsh harriers quartering the reed marshes, plus sparrowhawks crashing audibly into blackbirds or pigeons. This is indeed a most lonely pursuit, during the coldest winter months, highlighted every so often by one of the rod tips knocking, as down there on the silty bottom, a pike hoovers up our smelt or lamprey head dead baits.

BROADLAND PIKE

Here among the marshes of the Lower Waveney or Yare river systems, or up on the River Thurne with its interconnecting expanses of Hickling Broad, Heigham Sounds, and Horesy Mere, is an entirely different world from Norfolk and Suffolk's estate lake and gravel pit pike fishing. A quick fix, for instance, is rarely going to happen like it does in much smaller waters with easier access. Within Broadland there is so much pike-holding ground which all looks 'fishy'; you need to spend a disproportionate amount of time in research by simply fishing and trying various spots. With newcomers enduring countless blank sessions before gold is struck, and even then, not everyone strikes it rich.

History has it that many of those truly monstrous Broadland pike have been caught from the Upper Thurne Broads. Whether this is due to brine shrimp, which because of a ten per cent salinity in these waters, account for an extra, and most valuable food source always available to young pike in their early life, I am not sure, although I think it possible. Upper Thurne pike are certainly known for their huge heads, but either way, you cannot escape the fact that most monstrous Broadland pike, those topping 40lbs, have been caught from the Upper Thurne watershed, which is unique. Add Somerton (also called Martham) North and South Broads to the equation and you have the most prolific pike hot spots in East Anglia, as proved by that phenomenal, completely out of the blue, 45lbs monster caught by John Goble from the River Thurne's watershed in 2009.

I've concentrated on the Broads these last 40 years, and I've been fortunate enough to have sampled them all, accounting for 20lb-plus specimens from the majority, plus the occasional monster over 30lbs. They have taught me so very, very much about pike behaviour which, just as it differs in one type of gravel pit fishery to another, does so on the Broads. For instance, folklore has it that pike love to lie in wait between the reeds to pounce upon passing shoal fish, and so presenting a bait beside the reeds produces top results. In really shallow waters such as the Upper Thurne Broads, from Hickling through to Martham Broads, this can prove perfectly true, even throughout the coldest winter months, because the bottom changes little in depth from the reed lines to out in the middle, except for the commercial boat channels. Pike certainly don't like sheltering among reed stems which are continually clanging against their bodies during strong winds, though. I think it irritates them intensely, and they don't like continually moving position, so in these conditions they will be out from the reed lines,

It's back to the 1980s and a very much younger Wilson with this shot of an incredibly long 30lb-plus pike, 49 inches from snout to the fork of its tail. I caught it from the Upper Thurne area and its head alone was a foot long, with those characteristic, bream-munching jaws. What a fish!

and probably sniffing out food from the undertow.

In cross-section, the deeper Broads are much like a saucer or pudding bowl, with shallow reed lines shelving gently into a deeper bowl. Once winter has set in, it has been my experience that presenting baits in the bowl, where much of the small fodder-fish shoals will be concentrated, invariably produces top results, and being aware of that all-important undertow caused by windy conditions will put more pike in your net. When anchored in a boat on the Broads during windy weather, drop a piece of pinched bread flake beside the boat and watch it sink. Initially, it will go with the wind and surface flow, and then suddenly, set off in the opposite direction, carried by the underwater tow. This is why I much prefer a good wind when fishing the Broads, as opposed to an infinitely more comfortable, flat calm day. When nothing predator-wise seems to be moving, you need to wobble small, whole dead baits and move to the pike. Now, almost exclusively, I use static dead baits for the bigger fish. The aroma of a freelined or float-fished dead bait will be picked up by pike via the all-important subsurface tow, sometimes with incredible speed, and runs can come within minutes of putting the bait out.

To pike, the smell of a dead bait drifting along to them via the tow, must be like the smell of frying bacon and sausages to you and me. I like to get a pan full of both on the stove post-haste, as soon as all the rods have been positioned, because only very rarely does a good chop on the surface not produce results. Hence, my anchoring plan of putting a weight down at each end of the boat at the furthest point upwind, say, in a line with the middle of the Broad, with the bow anchor on a long rope, and the stern on a short, steadying rope. I fan the baits all around the boat covering as much water as possible, with a view to moving downwind and repeating the process, simply by lifting the weights and using the wind to move the boat for minimum disturbance. I do this every three-quarters of an hour unless regular runs develop. It really is a lovely, most effective, grid-searching way of luring pike to static dead baits, and I will probably reposition each bait once or even twice during that three-quarters of an hour. (see diagram) You can then explore on either side of your original 'down the middle' line if action is slow and you have enough of the day left, but as I have already said, runs are more liable to come from that slightly deeper bowl of the Broad.

One mistake many make when positioning their rods, is that they tend to present all their baits beneath floats, so that within minutes all the floats have swung around to the lee, stern end, of the boat and lie close together covering only a minimal amount of the bottom. Assuming the boat is anchored 'bow-on' into a strong wind, this is rarely the best policy. Far better to present the upwind and across-wind baits on a simple freeline, cast 25-50 yards out, with just three or four swan shots on the trace immediately below the swivel, to keep the baits static exactly where you want them, and to give a pike just a little resistance to pull against, in order to make it run off away from the rod. Present baits beneath floats, only in the area of water in lee of the boat, so they are not pulled out of position.

This technique really does cover the absolute maximum amount of water, and has no doubt produced numbers of fish that would not otherwise have come across the baits. With two anglers sharing a boat that is anchored bow into the wind, simply draw an imaginary line lengthways down the centre of the boat, with one angler covering one side and the second angler the other. (see diagram) It's really all about covering the maximum amount of water. Pike fishing the Broads will perhaps then not seem so daunting.

I usually fish a small multiplier outfit (6500 size) loaded with 30lbs braid to cover both upwind and across-wind areas, and leave the ratchet on with the reel out of gear to provide audible bite registrations, although to be truthful I rarely take my eyes from the line where it enters the water on each outfit. I react accordingly by instantly clicking the ratchet off and allowing a little line to pass under my thumb as a fish moves off with the bait, prior to putting the reel into gear, waiting for the line to fully tighten and follow the line of the fish before heaving gently into it. Harsh strikes are simply not required with braid; that's the beauty of it.

On the downwind, bottom-end, slider float rig set at least twice swim depth to prevent the bait being pulled unnaturally up and down from the silt by the float on every wave, I like to use 15lbs test monofilament, because of its inherent elasticity, on a fixed spool reel, and use the free-spool facility in case I don't always instantly see the float move off. For reels without a free-spool option, open the bail arm and slip a loop beneath an elastic band around the rod handle opposite the spool. It's nice having at least one float to watch, I always think.

With both outfits, incidentally, the swivelled trace is 30lbs easy-twist wire around 20 inches long with a pair of size 8, semi-barbless trebles on the business end. I think larger trebles tend to impede pike turning the bait, and cannot say I've noticed fish coming off inexplicably. Well, I rarely use hooks larger than size 8 for big carp, so why pike? Besides, I do not use large dead baits on the premise that if the pike is any size at all it will have the 5-7 inch whole or half-baits that I prefer to use, far enough inside its chops to warrant an instant strike.

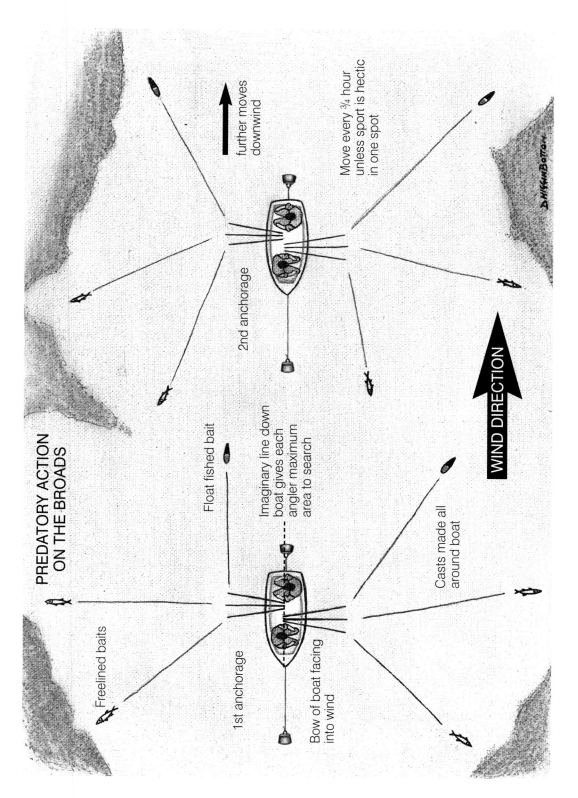

PREDATORY ACTION
ON THE BROADS

further moves
downwind

Move every ¾ hour
unless sport is hectic
in one spot

2nd anchorage

WIND DIRECTION

Float fished bait

Imaginary line down
boat gives each
angler maximum
area to search

Casts made all
around boat

Freelined baits

1st anchorage

Bow of boat facing
into wind

What are my favourite baits in order of effectiveness? Well, I would put the head end of a lamprey, say, six inches long, well spiked to let the blood ooze out, as my number one bait, with a six-inch whole smelt and the head end of an eel next. After that, both the tail and head end of joey mackerel attract brilliantly, as do 5-7 inch sardines and freshly killed roach and rudd. I've enjoyed great success with small rainbow trout, too, and when I can get them fresh from the market, and only then, herrings are always great attractors, not least for the kaleidoscope of iridescent scales that explode from the fish when it hits the surface.

One of my favourite little winter ruses to incite pike into sucking in static dead baits when conditions are difficult, such as when fishing clear water or over a carpet of bottom weed, is to pop them up several inches above the bottom. This not only prevents the bait becoming hidden in weed or suspended silt, it makes it plainly visible to patrolling pike from several feet away, which often rush at it, resulting in screaming runs.

It's a fact that Broadland pike regularly munch on eels, which from their hole in the bottom detritus tend to suspend half their body up from the bottom when looking around. I have observed this on numerous occasions during the summer months. Of course, to the pike this is like a red rag to a bull and provides an easy meal.

To simulate this, I use the head end of an eel or lamprey, six to seven inches long and mount as usual on a pair of size 8, semi-barbless trebles, fixed three inches apart and nicked into the tough skin at the end opposite to the head. To the shank of what will be the top treble when the bait is suspended, I twist on three inches of soft, multistrand wire with a three-quarter-inch diameter, green, Pro-popper soft foam, buoyant ball twisted to the end. This raises the bait the desired height off the bottom, and is easily adjusted by pinching on two 2XSSG shots on to the wire trace in the appropriate position; use larger diameter foam balls for larger baits. To ensure the reel line does not angle up sharply from those bottom shots to the rod and possibly induce line bites, I pinch a single 2XSSG shot five feet up the line to keep it ironed to the bottom. Small whole smelt or natural baits, and even half baits can all be fished in the same way.

In my experience, these three shots on the trace and line, though minimal in their specific gravity in water, are sufficient resistance to make the pike move off away from the rod and provide a most positive bite registration from either a baitrunner reel, the ratchet of a small multiplier, or a loop of line tucked beneath an elastic band on the rod handle just above the reel, with the reel's bail arm open.

My own boat, incidentally, though on some Broads I'm compelled to use the resident craft, is a beamy, 62-inch wide, 14-foot, aluminium, incredibly stable, Sea Strike with a semi-flat hull that has just two 14-inch square box seats, foam filled for buoyancy and positioned six feet apart. This allows for big fish like pike to be deposited in the middle on an unhooking mat, with plenty of room for unhooking all around. I just hate cramped conditions, sitting all day with my knees round my neck, and I'm not a particularly tall person. So, I designed 22-inch wide aluminium saddles, a top and two sides, which clip firmly in any position across the boat over each of the box seats, and on to which is bolted a comfortable, swivelled, American bass boat-style, padded seat with a fold-down backrest. These allow anglers to sit high up, and along with other refinements, are the best additions to what has become

Old pal, Jinx Davey, and I don't mess around when boat fishing the Broads for pike. He laces the coffee, I'm not saying what with, while I get the sausages burned to perfection. Lovely!

silt is not brought inside. Being heavy, these two weights allow me to anchor steadily and cannot suddenly be yanked from a particular spot by strong winds, just when the action is starting to happen.

There is also a manual bilge pump fitted and two banks of upright, aluminium rod racks. The first three feet of the bows are covered, providing waterproof storage for cameras, life jackets, drogue, unhooking mat, fire extinguisher, spare trailer wheel, tool box and other sundries, and I had the entire outside of the hull above the waterline sprayed green to alleviate glare in bright conditions.

As speeds throughout much of Broadland are restricted to just five miles an hour, an old 4½ horse, twin, two-stroke, Johnson outboard, that I just can't seem to part with more than suffices. I often wish it wouldn't start at times so I can replace it. In addition, I have an electric Turbo Minn Kota, 36lbs of thrust outboard that operates with power from a 12-volt caravan battery, for negotiating those shallow and clearwater areas with absolute silence.

an extremely efficient freshwater angling boat, whatever the species I'm after.

At the bow, for instance, is a pulley over which a 56lb steel anchor weight is easily lowered and pulled up, with a self-locking cleat for retaining the soft, half-inch diameter rope. The stern weight of 40lbs is also steel and both are merely pulled up when travelling, but not inside the boat, so that foul-smelling bottom

When targeting pike in the tidal rivers, a whole array of techniques will bring success. Around holiday areas like Beccles on the Waveney, Wroxham and Horning on the Bure, and Brundall on the Yare, where currents are minimal, massive concentrations of young roach and bream move into the boatyards during the colder months for protection.

Holding modest-sized pike hard as they start to run will invariably encourage them to tail-walk, as Martin Bowler's doing here, while sharing my boat on Suffolk's Oulton Broad. I remember this day well because, as we put the mud weights down just after dawn at our first anchorage to fish parallel with an enticing reedline, up popped the heads of three, yes, three otters! Enough said.

Simply trotting live baits close to the bottom with float tackle, alongside structures like moored boats, piled banking and in the entrances to boat dykes with the main river will produce well, as will static dead baits either presented beneath a float or just freelined. There is a strong case for fishing both early and late when movements on the river and around the boatyards cease, especially as dusk falls, should continual frosts render the water clear.

Things change drastically, however, in the powerful currents, where more coloured and noticeably deeper waters of the lower, tidal rivers at depths of between 10 and 20 feet are encountered. You need heavy mud weights, and to anchor bow-on into the flow, as opposed to sideways on which is not always possible. A long rope out to the bow's mud weight, and a short rope to the stern mud weight, not forgetting to alter them, particularly the stern weight, as the tide either rises or drops, will prevent the boat from swaying around too much. Personally, I then treat most swims as though I am searching the Broads. I endeavour to create an attractive scent trail across much of the river, by fanning dead baits at differing lines all around the boat, both upstream and across the flow, using a two-ounce bomb stopped with a rubber bead above the trace and dead bait. Incidentally, when fishing the tidals, I also have a 15-20 inch extra, up-trace of 15lbs mono, regardless of whether the reel line is braid or mono, between bomb and the wire trace, to alleviate the pike's head touching the reel line, bowed by current force, when it approaches the bait. I even think the greater length between bomb and bait allows the bait to flutter enticingly up from the bottom every so often.

Downstream from the stern, I then present dead baits on a 'through the middle' slider float rig, stret-pegging style, with the float lying perfectly flat on the surface, set at least twice that of swim depth, again, with the extra mono, up-trace (see diagram of stret-pegging for roach in Chapter Four, to understand how this deadly technique works). To keep the bait anchored, static to the river bed, again a running two-ounce bomb is fished on the line with a large rubber cushioning bead between it and the trace swivel (see diagram of the boat's rod plan).

Bites to the ledgered baits invariably start with a knock or two on the rod tip before line is taken from the multiplier's free spool set on the ratchet. Where the current is really strong, I clip the line up by pushing a loop beneath a rubber band wound tightly around the rod handle in front of the reel. With the stret-pegged baits, the float generally twitches and glides under positively, all in one glorious movement. An occurrence that happens fairly consistently with the ledgered baits, is to see a distinct knock on one rod, followed by the same on another rod, before one of the baits is taken. It's almost as if a pike is sampling each one before deciding which to take. Believe me, I am not imagining it, for boat partners have witnessed this too on numerous occasions.

On some days, particularly at the bottom of an exceptionally low spring tide when the river is as shallow as it's ever going to be with exposed mud banks, and the roots of reeds and even lilies clearly visible, it stands to reason that the pike, indeed all the fish, are far less spread out and can only be situated in the river's centre channel, because all those enticing bays and reed-lined dyke inlets simply screaming 'pike', become completely high and dry. It is essential to obtain a tide book when exploring these large, rather daunting, lower river reaches.

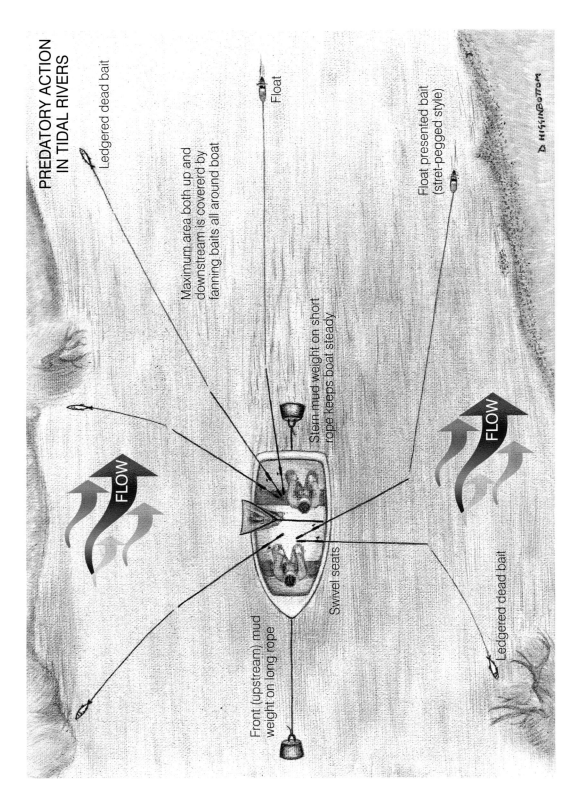

PREDATORY ACTION
IN TIDAL RIVERS

Ledgered dead bait

Float

Maximum area both up and
downstream is covererd by
fanning baits all around boat

Float presented bait
(stret-pegged style)

Stern mud weight on short
rope keeps boat steady

D HIGGINBOTTOM

Swivel seats

Ledgered dead bait

Front (upstream) mud
weight on long rope

In clear water conditions, trotting a live bait low down close to the bottom can now produce some spectacular action, usually for an hour or two either side of low water, searching different lines with each run down, rather like you would when exploring for roach. While we are at low water, and again at high tide, when the flow stops for up to half an hour before it starts to flow in the opposite direction, now is probably the best time to expect some action, particularly on slow days. That's because, while they may have moved little throughout the previous tide, pike, like all other species, are forced to move and change direction when it turns. Think about it. There is no better time for a big, old, lazy, 20lb-plus female to hoover up an easy meal, using minimum effort, and this is the time when the majority of my big, tidal river pike have come. It is certainly no coincidence.

During the 25 years that I ran a tackle shop in the middle of Norwich, many a young angler came in for advice on how to catch big pike from the Norfolk Broads, and I guess my advice today would be exactly the same as it was then. Freeline, ledger or float-ledger an aromatic, whole or half sea deadbait, 5-7 inches long on the bottom, perfectly static. All pike of 15lb-plus are big old girls (males rarely exceed double figures), and the females do like to suck up meals which do not attempt to get away. Being for the most part much more sedentary compared to jacks, big pike want their meals on the table, just like elderly people. They don't want to chase after hamburgers and eat on the run like teenagers; a point well worth remembering.

My advice was once taken too far by one young customer who, having purchased a couple of mackerel from his local fishmonger to follow my static, deadbaiting technique, accounted for a fine 24lbs pike from Ormesby Broads. When he came into my tackle shop and excitedly related the story of its capture and mentioned in passing that he had to open the reel's bail arm and to literally throw each bait out by hand because they were impossible to cast, I asked exactly how big they were. 'Oh, around two pounds apiece,' came the reply. I was flabbergasted to say the least. Pike are truly unpredictable, though, and my young customer was indeed fortunate to hook up positively using such a massive bait. Big baits do not necessarily catch big pike, believe me!

It is equally true that pike will have a go at almost anything on occasion. Using a three-inch diving plug along the margins of a deep gravel pit for instance, I once caught an 18lb pike that only minutes before had swallowed a young coot. How do I know? Well, I actually saw the unfortunate bird disappear beneath the surface in a huge swirl, which prompted my casting over the spot, and upon retrieval of my lure, the pike coughed up a wodge of sodden feathers. The event proved to me beyond doubt that there is, of course, no best bait size for pike.

They will, given the chance, attack virtually anything that looks like an easy meal. For instance, a friend of mine who for many years worked on the processing line at a famous local turkey factory, used to bait up with chunks of best turkey breast and accounted for numerous double-figure Broadland pike as a result. The fact is, pike are both predators and scavengers, and not likely to refuse a fresh meal or question how a chunk of pre-plucked fowl came to be resting on the bottom of a Norfolk Broad. I am certain that in their eyes, it is simply an easy meal, and not eyed with suspicion.

Martin Bowler captured this great action shot of my pike catapulting itself clear of the surface on a local lake. Like I said earlier, hold pike hard just when they start to make a run and you will enjoy all manner of surface acrobatics and explosions. You need a mega-wide angle lens for a photo like this, with the shutter speed on your camera set to a minimum of 500th of a second, and preferably faster, to help freeze the action.

During this strange day on Ardleigh Reservoir in Essex, when my boat partner blanked trailing live baits behind the boat, I whacked out over a dozen pike including two 20s like this deep-bellied beauty, all on big spoons. So never forget the effectiveness of artificials, particularly big spoons

Several years back, while playing what turned out to be my largest ever roach/rudd hybrid hooked on light float tackle in a deep, weedy lake, suddenly, just before being netted, it was grabbed and fortunately released after a few seconds by a pike that looked to be no more than around eight pounds. Yet, that huge hybrid tipped the scales at only an ounce below 4lbs, roughly half the size of the pike. In no way could that pike have swallowed it. Makes you think, doesn't it?

GRAVEL PIT PIKE

As this is far from an encyclopaedia of gravel pit pike fishing, let me outline how I personally attack gravel pit fisheries, when I'm not sure exactly what a particular pit contains in terms of fish and their ultimate size. Pits that have previously been, or still are, regularly stocked trout fisheries, for instance, have by far the best credentials for producing numbers of big pike, due to that all-important ingredient, and extra food source in the way of salmonid flesh. I have enjoyed some astounding catches from such well-fed waters, including three fish over 20lbs, totalling nearly 80lbs, in just a couple of hours fishing one late February afternoon.

This is far from the norm, though. Your average gravel pit, if there is such a thing, will in all probability contain no more than one or two double-figure fish per acre, unless it has enormous stocks of fodder fish. This, of course, is all part of the equation, working out whether or not a particular environment is worth much effort or not, and then plumbing its depths. This can be done either from the bank by counting down spoons while fishing (see Throwing Lures, Chapter Eight) or getting out in a boat to grid-search the water. An echo sounder can be used to locate accurately, those deeper gullies or holes created when the pit was excavated, where baitfish shoals over-winter and where the larger pike won't be so far away from their regular food supply.

My preference on large pits, say, 15 acres-plus, is to obtain permission to fish from a boat, and then after echo sounding the depths, grid-search like I would my local Norfolk Broads. This is by fanning static dead baits all around the boat in favourable areas like deep holes and gullies, while maybe wobbling a mounted dead bait on another rod. Alternatively, I wander the margins having first isolated in my mind the deeper areas found by careful plumbing, and then, particularly in mild weather when everything is on the move, play the roving game. I put out a couple of static dead baits presented over depth beneath bottom-end only sliding floats,

Yes, this is the same pike I'm chinning out in the photo on page 170. A magnificently spotted fish that I saw and to which I specifically cast my small spoon, among the clear weedy water of a Norfolk lake. Luckily for me, the action was captured by cameraman Tim Piper in the filming of my Artificial Lure Fishing video, made back in the mid-1990s.

so I don't need rod rests, buzzers or drop-off indicators, close to where I can easily keep an eye on them.

The rods are simply laid on the bank, pointed at the baits with fixed spool reels clicked into free spool mode. I then work the area all around them methodically, with a wobbled dead bait or large spoon, close to the bottom for say half an hour, before moving on and repeating the procedure, again and again. That way I get the best of both worlds, whether the pike want a static or moving bait and I get to cover simultaneously a large amount of the pit. It's a great and extremely effective roving routine. Try it and discover the benefits for yourself. It's a technique, as I have experienced on numerous occasions, that also works for assessing the potential of estate lakes. My routine here is to start at the deeper, dam end and then work along the lake gradually as it becomes shallower.

There will be days when being continually on the move, wobbling dead baits or working a spoon, provides continual action, and others when nothing seems to be on the move until, quite out of the blue a static dead bait or ledgered live bait gets nailed just as dusk starts to fall. There is one thing I am sure of, relating to gravel pit pike in particular, and that is by far the best times for action, especially in gin-clear pits, are immediately after dawn and again as dusk falls, so be prepared to arrive early and to stay late in order to wait for pike to start moving. This can often be a short window of opportunity, and I must admit that the majority of my own gravel pit, bank sessions are either early morning, or late afternoon stints in order to cash in on these moments.

This fat mid-20 came on wobbled smelt deadbait from a deep gully in a local gravel pit, when my two sleeper outfits, presenting static deadbaits beneath sliding float rigs, produced nothing. As the hooks were not dangling outside its jaws, I netted it but chose to unhook it in the shallow margins; far easier on the pike.

FRESHWATER STALKING

You know, as Isaac Walton said, you really do need to 'study to be quiet.' We are specifically talking about certain carp anglers in this instance, who after banging in their bivvy pegs with a mallet, think that because their baits have all been placed over 100 yards out, there is little point in bothering to be quiet. I guess I have a distinct advantage over most, in that my own two-lake carp fishery, which I walk every morning and evening with our dogs, the importance of being quiet and inconspicuous is brought home to me every single day of my life. I do study to be quiet, as I have for over half a century, by lifting each leg up like a chicken stalking worms (watch one and see) whenever walking beside water, so that my feet do not scrape the ground. I walk ever so slowly, too, keeping perfectly still whenever I wish to observe fish.

Contrary to popular belief, in most cases it is not the colour of your clothes that scares fish, although wearing drab clothes obviously helps, it is that sudden human movement, when the background of foliage all around you lies perfectly still, which initiates alarm to all wild animals. Just study a deer that has seen you but thinks you have yet to make the same observation. It will stand stock still for ages without moving so much as an ear, until you move on and break the spell. All this has almost become programmed into my brain, and yet I still cringe at the sight of a carp spooking off every now and again when I get it wrong, because I should know better. Clearly it was a fish that was feeding confidently close into the margins before I happened along, and which had heard or felt my footfalls. Strange too, how a carp will come up and look at the dogs crashing about through the undergrowth within inches of the water, but not take the slightest notice. The dogs do that every morning, though, and the carp have become used to it without any nasty recollections.

I remember back in the late 1970s when I bred and sold ornamental fish and lilies from the house before the one where I have now lived for the best part of 30 years. To encourage customers to look in the fish house, which was a few yards beyond a large koi filled pond I'd constructed a bridge. I always stamped over this bridge while throwing in a few pellets each time and the carp would then become not only accustomed, but attracted to, the noise and thus rise and show themselves every time a customer walked over the bridge. It worked an absolute treat, too. Of course, this conditioning can work both ways, positively or negatively, and certainly to the angler's detriment each time a fish grabs our bait and receives a headache from being hooked as a reward. Fish are certainly not stupid, as we are all continually experiencing; few animals are, once conditioned.

I can well remember back in 1990 when long time buddy Andy Davison and I filmed two programmes in series five of my Anglia TV's Go Fishing, along the Cauvery River in South India in search of giant mahseer. After three days, we had accounted for diddly squat, despite the river being in fine fettle, with all of our favourite big fish runs producing not a single bite regardless of how hard we tried. So, I got to thinking what was different to when we usually fished, and instantly came up with the answer. We had no fewer than seven people - the film crew plus angler and guide - clambering over the rocks adjacent to every run, instead of the usual two of just angler and guide. The following morning, I made the film crew stand way, way back from the river until I hooked into a fish, and it made all the difference. I just would not have believed that in such thundering water, and in such a wide river, that those mahseer would have been affected by a few extra people on the banks, but they were; big time. I could have kicked myself afterwards for treating the situation so lightly, and not sussing it earlier. Yes, everything's a learning curve.

I probably spend far more time in research, both fish and swim spotting, than I do sitting and waiting patiently behind a gallery of rods. I own neither bed chair nor bivvy.

It took a long time for the penny to drop when filming in South India for big mahseer in the thundering water of a wide river. There were too many bodies by far on the bank - a seven-man film crew - for those wily mahseer to bite. I should have sussed the problem earlier.

My tools of the trade are polarised glasses, yellow lenses for low light and amber for bright conditions, a pair of 10 x 42 Leica binoculars, and various wide-peaked caps to alleviate the need for continually holding my hand up to shield my eyes. Again, less movement; that sudden lift of the arm and especially pointing, scares all too easily. Over the years I have in all probability purchased more pairs of polarised glasses than I've had hot dinners. Well, perhaps not, but you get the idea.

My array of Polaroids and binoculars no doubt set me back more than the cost of at least three designer carp rod and reel combos, for argument's sake, certainly in excess of £1000. Yet, to my mind, it has been more than money well spent and an investment in fish location which stands me in good stead wherever and whenever I fish. After all, my reasoning is that providing I can locate the fish and then creep up and offer a bait at close range, I have far more chance of landing exactly the specimen and species I'm after. Okay, I do fish in large stillwaters and large river systems every so often, like Spain's massive Rio Ebro system for instance, where using a pair of rods and baits positioned over 50 yards out on bolt rigs is essential to obtain optimum results. However, I would say that at least 80 per cent of my fishing, and subsequently my catching, happens at close range where I can see at least the movements of the fish I'm after.

To illustrate this, let me recall an episode in series 16 of my Go Fishing TV programmes filmed back in 2001, when visiting a superbly landscaped gravel pit at West Stow in Suffolk. Film shoots, incidentally, are always a good example of what is not likely to happen, due to the sheer number of people involved. Initially, this was to be a 'feeder-fishing for tench' programme, but unfortunately we'd forgotten to tell the tench. They refused to move over the pre-baited area some 50 yards out, so by mid-morning I'd caught just a couple of small tench, and they were on float tackle from just a few yards out, something I could not possibly blame the crew for.

By now, I was in the mood for a complete species change anyway, so I told the film crew to take a rest while I took my binoculars and a bag of sweetcorn for a slow walk around the lake, which I had never fished before, hoping to come up with an alternative. Fortunately, I did, in the way of a dozen or so carp, seen easily with Polaroids at close range. Initially, I located their dark forms using binoculars from nearly 100 yards away. I could see them through the crystal-clear water as I worked along a steeply-shelving gravel bar, mere yards out beneath the shade of a large alder, not less than 50 yards from where two hours earlier we had parked our cars. Talk about changing tactics quickly!

As we approached the swim, I impressed upon the crew the importance of being stealthy where fortunately those lovely carp were still polishing off the carpet of sweetcorn that I'd left them. It must have been my lucky day; so intently were they feeding that one of our cameramen even managed to climb stealthily up the alder to capture both the carp hoovering up every single kernel of corn I'd thrown in, and my piece to camera about the situation, also from up the tree, before I actually made a cast. That was a trifle cavalier I admit, and rather milking the situation, but it worked nevertheless and I like to think it made great TV. Regular viewers of Go Fishing certainly always seem to mention that particular programme when I meet them at tackle shows and game fairs.

The rewards of stalking; a chunky grass carp approaching
20lbs that succumbed to float fished maize presented on
the bottom just a few yards out in one of the most
evocative old estate lakes I have ever fished. It's called
The Elms, in the Mississippi Delta in the state of Arkansas,
and dates back to the American Civil War.

My only regret, and I admit to being picky here, was not striking when a huge, silver-white metallic, or ghost-koi, sucked in my two grains of corn on an 8 hook. This particular fish, which was apparently caught later that year at over 32lbs, was facing me at the time. I envisaged the bait flying straight back at me, and the fish bolting off and taking all the others with it, so I bottled out and even allowed it to spit the bait out without scaring the rest, rather than strike. However, ten minutes later, I was to be more than compensated when a beautiful, big and deep bodied 31½ lbs plated mirror that I had been watching throughout, confidently inhaled my freelined corn, because the two cameras captured the lot. My cast, the line pulling tight, my strike and an unbelievably long and powerful battle, with me gibbering away as usual. Sometimes, it all does turn out happily, and I was simply over the moon!

Incidentally, I also have a small pair of Bushnell 8 x 25, polarised binoculars (available from JJ Vickers and Sons tel 01634 201284) which fit easily into my waistcoat pocket and are extremely handy for seeing where the carp in clear waters are situated, during spells of mild winter weather when fish spotting otherwise becomes difficult, and then capitalising on that knowledge. Yes, give me a pair of binoculars any time instead of the latest in designer rods, reels or buzzers. Knowledge catches you fish, remember that.

Of course, there are all manner of pointers to look out for when fish spotting and stalking, like the sudden appearance of a calm patch when the entire surface of the lake is rippled. A big fish doesn't even need to break surface to create this, it simply needs to move or turn over a few inches

Easily seen through yellow, polarised glasses, carp in my own two-lake fishery move beneath trees and between patches of lilies. They are easily catchable, too, by anglers who stalk stealthily.

beneath the surface chop, and just like a tail pattern rising to the surface, the waves will flatten out. Sudden calm patches do indicate fish movement beautifully.

What about movement down close to the bottom? Well, we have rising detritus bubbles to thank for portraying the fact that carp, bream or tench have been rooting about and they've released methane bubbles from the bottom silt. I have followed the movement of barbel in rivers, which will also sometimes provide details of their whereabouts by rooting through the bottom strata, sending clouds of bubbles to the surface. River carp, of course, do the same. In still waters, I reckon that those little, innocuous, swirly vortexes in the surface film denoting where carp are working really close into the margins just beneath the surface, are the best give-aways of all. They should be capitalised upon immediately with a freelined, free-falling bait, resulting in an instant hook-up on the drop.

Carp can be so very, very easy to catch at times, to those who spend more time in observation than bait making. A ruse I love trying during the warmer months, wherever the bankside allows, is lying flat down on the ground with my head just inches above the surface. From this prone position, the whereabouts of carp can easily be ascertained from the gentle humps in the surface film caused by big fish moving slowly mere inches beneath and displacing a noticeable amount of water. If you kneel or stand up, the same movements cannot be seen. Try it and see.

Patches of coloured water spewing up from the bottom, even in lakes where the water is already heavily coloured, can be distinguished more easily by wearing yellow-lensed polarised glasses. Even during the brightness of a summer's day, it is usually possible to distinguish the puffs of silt spewing up from the bottom or suspended in already heavily-coloured water, even if there are no bubbles to give away the presence of feeding fish. Clay pits, especially, fall into this category. Bubbles will be few and far between, but just you watch the bottom clouding-up when the carp start rooting about.

Even pike can reveal their presence by bubbles. For many, many years I have pike fished an extremely old Norfolk mere, where the sediment amounting to hundreds of years of leaf fall is several feet deep. While pike fishing there, I used to catch roach and bream from beside my anchored boat, to encourage predatory action. I noticed with regularity that whenever I wound one of my float fished live baits close to where I was actually catching baits and introducing loose feed, a great sheet of bubbles would suddenly erupt in the surface film, always just before the live bait was taken. Then the penny dropped. As the pike attacked the live bait, the powerful wash from its tail had obviously disturbed a patch of bottom silt, thus spewing bubbles to the surface. What a wonderful indication!

Stalking puts you up-close and personal with the fish you intend to catch. It allows you to be selective in the fish you target and it gives you the chance to observe and learn priceless information about their habits. Stalking fish is worth doing even without a rod in your hands, but when you get it right and you connect with a fish at close-quarters, all of that 'studying to be quiet' will be worth every minute you've put into it. As someone almost once said – it's good to stalk!

STREAMS AND BACKWATERS

These intimate, diminutive waters are among my favourites. They are probably so close to my heart because, when I was young, stalking the fish inhabiting the clear-flowing streams of Hertfordshire, sometime on all fours, Indian-style, taught me so much, especially in my teens, although I did visit further afield due to the convenience of a motorbike. Through the clear, flowing water, I witnessed how fish shoal up, and that was something not visually possible in the coloured water of my then local River Lea in Enfield, North London. I learned how they rely upon and relate to one another's reactions and caution at the onslaught of danger, like a pike invading their swim or a careless angler clumping along the banks of an overgrown stream in full view of its occupants. I saw how they slink off to disappear inexplicably and, if you get it right, how voracious and subsequently, how seemingly easy to catch, they can be, particularly to large baits when freelined through the swim naturally with the flow. By large baits I mean a thumbnail-sized lump of breadflake or cheese paste covering a size 8 hook, tied directly to a 5-6lbs reel line, or natural offerings, lobworms and slugs, maybe a minnow or a small, freshly killed bullhead presented on size 6-4 hooks. It is a legacy of knowledge that remains with me and is still often called upon to this very day.

Indeed, those wonderful, enlightening times totally influenced my angling life, and I often think that without those formative years, crawling on the banks and climbing high up into tall trees overlooking those lovely little rivers and streams such as the Rib, Mimram, Ash, Upper Lea, Beane and Whitewebbs Brook, I would certainly not be the same angler. Of course, this was a time long before the introduction of the voracious and destructive signal crayfish, massive cormorant, mink and otter predation, and prior to the levels of chronic water abstraction that we suffer today.

In the first chapter I mentioned how my brother Dave and I would catch our indigenous white-clawed crayfish from the shallows (now an illegal act) before dawn to ensure a good haul of chub from the tiny River Rib, many of which we spotted through Polaroid glasses long before they saw us. However, those chub were only readily catchable because we used watercraft, and wore waterproof trousers, enabling us always to kneel in dew-soaked grass and keep well below the skyline, regardless of bankside conditions. We took neither stools, holdalls, tackle bags nor rod rests, simply an 11-foot, Avon-style rod - quiver tips had yet to be invented - and a landing net apiece, with all bait and sundries being stored in our jacket pockets. Oh, how we could have done with one of the many designer waistcoats available today!

From the clear-flowing and weedy water of a winding Norfolk stream, Martin Bowler eases a fat chub over his landing net, having stalked the fish on all fours, Indian-style, before offering it a freelined slug. Lovely stuff.

Wearing Polaroid glasses and climbing trees provides wonderful views of possible swims and their inhabitants. You can see where the thickest weedbeds and clean, gravel bars are situated, and consequently, where your freelined bait needs to be placed.

When that first, all-important, cast into each swim was made, and the first cast, if accurate, is invariably the most productive, usually a low-trajectory underarm flick, to avoid any sudden shadows falling upon the surface, those chub had pounced aggressively and rushed at a freelined crayfish, sucking it in quickly and masticating it between those powerful pharyngeal teeth, in case another shoal member got there first. Often, this happened within seconds of it hitting the surface and starting to sink, the slack in our 5lbs test line suddenly tightening with alarming speed like the proverbial bowstring.

Big, fat and juicy, brown and black slugs that we gathered when creeping along in dew-soaked grass were taken with equal relish,

as were large lobworms, gathered by my dear old dad from his allotment patch. To this day, lobworms are among my very favourite baits when exploring streams and backwaters, and along so many stretches of the Upper Great Ouse and my local Rivers Wensum, Waveney and Yare, unless I am purely targeting big roach, when I think breadflake is unequalled.

Certainly, I cannot think of a species that won't chomp on a freelined lobworm. We caught some enormous summer dace, between 8-12 ounces, in those days, from such diminutive rivers, particularly the Beane and Rib, on lobs, regardless of the size 8 or even size 6 hooks we presented them on. Basically, we were chub fishing, but in so doing also accounted for the occasional good perch, brown trout, dace and even roach. Which is of course, exactly how I still fish to this day. I wish I had a fiver for every pike that chased and inhaled a lobworm as we enticingly twitched them back, and this is one of the secrets to presenting freelined lobs. If the worm is not taken, either instantly on the drop or after it has lain on the bottom for a few minutes, don't crank it back impatiently in order to make another cast. Lift it slowly off the bottom, in case a perch has been watching it, doing nothing just like a cat does with a mouse and it will pounce as soon as it looks like its meal might be escaping. Then, gently twitch it back upstream through the swim, allowing it to free-fall every so often, all the way back down to the bottom, imagining that at any moment something is following and about to grab hold. Be ready to lower the rod tip and give a little slack before tightening up as the line zings tight.

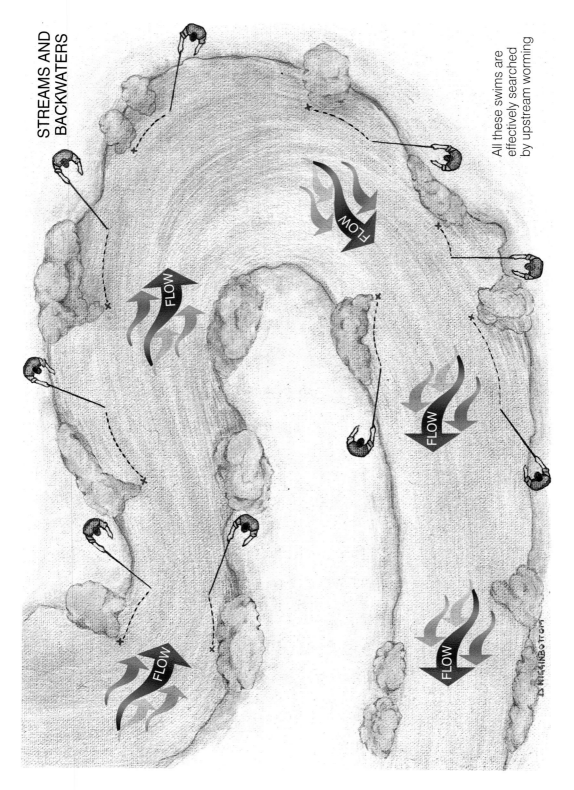

STREAMS AND
BACKWATERS

All these swims are
effectively searched
by upstream worming

FLOW

FLOW

FLOW

FLOW

FLOW

D HIGGINBOTTOM

Big perch do come from the smallest streams and backwaters. To tempt them from gaps among bulrushes or dark hideouts beneath part-sunken bushes and trees, there is no more effective bait than a large lobworm.

Upstream worming, assuming we have been thinking purely of casting downstream until now, is a particularly favourite technique and it's the only way of tackling fish in certain swims. I've caught double-figure barbel, 4lb-plus perch, and just about everything in between using this method. (see diagram) It is so successful because once the fish inhales the worm and immediately turns downstream with it, as the majority of fish do, it feels not the slightest resistance as your line suddenly falls slack, sometimes following an initial twitch or two, denoting an obvious bite. This is why it is so important to keep in constant touch with your upstream worm. At all times you should maintain a gentle bow in the line, whether it is being simply freelined back toward you along the gravel bottom by gentle currents, when you need to be constantly taking up the slack, or benefits from the

addition of a swan shot or two pinched on to the line 12 inches above it, for holding bottom in a strong flow.

Such is the fascination of working a lobworm, or it could be a large piece of cheese paste, slug, or breadflake, to the inhabitants of diminutive rivers, streams and backwaters, that I could happily lose myself in trying each and every swim between their source and end. I particularly love confluences where another stream or a side ditch enters, paying attention to working the bait through that noticeably slower and deeper 'filter lane' down the middle, through the crease where the larger specimens usually choose to lie because it is the prime holding spot.

In backwaters, where the main flow has been separated by a weir pool, with the lesser flow connected, often for a distance of several hundred yards, to a smaller, mill pool or over-shoot pool, there is every chance of contacting large roach, bream, tench even, and in these modern times of well-stocked

During the winter months, areas where streams and dykes converge with the main flow hold immense promise. In cold conditions, though, you do need to present a static bait on the bottom, relying upon a super-sensitive quiver tip for bite registration.

gravel pit carp fisheries, whose occupants escape into flowing water during heavy winter flooding, carp of even specimen proportions.

This all kind of makes tackle selection rather difficult. When I'm quivertipping for chub, say, along the mill streams and backwaters of my local rivers Wensum and Waveney, both of which, whether they want it or not, get regular winter stockings of carp from the numerous gravel pits adjacent to the rivers, I never go below a 6lb reel line and strong size 10 hook, because I never know whether the next bite might result in a long battle with a double-figure barbel, a 20-30lb carp, a chub, perch or big bream or even one of those exceedingly rare, nowadays, 2lb-plus roach. I guess this truly is the magic of exploring backwaters, which also invariably contain the biggest pike that particular stretch of river has to offer. It proves beyond question the old adage that pike thrive on neglect.

Confluences, where one ditch or stream meets another are great holding areas for species like dace, roach, perch, and grayling. Stret-pegging (see Chapter Four) is a great method of approach in cold conditions. During mild spells, try trotting.

Using a mobile approach, and wobbling small, light, whole dead baits such as smelts, or working a large flashy spoon, is my recipe for success with backwater pike, and incidentally, for the pike inhabiting the enormous, often interconnecting, network of dykes leading into and from most of the Norfolk and Suffolk Broads, most of which are accessible from the bank, though sometimes you may have a long walk. We are talking about shallow, 2-7 foot deep, man-made channels here (which is why I class them as backwaters), which are often ridiculously weedy in summer, but act as flood relief networks during the winter. Excessive water is pumped up into the higher levels but lower reaches of the adjacent tidal river by automatic diesel pumps, to drain the surrounding marshlands. There are thousands of acres of pike-holding waters that are very rarely fished, and moreover, free to all.

Just look at an ordnance survey map of the Norfolk Broads area, for instance, and you will see hundreds and hundreds of miles of these rarely fished backwaters, or dykes as they are perhaps better known. They are, indeed, the dark horses of all backwaters, containing good numbers of pike into double figures plus the odd 20, especially at back-end time. I'm talking about those last two weeks of the river season in the first half of March, when Broads monster females move into these reed-lined sanctuaries overhung by alder and willow, as an early grouping process prior to their eventual spawning, usually in April. So, early March is one hot period for the chance of producing a whopping great pike in all backwaters off the main river.

Yes, there is a lot of exploring to do, and remember, drains and dykes of an open nature are tailor-made for those who enjoy catching pike on the fly rod (See Chapter Six).

I've hit the jackpot here, with a 20lbs pike taken on fly, in March, from a network of shallow Norfolk dykes. What I don't like, however, is the fish's anal fin half bitten through. It is what otters do to immobilise their prey, and don't think for one moment that an otter won't attack such a big pike.

TELEVISION TRIALS, TRIUMPHS AND TRIBULATIONS

Wherever I go, whether it's to the waterside, a tackle show, exhibition or game fair, even when fishing abroad, I am always asked by both man and boy alike, and even the ladies, 'When are we going to see more fishing on terrestrial television?' I only wish I knew the answer. You would think that, as one in every 20 people in the UK goes fishing (that's over two million of us), the good old BBC, who gladly accepts our television licence money every year, would feel duty bound to screen at least one or two series per annum, wouldn't you?

After all, Auntie, as I believe they call the Beeb, was quite happy to spend our licence dosh flying no less than 437 of its staff to the Beijing Olympics in China, to film just 300 athletes representing Britain. Yet, what have we had in good fishing programs on the BBC during this last decade from 2000 to 2010? I'll tell you, one decent series only. The superb A Passion for Angling from the camera of someone I'm proud to call a good friend, Hugh Miles. This series of programmes accumulated countless accolades from the angling press and from anglers and non-anglers alike, and rightly so. It earned fabulous viewing figures, so why haven't the Beeb commissioned more? To date, they have even refused Hugh's latest series, Catching the Impossible, with Martin Bowler, and again, narrated by the great voice

of Bernard Cribbins. The film includes truly spectacular sub-surface footage and is, in several ways, more watchable than Hugh's first. It beggars belief, but there is light at the end of the tunnel here; a little bird has told me that Channel Four are to screen this fabulous series.

It's amazing really, when you consider the huge amount of money we anglers inject into the BBC with our television licences. Let's assume, for argument's sake, that there are just one million adult anglers, although we know there are substantially more, annually paying the £142.50 television licence fee. This adds up to a gnat's short of a staggering £150 million, and yet this faction of society, Britain's largest participant recreation, no less, cannot watch its own sport on BBC Television. It is utterly scandalous. It appears that costume dramas, soap operas, game shows, reality rubbish and continual football, football, football, are all anyone wants to watch. Which of course is simply not true.

It all seems totally out of proportion, like the supposed £6 million contract once forked out for talk show host Jonathan Ross, and £4 million for Graham Norton, plus the fact that no fewer than 37 top BBC executives actually earn more than the Prime Minister. Again, it's scandalous, but true.

Filmmaker, Hugh Miles, captures the action at my own two-lake Norfolk fishery of Bernard Cribbins endeavouring to put one of my carp on the bank using fly-rodding tactics. He did it, too! A lovely, big scale-perfect common.

Incidentally, do you know how many 12-part, half-hour fishing programmes could be made at today's prices for £10 million, the cost of just two trendy, BBC presenters? Well, as I have made more half-hour TV angling programmes for British television than anyone else, I should know, so I'll tell you. Approximately 50, 12-part series. Yes, that's around 600 half-hour programs, for the cost of £10 million which is/was the wages for just two presenters. Yet, what do we licence-paying anglers get? Diddly squat, that's what. It's perfectly true. The British Broadcasting

Corporation has certainly become far too big for its own boots. Who does anything about it? I guess you could say that at least the BBC makes its own shows, dramas, comedies, and wildlife documentaries, that would never be produced by commercial TV companies, as they would not actually be profitable. Sky, for instance, with the exception of news and sport, is merely a vehicle for transmitting programmes produced by someone else. If you are not confused by now, you certainly should be.

Today, when literally hundreds and hundreds of different commercial channels must all share the same pot, no one has any money to make great programmes any more. Back in the days when commercial television in the

UK commanded the giant's share of advertising revenue, though, things were not so different from how the Beeb is now, in that ITV grossly overpaid itself, due to one important reason, and that was union control.

I can well remember the very first programme I made for Anglia Television, which illustrates this perfectly. It was the first programme of the very first series of what turned out to be my long running Go Fishing, which lasted for 17 consecutive years, shot back in 1985. It was one of Anglia's longest running series ever, incidentally, until they stopped making local programmes.

The location was a lovely, shallow estate lake in North Norfolk, surrounded by beautiful tall trees and designed like so many in East Anglia, by Capability Brown, where I caught a dozen or so fat tench using both float and feeder-ledgering techniques in glorious summer sunshine. I certainly could not have asked for more. I had put an enormous amount of time and research into this, my first

go at fishing on the box, because I so much wanted it to be a success. For days beforehand, I walked the lake at dawn, with binoculars, to see where the tench would be bubbling, and to see what local wildlife was about and exactly what natural history slant I could slip into the half-hour Go Fishing show. I chose swan mussels living in the rich, organic silt of the lake, incidentally.

'Don't expect the crew to arrive before eight o'clock', was the reply I got from the director Peter Akehurst, to my request of a dawn start, when herds of deer came down to the lake to drink, accompanied by numerous herons and kingfishers, and of course those lovely tench bubbling their heads off. The prohibitive production cost at that time for getting a crew up and out on the bank before eight o'clock in the morning was five

I'm into a fat tench, one of a dozen I caught that day, during Anglia Television's very first Go Fishing program, filmed by Davey Jones, and watched by director, Peter Akehurst. It was all lovely stuff, but I hated the unbending rules and union control of my work.

times the going rate, would you believe, in overtime rates. Yes, a full five times the going rate! No wonder commercial television committed hari-kari.

What's more, and surely another nail in the ITV coffin, an outside broadcast unit like ours was compelled by union rules to have an electrician as part of the crew. Not another cameraman, which we could then have done with - the first series of Go Fishing was shot on just one camera until I insisted that further series needed two - but an electrician who merely sat around and occasionally made the tea.

What was even more bizarre in my mind, as someone who ran his own 'one man band' tackle shop, was that a couple of days after that first shoot, the director asked me to go back to the estate lake for another session to catch some more tench. Someone, no doubt a 'luvvy' at Anglia, had forgotten to send out a stills cameraman for their publicity machine, during our shoot. Naturally, I said that I already had more than enough colour transparencies of the action, trophy tench shots, the lot, including some lovely material that I self-took during the lunch break, when the crew had all disappeared to the pub, on my old 2¼ square format, Bronica S2A camera, using a 'bulb' shutter release, would you believe! I told Anglia that they were more than welcome to them, but oh no! As I wasn't in the union, I needed to go back to the lake so that their stills man could take exactly the same shots. I was not a happy bunny at all, because in those days I had to organise someone to look after my tackle shop in Norwich, so that I could swan off and make programmes in the first place. It was at the start of the fishing season, too, so there could be no worse time for me, but through sheer professionalism, and refusing to let them beat me, I did it anyway. What an absolute farce!

What an obscene waste of manpower it all was, too, but as we all know, Margaret Thatcher took care of that, and the rest is history. Today, as I type this in 2010, it seems that ITV do not have the money to spare to screen angling, unless it features a celebrity from another TV genre, who can't fish but is provided with a world-wide budget to produce crap that most serious anglers laugh at. Why, oh why, must everything we watch on the box be celebrity led? Thank heavens for Discovery TV!

Fishing, I might add, is not about 'high fives', fish dripping blood, yelling at the camera and continual cursing and swearing. It is about using angling presenters who can not only fish and be seen to fish with authority, but through a lifetime of the sport have a sensitive and deep understanding of natural history, while catching fish and explaining it all along the way; and who hook and play their own fish instead of repeatedly taking the guide's rod. Well, that's my take on it, anyway.

Television never hires football pundits who have never kicked a ball do they? You don't see Matt Hayes for instance, presenting a cricket programme, do you? If you did, cricket enthusiasts would have every right to voice their distaste. Paul Young doesn't present motor racing, or come to that, I don't present a football programme. God forbid! Like the rest of the viewers, two million anglers do not like having their intelligence insulted.

I'll say that again in the hope that at least one television-programming commissioner actually reads this. Two million anglers do not like having their intelligence insulted. So why, oh why have television's programming commissioners throughout the years insisted on wasting money by repeatedly trying celebrities to front fishing programmes? Is it because they think if a football celebrity fronts the programme, then not only anglers, but also all footballers will watch too? This is simply not the case. In actuality, nobody really likes watching a badly presented programme. Or is it simply that commissioners assume there is so little meat or general appeal in angling on TV that the subject needs a celebrity to spice it up? Well, I would have thought that programme makers like Hugh Miles and, dare I say, me, have long since dispelled any such theory, because quite simply nobody watches subject matter on television continually for over 20 years unless it is ticking most of the boxes and producing good viewing figures. That's something both Hugh's A Passion for Angling and my own Go Fishing series certainly did.

It is a subject which I am sure, dear reader, you realise, makes me sometimes truly despair. At times, I even feel like pulling my hair out, and I really do worry about how our wonderful pastime or fieldsport, call it what you will, is going to be portrayed on television in the future. Sorry, I'm on the verge of being an angry old man again.

Perhaps worse still though, as I mentioned earlier, as far as any future angling series are concerned, has been the complete dismantling of local broadcasting by all television companies, which was, in fact, the avenue by which my own 17 consecutive series of Go Fishing - in all a total of 108 half-hour programmes - came to be. It started off as local programming, and was then screened nationally for over 10 years, when Channel Four chipped in and paid half the budget to show it. Of course, now no one makes local programmes apart from the news. Once upon a time, when I first got into TV, Anglia Television employed over 1000 people that kept Norwich businesses alive during their lunch hours. Now I dread to think how few there are manning just a news station, so there is no platform from which anyone can now start. Should there be another budding John Wilson out there wishing to take the same route I did, sadly, he hasn't got a chance. It's all so very, very disillusioning and most disheartening.

Going back to the greed of commercial TV, which kind of makes me at least understand Margaret Thatcher taking the stand she did of dismantling the unions, I can well remember a film shoot that depicts and perfectly illustrates how obscene things were in those days, moneywise. Organised by Eagle Moss, the London based part-work publishers for whom I provided extensive copy and colour transparencies back in the early 1990s, the shoot was arranged for a London production company to film me holding and returning a sizeable fish to my local River Wensum, at a local mill-pool, while speaking to camera. I was well into several years of presenting Go Fishing for Anglia TV by then and so considered what they wanted as a bit of a doddle. This was for a television advert to showcase their new part-work series called The Art of Fishing, and I was told the producer's assistant would ring for directions. Indeed, she did, but her questions went on and on and on, and included acquisition of the menu from the local pub and how far away in miles it was from the local hospital, in case someone got hurt, and so on.

All this got the old alarm bells ringing and I doubted they would allow much time for yours truly to catch anything decent. That's always the problem with TV cameras. 'Okay John, catch one now'. So, I popped across to the mill-pool three hours before the crew's arrival and soon had a nice tench and a big bream on quivertipped breadflake, which I

Pete 'Yorkie' Wright (sound) and Paul Bennett (camera) record the action at picturesque Sywell Reservoir in Northamptonshire, of me displaying a nice pike that had grabbed a small roach on the way in, during what was in fact a specimen tench programme in series eight of Go Fishing in 1994

retained in a large sack at a pretty spot where I thought they might like to film - and was I glad I did.

When the crew finally arrived, for a 'fish-holding and returning' piece that I could have knocked off with a single cameraman and sound man in less than half an hour, I just couldn't believe my eyes. Instead of just two people, there were nine! From the proverbial tea boy up to the director, resplendent in a pink - yes pink - Pringle cardigan, with a stopwatch around his neck. Below him were his assistant and I believe another assistant, plus producer and her assistant, plus sound man and two cameramen. Talk about a waste of manpower. I laughed silently behind a smile, during the introductions.

It illustrated perfectly how commercial television at that time was grossly overpaying itself. Of course, none of this is in anyway as detrimental to how the greed of both TV and football frittered away hundreds of millions of pounds with the proposed commercial, digital/satellite fiasco that never was – pay-per-view soccer. This is partly why most big clubs in the land owe millions and millions that they never had in the first place, from purchasing new players, and (mega-rich owners apart) they have not the slightest chance of ever repaying. It's all so very sad, for everyone who likes to watch his or her particular sport or pastime featured on the box. Now, at the beginning of 2010 as I write this, it has gone full circle again, as many things in life do, with very few knowledgeable fishing presenters being awarded sufficient budgets to make the kind of programmes they would like, and more to the point, what experience has taught them viewers, including me, would like to watch.

WHENEVER

Whenever you see swans upturned with their heads and necks completely beneath the surface, chewing weed, you can be fairly sure that depth is around four feet, or shallower, or that weed is spewing up from the bottom in deep water to within four feet of the surface.

Whenever you fish in the tropics, in fresh or salt water, don't forget polarised sunglasses. Wear yellow lenses for dull, early mornings and at dusk, and either amber or grey for strong, bright sunshine.

Whenever you see a carp, bream, or tench roll during a slow session, even though it's far away from your ledgered baits, quickly wind a rod in and get a bait over it pronto.

Whenever you are stream or river fishing miles from anywhere and have forgotten or run out of bait, grub about in the marginal shallows for the protective cases of caddis grubs - the larvae of the sedge fly - which cling to pieces of flint and sunken logs. Its head and legs protrude from the front, so pinch the tail end, and out will come a superb natural bait slightly larger than a maggot, which all cyprinid species adore.

Whenever you visit a new, previously unseen, lake, pond or mere, and are unsure of the depths, remember that most varieties of cultivated lilies will not grow in depths beyond five or six feet. The common yellow 'brandy-bottle' water lily, though, the only lily with subsurface, cabbage-like leaves, flourishes in an optimum depth of between eight and nine feet.

Whenever you're finally connected with a monstrous fish, be it a giant white sturgeon, tarpon or huge wels catfish, when you could be in for up to an hour's hard work, try to relax and only wind to regain line when the rod tip starts to slacken after pumping, but never allow it to straighten.

Whenever you peer through polarised glasses into the clear, running water of a small river or stream where a willow overhangs an acute bend, and see clumps of those fibrous and reddish-brown subsurface roots down below, expect an undercut bank/cavern beneath. It is into these silent havens that big chub, trout, perch or barbel sometimes retreat during the brightness of a summer's day. This is why you sometimes cannot see them when you expect to.

Whenever adventure angling in foreign parts, always take sundries including a small torch, matches, Superglue, a multi-use knife, needle and cotton, both lip and body protection from the elements, Ibuprofen, a compass and a first aid kit. You never know when you might need them.

UNDERCUT BANKS
WHERE CHUB AND BARBEL HIDE

Willow

Angler looking - but sees nothing

Fibrous matting of sub-surface willow roots

D HIGGINBOTTOM

Undercut created through erosion of soil by current force supported by root structure of tree

Most undercuts have narrow entrances and open up inside, often several feet deep

FLOW

This is a quiet corner of picturesque Homersfield Lake, situated on the Norfolk/Suffolk border, adjacent to the upper reaches of the River Waveney. The patches of cultivated white and red lilies denote that the depth beneath them is less than five feet.

Whenever concentrating your eyes upon a float tip, the end of a fly line just beyond the rod tip, or a quiver tip, reduce glare and, more importantly, narrow your 'viewing screen' down by wearing not only Polaroid glasses, but also a large-peaked baseball cap.

Whenever fishing in the tropics, don't fill your suitcase full of clothes. You may well want the space for tackle. Wear and take along quick-dry shirts and shorts and wash or rinse them daily.

Whenever river swims have beds of dark green bulrushes protruding from the surface, quivering with the current force as they do, the bed of the river will be hard and of gravel. Which is why bulrushes are so attractive to barbel, and to perch, which use the vertical stems as effective, blend-in camouflage against their own stripes. True bulrushes have tapering, onion-like stems with a tiny brown seed head 18 inches from the pointed top. Do not confuse them with the cigar-like seed head of the reed mace, often wrongly called bulrush.

Whenever fishing in far-off locations don't ever be tempted to lift unknown species by hand. The electric catfish, for instance, inhabiting the River Nile and the Zambezi, plus Lake Nasser and Lake Kariba which these two rivers feed, may look a dull, innocuous grey colour, covered in large round, black spots, but it gives out up to 300 volts!

Whenever dense, floating beds of watercress protrude and hang out from the margins along diminutive rivers, the area beneath might stretch back as much as three to four feet into the bank. It could be concealing sizeable groups of chub, in a stretch which even when viewed through polarised glasses, at first appears barren.

Whenever gulls, and particularly terns, are dive-bombing the surface of either lake or ocean to gorge upon baitfish, especially when well offshore and there are no other pointers as to where big fish could be situated, keep well back from the mêlée and cast among the often fast-moving feeding fracas. Bass could be pushing up sand eels or small mackerel and sardines might be chased unmercifully to the surface by kingfish and tuna, where they gorge upon them, with gladiators like sailfish, marlin and sharks situated below them.

Whenever river fishing and you require small live baits for perch or chub, turn over large pieces of flint in the margins to gather the stone loach and bullheads lying beneath.

Whenever angling within the continent of Africa, remember that items like spools of line, split rings, replacement treble hooks of the right strength, swivels, wire traces and rubber beads cannot be bought in the jungle, so take plenty with you.

Whenever you pass elder trees stacked with bunches of ripe fruit during the early autumn, it takes but minutes to fill a carrier bag. The juicy, dark berries much loved by dace, roach and chub, even barbel, can be used straight away. They are deadly for trotting when loose feeding with stewed hempseed. Alternatively, you can also preserve them in a large, screw-topped jar, in a weak solution of formalin, for future use. Don't try to pull the berries from the stems; they only burst. Simply use scissors to remove golf ball-sized florets and pop these into the preserving jar.

Whenever a huge tail pattern erupts deep down and spews up to the surface as you lift your artificial lure or wobbled dead bait out for another cast, make sure next time, that you speed up during those last few yards, working it right up to the very edge of the bank.

Turning over large pieces of flint along the margins will reveal great natural baits in the way of caddis grubs, stone loach and bullheads, so you can fish for species like roach, chub and perch for free.

A big pike obviously wants a chase and will subsequently nail any meal that appears to be getting away, so be on your toes.

Whenever downtide or uptide fishing for tope using mackerel flappers, but you find that dogfish rip them to bits within minutes, cone a large mackerel by cutting it neatly in half and removing the tail. Hook once only through the muscles of the tail end. It will outlast a flapper by two or three times.

Whenever trotting maggots and casters beneath a stick float rig for dace of mixed sizes, the better quality fish will invariably come to the heavier sinking casters presented close to the river bed. Try it and see.

Whenever you want to offer a fair-sized live bait 20, 30 or even 40 feet down close to the rocky bottom and among the fast cross currents beneath waterfalls of big, deep rivers for monstrous freshwater fish like wels catfish, Nile perch or vundu and sementendu catfish, even mahseer, then remember two things; firstly, a large, single hook gently nicked through immediately behind the bait's dorsal fin, will not only snag up less, it allows the bait

to get its head down and reach the desired depth band on a simple freeline. So, don't put any lead above it, or it will snag in the rocks. Secondly, on no account present it with the hook through the lips. Upon any kind of control, it will be pulled upwards and away from your target species and intended depth band.

Whenever you are out in a boat, drift fishing in fresh water, working wobbled deadbaits or artificial lures for pike, and want to slow the boat down but do not own a drogue, (so buy one!) improvise. Hang a keep net out over the windward side of the boat, tied on tightly, roughly in the middle and preferably with some weight inside, to keep it down.

Whenever freelining while stalking along an overgrown river for chub or perch, and the weight of a single, large lobworm is insufficient weight to reach a particular lie - put two on!

Lobworms are the very best bait for freelining in overgrown streams for species like perch and chub.